D1171752

CRIMINAL JUSTICE HISTORY

AN INTERNATIONAL ANNUAL

CRIMINAL JUSTICE HISTORY is an international forum for the history and analysis of crime and criminal justice. It annually publishes research and historiographical articles, comparative and interpretive essays, book review essays, and shorter reviews. The Annual encourages submissions from authors in any part of the world in disciplines such as history, law, anthropology, sociology, political science, and the criminal justice sciences that relate specifically to the history of crime and criminal justice and to its broader social, historical, legal, and institutional contexts in any geographical area or period.

CRIMINAL JUSTICE HISTORY

AN INTERNATIONAL ANNUAL

Volume V

1984

Meckler Publishing
11 Ferry Lane West, Westport, CT 06880, USA

3 Henrietta Street, London WC2E 8LU, UK

ISBN: 0-88736-019-X
ISSN: 0194-0953

Manufactured in the United States of America.

Contents

Thieves in Medieval Icelandic Laws

Martina Stein-Wilkeshuis
Nuenen, The Netherlands

In the course of the Middle Ages important changes took place in nearly all areas of Scandinavian society. These changes originated mainly from Christianization and concomitant modifications in the conception of monarchy, whilst economic and social factors were instrumental. New ideas set in more gradually in the domain of juridical thinking and the treatment of criminals. Whereas in the early medieval period the accusing of criminals and the execution of sentences were the litigant's private affair, in the second period (from about the eleventh and twelfth centuries) we can observe the beginning of an executive power under royal auspices. Punishments also underwent a change, for revenge and outlawry were gradually replaced by the death penalty, detention, and corporal punishments.

In Norway, Sweden, and especially Denmark, these changes came about piecemeal. Iceland, because its isolated position made it less accessible for foreign influences, maintained the old situation for a longer period. Christianity and the monarchy were introduced in the island in the years 1000 and 1262, respectively, and the changes which resulted (especially from the last event) were more radical than elsewhere. The way these alterations affected juridical thinking in relation to theft, and the treatment and punishment of thieves, will form the focus of this article.

Introduction

A short survey of Iceland's history is indispensable for a proper understanding of these developments.[1] Iceland was a practically uninhabited island until its colonization in the period 870–930 by mainly Norwegian settlers. The exodus from Norway had several causes, and the main ones were supposed to have been a threatening overpopulation of the Scandinavian area and King Harald Fairhair's authoritarian behaviour. Many prominent men felt themselves threatened by the increasing regal power and left the country rather than to submit to the new order. They settled, sometimes after many wanderings, in Iceland. A new democratic state was founded, populated by free men

1

and slaves, like the rest of Scandinavia. People were heathen and the most important means of subsistence were cattle-breeding and trade.

Generally in the early societies of Germanic peoples the standard unit was the family, not in the sense of household but in that of kinship. An individual was not considered a separate being as much as he is today, but he was looked upon as a link in the long family chain. This attitude can also be observed in early medieval Iceland. Lengthy genealogies occur in many Icelandic sagas, and as a rule it is the family that bears responsibility, not the individual. It is up to the family to care for poor relatives—a duty regulated by law in full detail—and to uphold the family's honour and property. Honour was very highly estimated and closely connected with blood revenge. The duty to take revenge for any insult was an unwritten law that ultimately was based on the conception that under all circumstances a man's honour and that of his family had to stay intact. If, for instance, a family member had been offended or killed, the injured family had to inflict a similar offence on the opposing one. As long as no revenge had been taken this was considered a "shame." A free man's legally guaranteed immunity was called "mannhelgi," and by committing unlawful deeds the offender automatically forfeited his immunity partly or totally. If revenge was taken on him the law required demonstration that he had lost his immunity and his right to legal redress. Crimes committed secretly, like murder and theft, were particularly detested because the victim was given no chance to defend himself.

The cornerstone of the political and juridical organization of early medieval Scandinavia was the local 'thing', an assembly bound to be attended by all freeholders. Here laws were issued democratically, and each participant could bring a charge against his enemies and defend his case in the presence of his equals. Sentences were passed by a court formed by lay judges, and no action was legal without witnesses being present, a situation characteristic for times when writing was not known. The early medieval Icelandic society was modeled on this organization.

Iceland since its colonization was divided into thirty-six "goðorðs" (chieftaincies), each one under the leadership of a "goði," a chieftain who besides his secular task also held the office of priest in the heathen temple. Groups of three goðorðs met at the local "þing"—meetings in spring and autumn attended by all freeholders of the three chieftaincies. Already in 930 a national assembly, the Alþing, was instituted, and to minimize inevitable differences in legislation, new laws were introduced modeled on the Norwegian Gula-thing law, which was adapted to Icelandic conditions. The local þings remained beside the Alþing for handling local affairs and cases of first instance, but they did not possess legislative power. The newly established Alþing had legislative power that rested with the "lögrétta" (Law Council).

The Council comprised the thirty-six chieftains, each of whom brought two men to advise him, and was presided over by the "Lögsögumaðr" (Law-speaker). After 960 the Alþing's judicial power rested with the four Quarter Courts, a reflection of the island's division into four jurisdictions. Each court had thirty-six judges, one nominated by each chieftain. An executive power did not exist, and the execution of sentences was left in private hands, although sometimes the chieftains gave assistance.

As a rule Christianity in the north European countries was introduced by a king who, not without political aims, was converted to the new religion. In Iceland, the Alþing in the year 1000 established Christianity by law as the national religion. This happened on instigation of the Norwegian King Olaf. Initially the new faith was very pliant. Rome was far away, the vernac-ular became the church language (both in Iceland and in Scandinavia) and the Icelandic clergy helped to put the heathen literature onto parchment. In the first hundred years or so there was no question of a profound Christian influence on the Icelandic society. In general Christianity, by founding monas-teries and by emphasizing individual responsibility as opposed to the family responsibility of former times, brought about a weakening of family ties. In Iceland, where family ties had lost some of their strength as a consequence of the colonization, the new religion undermined them still more.

In the course of the twelfth and thirteenth centuries social and economic conditions in Iceland deteriorated as a consequence of three factors. First, internal political troubles resulting from corruption among the chieftains brought poverty and unrest among the population and caused a spread of criminality. Second, the shifting of sea routes adversely affected Iceland's economic position and caused an almost complete isolation of the island. Third, the growth of population (Christianity declaimed against exposure of children) led ultimately to the island's loss of independence and its sub-mission to the Norwegian crown in the year 1262. The Norwegian king took advantage of Iceland's internal political instability and its economic depen-dence to lay his hands on the island. The Gamli Sattmáli[2] (Old Covenant) was concluded, settling the rights and duties of the Icelandic people with respect to the Norwegian king. According to the treaty, Icelanders were obliged to pay taxes to King Håkon Håkonsson and his son Magnús. One of the obligations the king entered into was to restore the internal peace and to maintain the Icelandic laws. It would soon turn out that the first promise could be realized only at the cost of the last one.

Before long the country's government and administration were funda-mentally altered. A royal governor was appointed, and the land was divided into twelve districts ("sýslar"), each one coinciding approximately with the groupings of three chieftaincies of former times. The function of chieftain was abolished, and the Lawspeaker was replaced by the "lögmaðr," a royal functionary. Royal agents were charged with the government of one or more districts; these "sýslumenn" (sheriffs), were invested with all offices of public authority — police, public ministry, and executive and judicial power. In executing these tasks assistance was given by the "umboðsmaðr," a kind of policeman. With the submission to Norway a period of independence and originality in many fields came to an end, and Iceland's society and culture became directly subject to the West European sphere of influence.

Sources

Until about 1100, laws and law lore in Iceland were transmitted orally. The art of writing followed in the wake of Christianity and with it the production of books. In the year 1117 a decision was taken by the Alþing to have the laws written down and revised, with the intention of making a unified codification of the Icelandic laws. We do not know whether the undertaking was ever carried through completely, but it is certain that the recording of laws continued after that date, and that in the course of the twelfth century in addition to whole books of laws there were many parts of laws in existence. Two great codices of customary law have been preserved — the "Konungsbók," supposed to date from about 1250, and the "Staðarhólsbók,"[3] thought to date from 1260. All these laws, written in the vernacular, are known by the collective name "Grágás" (Grey Goose). It is presumed that all the provisions in this collection were once law in Iceland. The Grágás contains, in addition to the Christian section, many articles that date back to heathen times when legal knowledge was transmitted orally. It is this lawbook that forms the base of our investigation of the period until the year 1262.

King Håkon died in 1263 and was succeeded by his son Magnús, who afterwards was nicknamed by the Icelanders "Laga-boetir" (the Lawmender). During his reign all the laws of Norway were revised, and it was expected that the Icelandic laws should receive the same treatment. A new lawbook called "Járnsíða" (Ironside) was introduced in Iceland, in essence identical to the Norwegian code of the time, and scarcely if at all adapted to Icelandic conditions. Although it was ratified by the Alþing in 1271, it was highly unpopular and in many cases it was silently replaced by the Grágás. In our investigation the Járnsíða therefore is left out of consideration. A revision was quickly undertaken, and in the year 1281 the Alþing reluctantly accepted a new code, a creation of Magnús Lagaboetir, who took the Norwegian Landlov as a starting point but adapted many articles to specifically Icelandic conditions by using, among others, the Grágás.[4] The code was called "Jónsbók," after the Icelandic lawyer Jón Einarsson, who brought the book to Iceland and was probably involved in its compilation. This lawbook is the major source for our investigation of the period after 1281. Although the Jónsbók was ill-received, it came to be popular in Iceland and very much respected. Parts of it are still in force today.

Thieves In the Grágás

Theft was considered one of the most detestable crimes because it was committed secretly, as opposed to robbery, which was committed openly. The most severe punishments seemed appropriate for thieves in Roman, Greek, and Celtic tradition. It is assumed that in heathen times theft, like murder and violation, was punished by sacrificing the guilty to the gods. The north European sources, however, do not mention this measure.[5] The Old Icelandic lawbook Grágás contains one section that is devoted to theft and thieves. It is called Rannsóknar þáttr (Searches Section), and runs as follows:

> Everybody in our country shall keep what he owns, unless he wants to give it up as a present or for payment. If a man without permission takes something belonging to somebody else then this person can accuse him of "görtæki" [minor theft], if the value amounts to one penny or more. He who owned the goods has to summon him for minor theft and claim a double compensation on the ground of a valuation made by the neighbors and fix the fine at three marks, and call five neighbors to serve on a panel at the þing of the man prosecuted. If a man takes another man's properties worth half an ounce or more and does not hide them, then he is liable to be punished by outlawry. And he has to be summoned for taking in order to make use of it, but not for theft. If a man takes another man's properties to the value of half an ounce or more and he hides it with thievish concealment, then it is right to bring an action for theft and to summon him and get him condemned to outlawry if the panel declares him guilty of the charge. A panel of twelve has to be called.
> . . . If a man summons another man without scruples and reserve because he should have stolen something, and the panel declares him not guilty, then it is right to prosecute for malicious speech. He [the new plaintiff] is allowed to call witnesses as soon as he hears it, and summon for malicious speech and claim lesser outlawry and prosecute with testimony . . . .
> He who knowingly receives or buys stolen goods is punished in the same way as the one who stole. He is an accomplice. And the same applies to him who egged on to theft. In these cases they will be prosecuted with the same formal means of proof as in thieving cases . . . .[6]
> Whether there is stolen a greater or a smaller amount of food: if a man steals something eatable, or raw meat, then it is right to summon to outlawry.[7]
> If a man loses his property, worth two ounces or more, through one man in twelve months, then it is right to summon him for theft and have him sentenced to thralldom if he has hidden the stolen goods with thievish concealment. He will be a thrall as though his father were a thrall and his mother a bondwoman, and he himself had fallen on the earth as a slave. He [the prosecutor] shall claim the whole of his property. Nine neighbors shall be called to serve on a panel at the þing of the prosecuted to declare whether he has stolen the goods in those twelve months, and summon him, whether he has

hidden the stolen goods or not. If the panel verdict declares him guilty, he must be sentenced to be a slave whose feet are bound, and the prosecutor gets his properties. . . . [8]

House-searches. If a man loses his property he can search the house if he wishes to do so. He must ask people from his own house or from the neighbouring farms for this house-search until he has thirty men. . . . These people must go to the fence of the farm they will search. Only three of them shall enter the yard and go to the farm, the prosecutor or his man of business, and two others. For witnesses he must request the farmer, who lives there and the other people present, to make a truce and give a formal guarantee according to the law of the searches. . . . When house-search is permitted three men of the company that will search the house have to go in, and one man of the other party. He has to go ahead, carrying a light and open the locks. These four people enter the house. They must have themselves searched before they set foot in the farm in order that no stolen goods are carried in as a charge for the inmates, and the same when they go out again. If no keys are made available the locks forfeit their immunity when being prized. The same people have to search in all places inside and outside the farm. . . . When searching they are not allowed to do damages causing injury or losses for the inhabitants. . . . Even if they find stolen goods inside, they are not allowed to kill the people or hurt them unless it is found in their hands. Prosecution has to be carried out as if no house-search had taken place. [9]

The Staðarhólsbók[10] gives the following provision for avenging a theft:

If a man takes another man's property and commits theft thereby, or it is found in his hands, then the one who took the property falls at that place of action with forfeit immunity if killed by the man who owned that property that was stolen, and also if killed by anyone who gives the latter help in this. They are not to avenge anything but the theft committed by the man who took the property found there in his hands at that place of action.

The following cases of theft or unlawful appropriations are especially mentioned by the Grágás:

If a man without permission and on purpose appropriates the milk-yield of someone else's cattle, not his own, then the owner must choose to summon him and have him sentenced to outlawry, or rather for minor theft. [11]

If a man marks another man's livestock in order to appropriate the animals, and he hides it with thievish concealment, then the owner has to decide on the summoning. [12]

Whale hunting was subjected to strict rules. If for instance a whale hunter's harpoon was removed secretly from the whale, so that the hunter missed his share in the catch, the owner was allowed to bring an action for minor theft with a fine of three marks or to claim the offender's outlawry. [13] Next an example of embezzlement:[14] If a man had lent something to somebody else or entrusted it to his keeping, and the first one embezzled it denying to have received anything, then the first one could bring an action for major or for minor theft. Whenever there was a question of taking more sheep from the pasture than one owned[15] and keeping this secret, of secretly slaughtering borrowed animals, or of fishing and catching fowls on another man's ground,[16] in all these cases the owner had to choose whether he wanted to summon for major or for minor theft.

Interpretation

The Grágás provisions teach us that theft was considered a most serious crime because it was seen first of all as a violation of another man's right to property. The articles focus on the injured, as he is the one who plays the lead. He has to call the neighbors for the appraisement and for the panel; he must summon the offender, claim compensation, and undertake house-search; and finally, he has to look after the execution of the sentence. Theft was also considered a dishonest crime, the more so when the stolen goods were hidden or the tracks covered up. The laws stipulated that every injury be published for witnesses at the þing, both by offender and by offended, and it is clear that a thief omitted this by committing the offence with secrecy. In the saga literature the same attitude toward theft prevails. A thief generally is considered one of the most detestable criminals, one to whom no mercy was shown. Here too it is the secrecy of the crime that generates aversion. Robbery as a rule was less despised, for it was committed openly and the victim got a chance to defend himself. Robbery was looked upon as a fair crime. A well-known saying illustrates this attitude:[17] "Vikings have the habit to gather boot by robbery, thieves on the contrary are used to conceal it afterwards."

The Grágás, no matter the circumstances of the crime, distinguishes two limits: one penny or more, and half an ounce or more.[18] No limits were applied to theft of food and slaughtered animals. Even theft of the smallest amount was liable to outlawry, an indication that this form of the crime was considered the worst one. An accomplice was liable to the same punishment as the thief himself, and the same applied to the person who put him up to theft. That sometimes the accomplice was considered to be even worse than the thief himself can be deduced by the saying: "A thief may thrive, but a thief's accomplice never."

The verb "rann-saka" (to search a house) is composed of two elements, a Germanic word "rann," which in the Icelandic language still has the meaning of "house," and the second part, "saka" (to search), which is etymologically cognate with the English "to seek," and the Dutch "zoeken." House-search, undertaken on the initiative and under the leadership of the prosecutor, is known in all Scandinavian lawbooks, and according to the legal provisions a person who had fallen a victim to theft was entitled to undertake house-search. Sometimes distinct provisions are given in relation to the clothes of those who wanted to search a house. Swedish laws, for instance, stipulate: "They shall wear no coat, have their girdle undone, be barefoot and have their trousers tied up to the knees."[19] These rules, as much as the examination prescribed by the Grágás, are meant to prevent the searchers from secretly carrying into the house the very object they were looking for. In general, a domicile was considered essential in early Scandinavian society. Without a fixed residence, a man did not exist legally, as he could not be summoned. A man without a house became more or less rightless. In the lawbooks constant attacks on beggars and vagabonds can be observed.[20] They were people without a domicile, and for that reason it was difficult for others to obtain legal redress against them. House-search is an act that marks the seriousness of the crime of which the inhabitant is suspected, for it is virtually a disturbance of domestic peace. Domestic peace is a common Germanic concept, originally closely linked with the heathen cult, like thing-peace. Several north European lawbooks devote provisions to the subject.

The Grágás takes a theft to the value of one penny or more as a minor theft, and at the same time the lawbook mentions several cases of deceit, pilfering, unlawful appropriations, and embezzlement that can be judged as minor or as major theft, leaving the decision to the prosecutor. In the case of a minor theft, the injured person always had a right to double compensation, and a fine of three marks[21] was imposed on the criminal. This was the standard penalty for minor offences in general.[22]

Major theft entailed for the thief a loss of all his rights. According to a number of provisions, revenge was permitted when the thief was taken red-handed. The injured person was entitled to kill the thief on the spot if he was caught in the very act, or if stolen goods were found in his hands. The thief who by his unlawful act had lost his immunity was "óhelgr," which means that in case of his death by killing, his next of kin were not entitled to legal redress. These Grágás rules, which permitted revenge on the thief exclusively to the injured person or his helper, and on the spot of the offence at the very moment the criminal was taken red-handed, meant a clear restriction of the original vengeance conception. Originally, the right of vengence knew no boundaries; it was family against family, for any crime could be avenged by the injured person or one of his kinsmen on the offender himself, or one of his relatives, at any time and anywhere. In their turn, the offender's kinsmen could revenge themselves on the opposing family, and so on, with the result that feuds could rage generation after generation. These feuds form the focus of many Icelandic sagas. The restriction of the right to revenge we observed in the Grágás is due to the influences of canon law, for Christianity preached against bloodshed and stressed individual responsibility as opposed to the former collective family responsibility.

Revenge for theft was permitted among many Germanic peoples. Danish laws contain remnants of provisions that permitted avenging theft. As a rule these prescriptions disappeared when the laws were codified. In Sweden the Västgötalagen[23] permitted revenge on a thief who was taken red-handed if the victim could not otherwise get back the stolen goods. The Norwegian Gulathing Law contains an article according to which a thief taken in the very act could be killed with impunity.[24] Blood revenge in Norway was legally forbidden in the year 1273 by the Landlov of King Magnús the Lawmender.

A thief could be enslaved and the whole of his property confiscated by the prosecutor. This article too shows that a thief lost all his rights, for a slave had no rights, not even to property. Enslaving of thieves is also known from early Anglo-Saxon laws.[25] The Skånelagen postulates that a man caught for a minor theft should be a slave in the king's palace.[26] Enslaving according to the Grágás took place after a judicial sentence.

The most common and appropriate punishment for theft was, according to the Grágás, outlawry.[27]

The Icelandic word "skóggangr" (wood-going) is of Norwegian origin. Banishment to the woods was in medieval Iceland hardly possible because of the almost total absence of forests on the island. This penalty also shows that a man by committing theft lost all his rights, became an outlaw, was cast out of society, and forfeited his property, family, and civil and ecclesiastical liberties. He could not lawfully be given any assistance, or saving advise; he had a price on his head and might be killed by anyone with impunity. All this applied forever, even if he escaped abroad. Children procreated after his condemnation had no right of inheritance. Confiscation of an outlaw's property was done by a confiscation court that adjudged what was due to his wife, creditors, chieftain, dependents, prosecutor, and assemblymen.

In certain cases an outlaw could win reprieve by killing other outlaws, but not if he was outlawed for theft, murder, killing, or other grave crimes. A remarkable passage in the Landnámabók[28] gives an account of the severe winter of 975 or 976, when many people in Iceland died of starvation. "But some went stealing and were therefore sentenced or killed. Then outlaws killed one another, for a law was accepted at the advice of Eyólfr Valgerðarsonr, that everybody redeemed himself if he killed three condemned." This does not quite fit in with the Grágás article just mentioned, but the extraordinary circumstances would have increased the number of outlaws greatly. Outlawry was not identical with a death sentence, but it was considered a judicial sentence that invited the offender's death to be executed by private hands.

In the introduction it was pointed out that a person's honour was estimated very highly among Germanic peoples. Consequently, this honour was very vulnerable, and, for instance, all kinds of abusive words were regarded so offensive that it was appropriate to take revenge. Severe punishments were inflicted on persons who committed libel or used abusive language: The word "argr" (coward) usually resulted in three years' outlawry. Against this background we can understand the measures taken by the law against people who, without sufficient ground, accused someone of theft and called him a thief. In several Icelandic sagas we find a confirmation of the law's great concern for a person's honour.[29] Summoning for malicious speech in relation to a charge of theft entailed lesser outlawry, sometimes even a total loss of immunity. A sentence of lesser outlawry meant payment of a "fjörbaugr" (an amount of money) and banishment for three years. Lesser outlawry was a typically Icelandic penalty not occurring in other Scandinavian countries.

As previously stated, according to the provisions of the Grágás, every injury had to be published by the þing before qualified people. The offender should publish his act, and the injured party the charge against him. It is self-evident that a thief omitted to make his act public knowledge, one of the reasons why he was so much despised. Summoning usually was done at the offender's home or the assembly on the prosecutor's initiative. The court was nominated by the chieftain and consisted in all probability of thirty-six lay judges. Men present at the time of summoning might be formally called as witnesses to take note of the offence and to give testimony under oath before the court of what they had seen and heard. In general witnesses had to be present at every stage in the procedure and were named to witness that formal means of proof had been brought. Then there was the panel of neighbors, consisting of qualified people living closest to the legal home of the prosecuted or of the prosecutor. Depending on the nature of the case, five or nine neighbors were called. They had to deliver verdicts under oath on circumstances, motives, and facts before a court and to declare that formal means of proof had been produced. The panel of neighbors was a typically Icelandic feature. In other Scandinavian countries a panel of family members had to act as oath-helpers, or compurgators, to support an accused man's denial. Because of the settlement the Icelanders did not have many relatives ready to hand, and the new form that developed in Iceland was the panel of neighbors. Major theft cases, like other cases where a greater degree of public interest was involved, required a panel of twelve, formed by the chieftain and eleven men nominated by him to provide formal means of proof.

Thieves in the Jónsbók

In the year 1281 the Alþing ratified the Jónsbók, based for the greater part on the Norwegian Landlov. The new lawbook also contained a special section devoted to thieves and theft called "þjófabálkr." It runs as follows:

The first thing is that nobody among us shall steal from the other. An exception has to be made for a man who steals food because he is not able to earn himself a living by work, and who steals out of starvation. That theft is by no means punishable. . . . But if a man who is capable to earn himself a living, and who was not known as a thief before, steals something to the value of one ounce, an action of theft has to be brought at the þing, and he can redeem flogging by paying three marks to the king. If he steals a second time to the value of one ounce, he can redeem flogging by paying six marks. If he does not pay this amount he will be flogged, and with a key he is branded on his cheek [see Figure 1]. If he steals for the third time to the value of one ounce, he will be flogged and the king takes six marks of his property. If the same man steals more frequently he will be killed. But if a man steals to the value of one mark and was not known as a thief before, an action has to be brought against him, and he can redeem himself by paying thirteen marks to the king or be outlawed. But if he steals more frequently he will be killed. If a thief steals to the value of two marks for the first time he has lost all his movables, but if he owns land he can pay thirteen marks of it and be punished in a way the royal agent thinks appropriate, but save his life. If the same man is more frequently charged with theft, he has lost his hand, his movables and his life. Equally guilty as the thief is the one who knowingly accepts stolen goods as a present, buys them or hides them, and keeps them secretly, only he will not be killed for that. He is called an accomplice. Only half so guilty as the thief is the one who eggs on to theft, unless he advises his dependents under sixteen years of age to go stealing. In that case he will be punished fully as though he had stolen himself.

Chapter 2. How a thief has to be caught and sentenced. If a thief has been caught one has to bind the stolen goods on his back in the commune where he was caught, and take him tied to the policeman [see Figures 2 and 3]. The policeman detains him until the þing takes place, and afterwards he takes him to the coast or a lavafield or some other place that seems fit. And the policeman charges a man to kill him, and so it applies to all thieves. The farmers are obliged to follow the thief to the execution; that is their responsibility. If they refuse to follow, each one of them pays half a mark to the king. The one who refuses to have the thief sentenced according to the law pays half a mark to the king, even if the sheriff does not want to inflict punishment. All property taken from the thief is for the one who caught him, unless other people claim it for witnesses, but all the other movables are the king's. The one who binds the thief is responsible for him on paying four marks to the king until he delivers him bound at the house of the policeman, witnesses being present. But if the thief offers resistance he will be banished. If a man let go a thief, then he has to pay four marks to the king, and this applies to the policeman and anybody else.[30]

Where the procedure is concerned, the neighbors do not appear anymore in the Jónsbók, for they have been replaced by a panel of compurgators, appointed to support the accused man's denial. Theft cases normally required a "séttareiðr" (an oath of six).[31] The articles on house-search are virtually unaltered.[32] New provisions concerned the following thefts:[33]

If a man steals a hawk, tied to its nest, and hides it, then he is a thief if the man who owned the bird publishes it. If a man steals a seal from somebody's

Figure 1. A thief is branded on his cheek. This woodcut from the Skarðsbók, a fourteenth-century Jónsbók manuscript, appears in a section relating to theft.

Figure 2. A thief with a stolen ram on his back, and, subsequently, the thief on the gallows. This woodcut is from a fourteenth-century Jónsbók manuscript, Gl. Kgl. sml. 3269a 4to.

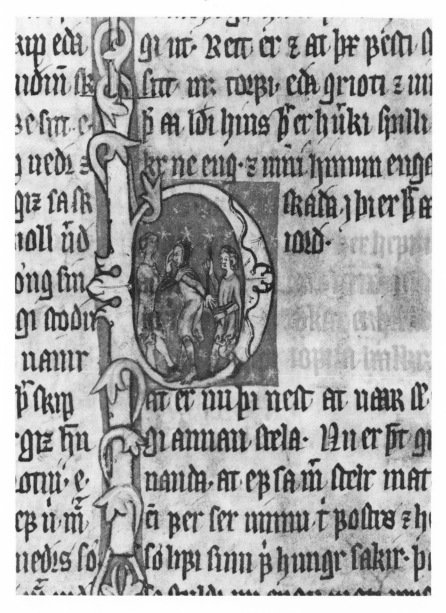

Figure 3. In this woodcut from the Svalbarðsbók, a Jónsbók manuscript from the fourteenth century, a captured thief is taken to the policeman.

land, then he is a thief if it is so big that an action is brought. He can deny it with an oath of six, but pays a fine of three marks if he fails in taking the oath, and the same applies to the hawks. The king gets the fines.

To sell the king's lands without his permission is punished in the same way.[34]

Comparison of Old and New

The Grágás was a collection of customary law that arose in a society where the free farmers at the Alþing decided what was and what was not law. Rights were personal, and it was necessary that every free adult of twelve years and older had a profound knowledge of his rights and duties because there was no central authority to see that the laws were being respected. In view of this origin it is not surprising that the lawbook focuses on the rights and duties of the freemen, that in the "Searches Section" the starting-point is formed by every free farmer's right to property, and that theft is considered a violation of this right. This attitude is perfectly illustrated by the section's opening sentence: "Everybody in our country shall keep what he owns." The injured person plays the lead and his task is comprehensive; he has to catch the thief, summon him, call the neighbors for valuation and to serve on the panel, distinguish between minor and major theft, and execute the sentence. Throughout the Grágás the duty to publish crimes is stressed, and this makes it comprehensible that anyone who omitted this was seen as an unworthy member of society. Concern for the criminal and the motives of his act was fully absent.

The Jónsbók was promulgated by the central authority in the person of the Norwegian king. The opening line of its section on theft reads: "Nobody among us shall steal from the other." This contrasts sharply with the Grágás, reminding us of one of the ten commandments. In the new lawbook the sinner comes to the fore, and attention is paid to him and to the motives for his sin. Extenuating circumstances are considered, especially in relation to food theft. If somebody steals out of hunger because he is unable to work, he will not be punished. Not only the stolen goods' value, but also the number of times a theft was committed are taken into consideration when fixing the penalty. Punishment obtains a preventive character, and the thief is given a chance to mend his ways. The injured person sees his role very much reduced. He has to deliver the thief at the policeman's house, and after the condemnation he has to accompany the criminal to the place of execution. "That is their responsibility," the Jónsbók states expressly.

This change of conception involving concern for the thief as an individual, and for the motives that influenced his act, originates from the

Christian way of thinking. That these ideas were not new in Iceland is shown by a statute issued around the year 1178 by þorlákr helgi, bishop of Skálholt, that pays attention to thieves and theft and distinguishes between theft out of wickedness and theft out of poverty.[35] It is one of the oldest statutes, issued by the bishop in his attempts to reform the Icelandic church. Some provisions of the statutes were ratified by the Alþing, for until about 1200 the ecclesiastical legislation formed part of the secular. The deterioration of economic circumstances during the twelfth and thirteenth centuries, causing doubtless more hunger and poverty than in previous times, may have added to the new point of view. The Grágás considered a thief's accomplice and the one who put him up to theft to be as bad and punishable as the thief himself. The Jónsbók, on the contrary, held that the person who counseled theft was only half as guilty as the offender. This change also gives evidence of Christian influences stressing individual responsibility as opposed to the collective responsibility of former times.

The introduction discussed the important role played in the early Icelandic society by a man's honour. In the Grágás the enumeration of many transgressions as being offensive to someone's honour provides evidence of this high estimation. One of these is the provision of a prosecution for malicious speech involving a charge for theft. The role of honour was considerably deemphasized in North European societies after the spread of Christianity. The new faith preached obedience and toleration, and it was sustained in this attitude by the monarchy which, in close co-operation with the Church, had undergone profound changes since the early Middle Ages. No longer lacking legal and illegal masculine descendants, kings were chosen on the basis of their ability to act as leaders in times of war, although kingship was made hereditary and monarchs were considered God's representatives on earth. Among the people obedience gradually took the place of self-consciousness, and honour gave way to subordination. The lawbooks reflect these changes by focusing not on a man's honour, but rather on the king's, and by making lese majesty liable to severe punishments. The Jónsbók inserted far fewer articles than the Grágás on violations of a man's honour, and the prescription on malicious speech relating to a charge for theft was omitted.

In general a thief was looked upon by the Grágás as a man who by his act had lost his right of immunity; he might be killed without redress, and he could be enslaved or outlawed. The original conception of vengence underwent a restriction under the influence of Christianity and the development of the monarchy. Both pleaded strongly against blood vengeance, but in Norway King Magnús did not succeed until 1273 in abolishing it by law. Vengeance has disappeared totally from the Jónsbók, and the same holds true for the idea that a thief is a man without rights. The number of penalties of outlawry is significantly reduced. Instead, a new system is introduced that is deeply influenced by medieval West European culture. Punishments from now on are directed completely against the offender, and they are more differentiated than before, according to the crime's proportion and the number of times the crime involved was committed. Thus, punishment obtains a preventative character.

Corporal punishments were practically unknown in early medieval Scandinavia, and in all probability the oldest written laws did not contain any provisions on detention or a public death penalty. In Iceland the lawbooks and the saga literature do not mention corporal punishments with the exception sometimes of those practised on slaves. Detention is unknown either in daily life, where the locking up of children as a punitive measure was completely unusual,[36] or in the sphere of law. A freeman's right of immunity and of freedom, together with the high estimation of honour, were incompatible with a penalty system where personal freedom was at stake. The Jónsbók, under West European influences, introduced corporal punishments, detention, and a public death penalty. The corporal punishments involved whipping and branding, the last usually practised by marking the thief's cheek with a glowing key. Detention in the Jónsbók did not yet have the character of a penalty, as the criminal was locked up only temporarily by the policeman, pending the lawsuit. To a certain extent, corporal punishments could be redeemed by paying a fine to the king.

Although in medieval Europe the death penalty for a thief meant an execution by hanging, it is by no means certain that in Iceland this was the common way of execution. The Jónsbók used in this connection the word "drepa," which means to kill, to slay. The places summed up to be "most appropriate" for execution, a lava field or the coast, are not naturally the regions in Iceland where a tree or some wood was ready at hand for an execution by hanging. Fourteenth-century annals report that thieves as a rule were beheaded. Manuscript illustrations suggest that in later times execution was by hanging.

The ecclesiastical statute mentioned before shows that by 1178 the church had launched new ideas on punishment. Bishop þorlákr advises "a penance of five years. . . for a theft that cannot be paid back." He stresses compensation to the injured person and continues: "Punishment for a major theft should consist of fasting, chastisement, pray and kneel, and penance, depending on whether the thief has stolen out of wickedness or out of poverty until there has been [repayment] for the theft."[37]

Remarkable, too, in this connection is a letter from Pope Innocent IV in the year 1243, expressing his concern at the increase of criminality in Iceland, which is "situated in a so far remote part of the world that people from there seldom or never visit the Apostolic See." The Pope charges the abbot Björn at Nidaros (the archbishop of Nidaros, or Trondheim had jurisdiction over the Icelandic church) to examine secular and ecclesiastical criminals in relation to incendiarism, plunder, and sacrilege. The abbot had to give absolution on the condition that the offenders would pay the estimated traveling expenses for a journey to Rome and back, lodging included, in support of the Holy Land.[38]

We noticed that in cases of minor theft in Commonwealth times the prosecutor had a right to double compensation. The fine of three marks that was paid by the criminal was divided among the prosecutor, the lawspeaker, and the men of the spring assembly. The outlaw's confiscated property was allotted to his wife, the chieftain, the creditor, dependents, the prosecutor, and the men of the spring assembly. The Jónsbók also recognizes the prosecutor's right to a double compensation for minor theft. But the number of fines has increased enormously, and without exception these fines go to the king.

The Jónsbók has added some provisions that reflect political changes. This is in particular the case with the prescription relating to the theft of hawks. The word "haukr" is a collective noun for hawk and falcon. Of these birds it was especially the Icelandic gyrfalcon that was much sought after in medieval Europe, and there are many references to gifts of gyrfalcons made by Norwegian kings to the kings of other countries.[39] From time to time the church in Iceland and the Norwegian kings contested one another's right to the falcons,[40] but since 1262 the Icelandic falcons belonged definitively to the king's variable income from the island.[41] A way of catching young hawks and falcons was to tie them to their nest shortly before they flew out. At the same time the ownership of the falcons was established, the king acquired the monopoly of the Icelandic trade, and no doubt the sealskins formed an important article of commerce.

Judicial procedure likewise underwent some changes and was modeled after the Norwegian example. The typically Icelandic panel of neighbors gave way to panels of compurgators, or oath-helpers, who had to support the accused man's denial. A "lyrittareiðr" (oath of three) was required for minor crimes, and a "séttareiðr" (oath of six) for cases where grave offences were involved. It is clear that by the abolition of the function of chieftain and the appointment of royal officials the procedure as a whole gradually became a matter of the government.

Conclusion

In the preceding pages we have examined the laws on thieves and theft in a society that during the Middle Ages was exposed to important changes.

The submission to Norway entailed the establishment of a public authority. The sheriff, the policeman and the executioner made their appearance, and two of their tasks were to fight theft and punish thieves, tasks that previously had been in private hands. Doubtless this was favorable for the public security. The confiscated properties of criminals and the fines that passed into the hands of the public authority and from there to the king brought a situation that diminished the endless feuds between families and reduced bloodshed. But there is another side of the picture. The developments must have caused a growing impoverishment of the population because the price paid for the benefits of more public security was very high. In commonwealth times fines were divided among prosecutor and chieftain, and an outlaw's property was adjudged to his family and to society. Now, money, movables, and the land of condemned criminals fell into the king's hands, a situation that furthered a subordination of the farmers. The establishment of a public authority had earlier caused similar developments in Norway, Sweden, and Denmark.[42]

It was not only a matter of material decline, however, for by the political changes the farmer lost part of his responsibility. No longer was he supposed to have a role in lawmaking and in jurisdiction in general; no longer was he the central figure in the articles of law. His task in the prosecution of thieves and other criminals was strongly reduced and taken over, for the greater part, by the public authority that had to look after the execution of the sentences and whose share in the trial of criminals was increasing.

Great changes came about in the penal system, where a public death penalty, deprivation of liberty, and corporal punishments came to replace revenge and outlawry. The role played by the church in this process should not be underestimated. By stressing concepts like humility, tolerance, sin, and mercy, the church greatly contributed to a change of mentality, a change that we find reflected in the new ideas on punishment and the treatment of criminals. The thief was no longer a practically rightless individual. As a sinner he had a right to mercy, he could claim a differentiated judgment, and he had a new chance to mend his ways.

The changes sought by the Jónsbók were radical, and one can wonder whether the Icelanders were pleased with the introduction of the new lawbook. We are fortunate to have at our disposal an authoritative report on the discussion that arose when the Norwegian king's delegate, Loðinn Leppr, tried to persuade the Icelanders to accept the Jónsbók.[43] It was during the summer of 1281, when the Icelanders gathered at the Alþing, that the new lawbook met with much resistance. The penal provisions were thought too severe with regard to confiscations. The new laws did not fit in with the country's conditions, and they were in conflict with church laws. Three groups of people — royalists, clergy, and farmers — had written "on the roll" their objections after having studied it during the preceding winter. The objections of the royalists are not known with certainty. The clergy objected mainly to secular authority in church affairs. From the farmers' criticisms it is evident that they felt themselves deprived of their right of self-determination. They stipulated that "all people in this country are free to manage their own business." They criticized the removal of thieves. Moreover, they felt themselves deprived of their right to property, "everybody will rule his own property."

> Then the men went to the Law Council and everybody read what he had written down. Mr Loðinn grew very angry and said that the farmers puffed themselves up that they imagined they had to arrange the laws in the country on which only the king had to decide.

In spite of much resistance Mr. Loðinn managed to have the Jónsbók for the greater part accepted by the Alþing, and with that event a period of independence had definitively come to an end.

Notes

1. For general information, see P. G. Foote and D. M. Wilson, *The Viking Achievement* (London, 1973); G. Jones, *A History of the Vikings* (London, 1973); L. Musset, *Les peuples Scandinaves au moyen âge* (Paris, 1951); and *Kulturhistorisk Leksikon for Nordisk Middelalder* (København, 1982), 22 vols.
2. *Diplomatarium Islandicum*, ed. J. Sigurdsson (København and Reykjavík, 1857–76), 1:602.
3. *Grágás Konungsbók*, ed. V. Finsen (København, 1974) and *Grágás Staðar-hólsbók*, ed. V. Finsen (København, 1974). An English translation of the *Grágás* is in progress: *Laws of Early Iceland, Grágás I*, transl. A. Dennis, P. Foote, and R. Perkins, vol. 3 of *University of Manitoba Icelandic Studies* (Winnipeg, 1980); Aa Gregersen, *L'Islande, son Statut à travers les Âges* (Paris, 1937).
4. O. Lárusson, "Grágás og Logbækurnar," *Fylgir Árbók Háskola Islands* (Reykjavík, 1922); and *Jónsbók, Kong Magnus Hakonssons Lovbog for Island, vedtaget paa Altinget 1281*, ed. O. Halldórsson (Odense, 1970).
5. K. von Amira, *Die Germanischen Todesstrafen. Untersuchungen zur Rechts- und Religionsgeschichte*, Bd. 31, Abh. 3 of *Abhandlungen der Bayerischen Akademie der Wissenschaften*. Philosophisch-philologische und historische Klasse (München, 1922); and P. Merker, *Das Strafrecht der Altisländischen Grágás* (Altenburg, 1907).
6. *Grágás Konungsbók*, ed. Finsen, Chap. 227.
7. Ibid., Chap. 228.
8. Ibid., Chap. 229.
9. Ibid., Chap. 230.
10. *Grágás Staðarhólsbók*, transl. Dennis et al., in *Laws of Early Iceland, Grágás I*, 231.

11. *Grágás Konungsbók*, ed. Finsen, Chap. 224.
12. Ibid., Chap. 225.
13. Ibid., Chap. 215.
14. Ibid., Chap. 221.
15. Ibid., Chap. 224.
16. Ibid., Chap. 208.
17. *Flateyarbók*, ed. G. Vigfússon and C. R. Unger (Kristiania, 1860–68), 1:412.
18. A penny is a subdivision of an ounce, but the value varies from one-tenth to one-sixtieth of an ounce. An ounce-unit represents in Iceland normally the value of six ells of two ells wide cloth.
19. *Äldre Västgötalagen*, ed. E. Wessén (Stockholm, 1965), Tjb. 5:1.
20. Martina Stein-Wilkeshuis, "The Right to Social Welfare in Early Medieval Iceland," *Journal of Medieval History* 8 (1982): 343–52.
21. One mark equals 8 ounce-units. See also note 18.
22. L. Ingvarsson, *Refsingar á Íslandi á þjóðveldistímanum* (Reykjavík, 1970).
23. T. Wennström, *Tjuvnad og fornaemi* (Lund, 1936), 94 and *Äldre Västgötalagen*, ed. Wessén, Af Mandrepi 8:2.
24. *The Earliest Norwegian Laws, Being the Gulathing and the Frostathing Law*, transl. L. M. Larson (New York, 1937), Gulathing Law, Chaps. 160 and 253.
25. Dorothy Whitelock, *The Beginnings of English Society* (Harmondsworth, 1965), Chap. 7.
26. Von Amira, *Die Germanischen Todesstrafen*, 59; *Danmarks gamle Love paa Nutidsdansk*, ed. E. Kroman and S. Iuul (København, 1948), 3, Skånelagen, Chap. 151.
27. J. Spoelstra, *De Vogelvrijen in de IJslandse letterkunde* (Haarlem, 1938).
28. *Landnámabók Björns Jónssonar*, ed. Jakob Benediktsson (Reykjavík, 1958), 189.
29. Gunnar Thoroddsen, *Fjölmæli* (Reykjavík, 1967), 16, 17, 18; *Reykdælasaga ok Víga-Skútu*, vol. 10 of *Íslenzk Fornrit*, ed. Jóhannes Halldórsson (Reykjavík, 1933), 155–59; *Víga-Glúmssaga*, vol. 9 of *Ísl. Fornrit*, 20–24 and *Laxdælasaga*, vol. 5 of *Íslenzk Fornrit*, 239–47.
30. *Jónsbók*, ed. Halldórsson, Book 10, Chap. 1.
31. Ibid., Chap. 19.
32. Ibid., Chap. 6.
33. Ibid., Chap. 9.
34. Ibid., Chap. 10.
35. *Diplomatarium Islandicum*, ed. Sigurdsson, 1:242.
36. Martina Stein-Wilkeshuis, *Het kind in de Oudijslandse samenleving* (Groningen, 1970).
37. *Diplomatarium Islandicum*, ed. Sigurdsson, 1:242.
38. Ibid., 720.
39. Richard Vaughan, "The Arctic in the Middle Ages," *Journal of Medieval History* 8 (1982): 313–42.
40. *Árnasaga byskups*, vol. 1 of Byskupasögur, ed. Guðni Jónsson (Reykjavík 1948), Chap. 29.
41. *Diplomatarium Islandicum*, ed. Sigurdsson, 1:602.
42. Musset, *Les peuples Scandinaves*, Chap. 3.
43. *Árnasaga byskups*, ed. Guðni Jónsson, Chap. 29.

The Self-Image of the Magistrate in Sixteenth-Century France

Raymond A. Mentzer, Jr.
Montana State University, Bozeman

Esteem for continental Europe's criminal justice system had declined noticeably by the mid-eighteenth century. Cesare Beccaria's *Trattato dei delitti e della pene* of 1764, as well as Voltaire's defense of Jean Calas and subsequent commentary on Beccaria, seriously challenged the legitimacy of existing procedure. Others joined Beccaria and Voltaire in voicing grave doubts centering on the use of torture, the frequency of brutal corporal punishments, and the lack of uniformity within the law. These enlightened critics were, on the whole, careful and specific in their remarks. Yet the eventual result was a popular and often half-enunciated notion of early modern justice as overly harsh and cruel. According to a standard textbook judgment, the jurists and *philosophes* of the Enlightenment sought, in their advocacy of reform, to "humanize the criminal law."[1]

This brief essay is certainly not an adequate forum to weigh the humane and inhumane aspects of pre-Beccarian justice. Rather, the analysis that follows concentrates on the figure and self-image of the early modern judge. It describes the criminal procedure and details the judge's role within the process. The basis for the analysis is a series of mid-sixteenth century French woodcuts that suggest that the magistrate and other court officials by no means viewed themselves as principals in an unusually rigorous or dreadful system. They would not have identified with the flail-bearing Talus of Spenser's *Faerie Queene*. They carried no swift sword and showed little interest in weighing souls on a balance. They preferred instead the attributes of benevolent justice and emphasized their own temperate and merciful qualities.

The illustrations appear in Jean Milles de Souvigny's *Praxis criminis persequendi*, first published at Paris in 1541.[2] The author was a knowledgeable jurist associated with the administration of the king's waters and forests (*eaux et forêts*) and attached specifically to the multi-faceted Parisian court known as the *table du marbre*.[3] The treatise takes the form of an imaginary trial and allows Milles de Souvigny, thoroughly familiar with legal practice, to comment on criminal process in the tradition of the medieval glossator. On each page there is a central text surrounded by an elaborate gloss. The illustrations are the novel feature. Thirteen in number, they portray criminal justice from the commission of a crime through inquest and apprehension, interrogation and torture, condemnation and execution. The adoption of this inquisitorial procedure, or more precisely its uniform practice by French courts, was a fairly recent development—hence the value of the handbook, with its comprehensive explanations and meticulous woodblock prints.

The format employed in the *Praxis*, a combination of legal commentary and didactic illustrations, did have contemporary parallels. The *Bambergische halsgerichtsordnung* (Bamberg criminal code) was issued for use by that city's courts in 1507. Though considerably less ornate, the Bamberg woodcuts are similar in spirit to those of the *Praxis* and may have served to inspire de Souvigny and his artist. Representations of the recording of depositions, torture, and final sentencing display the same essential elements. The choice and treatment of subject matter, on the other hand, tend to be more allegorical. A depiction of the abuse of justice, for example, has the magistrate and six associates sitting blindfolded and dressed in fool's costumes. A half-century later, in 1564, Joost Damhouder's *Practique iudiciaire ès causes criminelles*, a commentary on Flemish procedure, also included illustrations. They provide little iconographic detail, however, and concentrate more on criminal acts than trial procedure.[4]

The publication of these various manuals was, in some ways, associated with the full reception of the Roman-canon model of inquisitorial procedure. The late fifteenth and early sixteenth centuries were a formative period in the evolution of the continental criminal system. And legislation such as the German imperial *Constitutio Criminalis Carolina* (1532) and the royal French ordonnances of Blois (1498) and Villers-Cotterets (1539) represent the culmination of a long and deliberate process. The ancient accusatorial procedure—characterized by the private complaint, the detention of accused and accuser pending trial, and the judicial duel—had fallen into disuse. The older imminent mode of proof, which in a feudal age often meant trial by battle or ordeal, left the issue of criminal intent unresolved—unresolved by the earthly magistrate. God distinguished guilt from innocence through the armed confrontation of two noble combatants and trial by fire or water for common folk. This judgment of God (*judicium Dei*) had little regard for what actually occurred at the time of the offense, proved less and less satisfying, and gradually disappeared.

The substitution of trial by inquest (*inquisitio*) for trial by physical ordeal and battle began with the twelfth-century revival of Roman law among the recently established Italian universities. The new method of proof soon found favor with the Church and the northern city-states of Italy. The Fourth Lateran Council of 1215 decreed it as standard procedure for all ecclesiastical tribunals. And when the system slowly spread beyond the Alps, it neatly coincided with the general post-feudal trend toward the centralization of royal power. An officer of the state, the magistrate, thoroughly and leisurely investigated criminal intention. He established the facts of the offense through the examination of witnesses under oath and the interrogation of the accused in secret. He gathered the evidence in a written dossier that, in turn, provided the basis for judgment and final sentencing. The burden of criminal prosecution shifted from private to public domain, the investigatory modes became far more precise and complete, and the role of the judge was measurably enhanced.[5]

The increased importance of the magistrate permitted, even required, the fuller development of his portrait, and de Souvigny's treatise serves this purpose. It begins logically with the commission of a crime, in this instance homicide (*Figura Homicidii Perpetrati*).[6] Five men, armed with knives and swords, engage in the killing of four others. The scene, an act of violence appropriate to the age, takes place at night within the confines of a town square. Two obviously awakened men, holding lighted candles, peer from upper-story windows of the surrounding buildings. Two details are especially noteworthy: time of day and number of witnesses. French customary law regarded slayings carried out under cover of darkness as unemendable. A killing that occurred at night was a hidden, rather than open, misdeed and therefore was presumed to be murder and not the more legally neutral act of homicide. Secondly, and in some contradiction to the nocturnal setting, two persons witness the crime with the aid of candlelight. The Roman-canon law of proof required two eyewitnesses for conviction of crimes the punishment for which involved death or mutilation. Anything less—one witness or circumstantial evidence—was inadequate for condemnation, although it could provide the basis for prosecution and the elicitation of a confession, either voluntary or through torture.[7]

The next step required that the competent magistrate possess knowledge that a crime may have been perpetrated. Numerous commentators have attempted systematic explanation of the ways by which the judge might take cognizance. The sixteenth-century modes can be summarized as three: flagrant delict, public renown, and denunciation. Flagrant delict was somewhat rare, for it necessitated capture in the act. Public renown was, in its own way, equally unusual. Rumors and hearsay, at times grave but never precise or traceable to a single source, occasionally warranted inquiry. The denunciation was the most common manner whereby the judiciary became aware of an allegedly criminal act. The denouncer was not an accuser in the strict legal sense. He merely reported what seemed to him to be a crime. He was not required to sustain the legal veracity of his allegation or bear the costs of litigation. The decision to investigate and prosecute rested with the bench. The informing party would probably be called upon to offer testimony and name other witnesses, but aside from this he remained in the background. Even if the denouncer wished to pursue the matter through private complaint, assuming for example that he was himself the injured party, he could only do so as a civil plaintiff joined to the public criminal action.

The structure of the denunciatory process naturally poses questions concerning motivation. Were there safeguards against malice and personal enmity? The conscientious and thorough magistrate would be expected to address this issue in his initial investigation. In his examination of witnesses, among whom the denouncer typically figured, he would seek to determine the reputation and reliability of those who offered testimony as well as their relationship to the suspect. Another discouragement to abuse was the threat of countersuit. The defendant would have the opportunity in the course of his trial to confront the witnesses against him and offer his personal objections to them. Such objections normally related to the capacity or motive of the witnesses. If the objections were sustained and the suspect released, he could bring suit against his denouncer for false witness and slander.[8]

De Souvigny presents a variation of the denunciation by having the bodies of the murdered men physically laid at the entrance to the court (*Figura Percunctationis Vulnerum*),[9] a striking example of *corpus delecti*. Several men inspect the lethal wounds, while mothers, wives, and children gather at the foot of the stairs to lament the slain. Women weep and clasp their hands in grief. A young mother comforts the infant at her breast. Another woman approaches the tribunal's entry with a small child in tow. Two older siblings kneel in supplication. The woman asks the court to initiate proceedings and presents a written petition to this effect. Her action kept with existing practice, for the judiciary frequently authorized inquiries upon receipt of such requests.[10] It was a form of denunciation. Certain architectural features of the courtroom and *palais de justice* stress the community's access to justice by recalling the Roman and medieval practice of holding judicial sessions in open air.[11] Though the members of the court are sheltered, the front of the chamber lets onto the exterior via an elaborate archway flanked by two spacious windows. The judge and his assistants face the mourners and stand ready to entertain their grievances.

Actual trial process began with the inquiry or inquisition whence this type of procedure takes its name. The ordonnance of Villers-Cotterets

Figure 1. The beginning of the trial process—the investigation (information). Woodblock print from Jean Milles de Souvigny's *Praxis criminis persequendi* (1541).

stipulated that the judge, upon notification of the crime, should himself investigate or order an assistant to do so. The information, its technical name in French law, consisted of the secret depositions of witnesses against the suspect in question. It occurred prior to the suspect's appearance in court, and he typically remained at large during its conduct. The subject of the investigation often had no knowledge of it, played no active role in its preparation, and was rarely apprised of its contents.[12]

The *Praxis'* depiction of the information (*Figura Quaestionis*, Figure 1)[13] reveals its basic characteristics. The court tended to question prominent members of the community as well as persons who had specific knowledge of the crime. Each witness (*testis*, pl. *testes*) was heard privately and separately by the judge or special officer called an examiner (*enquêteur* or *quaesitor*). Several witnesses in the right foreground await the opportunity to offer testimony. To the left, an examiner takes a deposition. Here there is a slight error in that the examiner would not normally record the testimony himself; a notary usually assisted in the task. Upon completion of the deposition, it would be read to the witness in its entirety, and he fixed his signature or mark to the document.[14]

The iconography fully expresses the solemnity of this gathering of depositions. The testor has his right forearm raised in confirmation of his oath (*fides levata*) to be truthful. At his feet sits a small dog, perhaps a reference to the requirement of faithfulness.[15] Finally, in a manner reminiscent of certain Italian compositions, the artist places the sequel to the inquisitory deposition in the upper right-hand corner. Assuming that the information revealed sufficient grounds for prosecution, the judge would order the suspect to be summoned or captured. Thus the guards escort the bound defendant into the courtroom. The enthroned posture of the magistrate, a theme repeated throughout the *Praxis*, is noteworthy. Given that the judicial function is a prerogative of sovereign political power, it is the king, or a magistrate officiating in his name, who presides. The judge sits upon a canopied throne, symbolic of royal dignity. The cloth of honor draped behind serves to enhance the image. And he holds in his right hand a scroll or rolled manuscript, a representation of the law.[16]

The testimony assembled during the informational phase became the basic document for the trial. It supplied the evidence for arrest, formed the framework for the interrogation of the accused, and contained the statements he was obliged to refute in order to establish his innocence. Yet the suspect did not participate in the preparation of this dossier, nor would its contents be communicated to him in any precise fashion during the trial. He had to rely upon the court's impartiality in gathering accurate and true evidence in a document to which only members of the judiciary had access.

If the magistrate chose to prosecute, he had at his disposal two types of decree: personal summons and bodily arrest.[17] De Souvigny gives examples of each. One woodcut (*Citatio per quatuor Edicta*)[18] places two mounted officials in a town square amid a growing crowd. One sounds the announcing trumpet, while the other reads the decree aloud. A personal summons, generally used for lesser offenses, required the accused to present himself within three days, lest he be declared contumacious. Compliance did not normally lead to imprisonment. The court usually granted provisional liberty, confining the defendant to the town in which the tribunal sat. For grave transgressions where the suspect might be tempted to flee rather than voluntarily submit, the judge could invoke a decree of bodily arrest. The depiction of this form (*Figura Praehensionis Reorum*)[19] gives the circumstances of a half-dozen or so captures. Men are seized in the countryside and the village, stirred from the bed and dining table, interrupted while engaged in conversation and tennis games. They are then placed in prison, the equivalent of preventative detention pending trial.

Once the suspect heeded the personal summons or was arrested, the magistrate immediately proceeded to a careful interrogation. He examined the defendant on the charges and evidence assembled during the inquisitorial phase. Most sessions began with a series of stock questions that established the accused's age, profession, residence, and the like. The judge then turned to those areas where he possessed detailed knowledge, basing most of his questions on incidents described in the information, the depositions recorded earlier by the court. Although the modern observer often finds the questions leading or suggestive, the prudent and patient interrogator left no issue unresolved. The appropriate illustration (*Figura Interrogationis*, Figure 2)[20] shows a jailed suspect entering from the right in the company of guards. Subsequently perched on the traditional stool (*sellette*),[21] he is alone with the judge, yet bound and shackled in view of the seriousness of a murder charge. The other principal is the clerk of the court (center foreground) who kept an abbreviated version of the questions and answers. The defendant swore to tell the truth and, upon completion of the interrogation, signed or marked the clerk's transcription.

Conspicuously absent is a defense attorney. The law denied the accused benefit of counsel on the theory that it would needlessly delay and obscure an otherwise honest and dispassionate investigation into the truth. The major exception occurred when a private party attached himself to the criminal proceedings by means of a civil suit.[22] In such cases, both plaintiff and defendant retained lawyers. One final handicap for the accused was the requirement that he respond to the judge's queries without knowledge of that which was contained in the information. He often had little more than a vague idea of

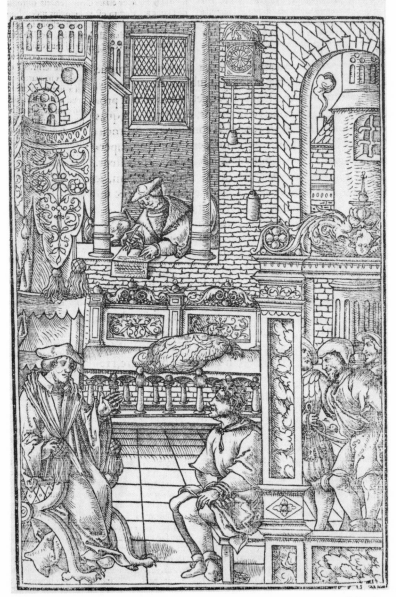

Figure 2. The magistrate's interrogation of the suspect. Woodblock print from Jean Milles de Souvigny's *Praxis criminis persequendi* (1541).

the specifics in the charges against him and was at a distinct disadvantage.[23]

The magistrate, here sitting amid the royal attributes of throne and ornate canopy, raises his left hand in an interactive, questioning gesture. He seeks to elicit further evidence and, if possible, obtain a truthful confession. Two iconographic devices convey the ideal of the protracted interrogation. Almost central to the composition is a large cushion, the emblem of mercy, and above it hangs Temperance's clock, suggesting moderation.[24] Justice, in this view, ought to be imbued with both qualities.

The confrontation of witnesses and the accused (*Figura Commissionis Testium*, Figure 3)[25] constituted the next stage of the trial. The magistrate first admits each witness individually and separately. The testor sits to the right of the presiding judge and with his right hand raised in solemn oath summarizes his original testimony. A judicial officer on the balcony above checks to be certain that the statements are subtantially the same as those contained in the earlier deposition. Afterwards, the deposition is read to the witness and he is asked in what ways he would confirm, alter, or correct it. Guards then deliver the restrained defendant from his cell, an act portrayed beyond the screen behind the magistrate. The accused sits facing judge and witness. To his right is an associate jurist and toward the left a notary records the proceedings. The dossier, now a thick book, rests on the scribe's desk, while above and in the background other witnesses wait their turn to appear. The judge raises one hand in a sign of speech and holds the scroll of the law in the other.

The confrontation had several purposes. It obviated the problem of mistaken identity. The witness had to affirm that the defendant was the person of whom he spoke in the deposition. It also permitted the accused, again without benefit of counsel, to state his objections to the person of the witness. This was his first and only opportunity to argue, for instance, that the witness was prejudiced. Yet the objections had to be offered prior to the reading of the deposition. The logic behind the requirement was to force the accused to disassociate his objections to the person of the witness from his objections to the substance of the testimony. Once the objections had been stated, the court proceeded with the reading of the deposition and permitted the defendant to contest it.[26] This procedure was repeated for each witness. And only upon completion of this phase of the trial would the court consider the question of release on bail and entertain a formal defense.

Prevailing statutes and theory provided that in cases of heinous crimes, bail was denied until completion of the confrontations and verifications of testimony. Not only did the judiciary desire a firmer notion of the gravity of the affair before granting bail, but it sought also to avoid falsification of the modes of evidence and in particular the subornation of witnesses. An

FIGVRA COMMISSIONIS TESTIVM.

Figure 3. The formal confrontation between the witnesses and the accused in the presence of the magistrate. Woodblock print from Jean Milles de Souvigny's *Praxis criminis persequendi* (1541).

obvious exception that permitted earlier release was an instance of critical illness or infirmity.[27]

The formal defense permitted the accused was restricted and indirect. Juridical theory held that a negative fact such as nonculpability required no proof. Failure to establish legal proof of the defendant's guilt rendered useless any countervailing proof on his part. He was limited, in fact, to raising objections to witnesses and offering peremptory facts favoring acquittal. Moreover, the rules of procedure seriously hampered these efforts. The accused was denied legal counsel in the organization and conduct of his defense, and the court provided no more than an oral reading of the testimony against him. He had no opportunity for a leisurely perusal of the written evidence in consulation with an attorney. He even needed the court's approval to summon witnesses on his behalf.[28] From de Souvigny's perspective the entire matter had little direct bearing on the magistrate's role as compassionate investigator of the truth. He dismisses it without illustration.

As the proceedings drew near their close, the trial could move in several directions. If nothing had been proven or if the defendant had successfully refuted the testimony against him, the case could be dismissed. If evidence was strong but insufficient for condemnation, it could move to torture. Finally, if adequate proof existed or a confession had been elicited, it could enter final sentencing. The *Praxis* illustrates the three alternatives.

In the case of dismissal (*Figura Publicati Diplomatis Gratiae*),[29] the defendant who had been pictured in the interrogation and confrontation is pardoned. Absolution pure and simple was rare and infrequent for sixteenth-century justice. The courts declined to acquit fully and preferred instead a verdict that amounted to culpability not proven.[30] The fate of de Souvigny's model defendant appears to follow this pattern. In the scene, the judge rests on his throne and six associate magistrates stand to his sides. It recalls earlier imperial and Christian representations of the political sovereign or Christ in Majesty (*Maiestas Domini*) along with the "guardians of the divine flank" (*custodes divini lateris*).[31] Below these wielders of royal justice sits a scribe engrossed in his transcription. Facing them are the relieved yet reserved defendant and the jailer who will soon free him. On the near side of the bar, which separates audience from participants in any courtroom, the accused's wife and small child anxiously await his release. Several bystanders casually watch, and a sergeant assures the reign of order. A sense of clemency and fairness prevails. Justice and those who serve its cause wisely and beneficiently separate innocent from guilty and return the former to the bosom of his family.

An alternative to dismissal, the continuation of process and use of judicial torture was a distinct possibility in the adjudication of serious crimes—

murder, theft, forgery and heresy — where condemnation entailed "blood sanctions" such as death or maiming. The Roman-canon standard of proof sufficient for conviction of heinous crime required either two wholly unimpeachable witnesses or the defendant's voluntary confession before the judge. Anything less did not constitute full proof. Circumstantial evidence, allowable under the English jury system, was inadequate on the continent, but under certain circumstances did suffice for authorization to torture. Coercion, in this case, secured the vital confession.[32]

The chief precautions against irresponsible use were the requirement of half proof, the right of appeal, and the necessity of subsequent ratification. A suspect could not be tortured unless there existed half proof, either one eyewitness or grave incriminating evidence. Although jurists' opinions varied regarding the exact constitution of this requirement, it did set limits for the invocation of torture. In addition, the defendant could usually appeal the decision. An appellate jurisdiction occasionally reversed the lower court's ruling and frequently moderated the terms of its application. Torture could be reduced to a psychologically forceful display of the instruments or an equally effective single "touch." Finally, the law stipulated that the defendant freely ratify his statements a day or so after the ordeal. No one could be condemned because of a confession made under torture if he did not persist in that confession thereafter. Voluntary repetition ratified it. Yet this requirement appears to have been circumvented. The jurist Jean Imbert reports that because many persons would totally deny whatever they confessed under torture, it became customary to condemn a person upon the confession made under torture if it conformed generally to the contents of the information.[33]

The frequency of torture is difficult to gauge and interpret. One study of criminal justice rendered by the Parlement of Paris during the first half of the sixteenth century finds wide variance according to the particular crime. Though the incidence of the application of torture averaged seventeen percent for the trial of major criminal offenses, it ranged from a low of seven percent in instances of heresy to a high of thirty percent for forgery cases.[34] This pattern suggests that much depended on the nature of the offense itself. Crimes such as homicide, theft, and forgery, where the frequency of torture was high, were typically committed by a single person or a small, tight-knit band of conspirators acting surreptitiously. The solitary and furtive character of these offenses left few eyewitnesses and increased the likelihood that the court would resort to torture in the absence of full proof. Heresy tended to be a more social activity. Believers frequently assembled for religious purposes, and proselytizing efforts, even when guarded, entailed incriminating contact with persons outside the group. Greater opportunity existed for personal testimony against heresy suspects and thereby diminished the necessity for

FIG. TORTVRAE COTHVRNORVM EXTRAORD.

Figure 4. Torture for the purpose of obtaining additional evidence from the accused. One of three woodblocks depicting methods of torture from Jean Milles de Souvigny's *Praxis criminis persequendi* (1541).

judicial torture.

De Souvigny and his artist devote three separate woodblock prints to torture.[35] Water torture (*Figura Torturae Gallicae Ordinariae*) was perhaps the most common and the strappado (*Figura Torturae Tholosanae*) the most barbarous, for it distended and dislocated the defendant's limbs. The depiction of another common device, the boot (*Figura Torturae Cothurnorum Extraord.*, Figure 4), contains the essentials of the act. The magistrate, standing near his throne, presides over the dungeon session. He holds the law in his left hand and lifts the other to interrogate. The questions he put to the defendant under torture were not meant to differ greatly from those posed in the original interrogation. This was an opportunity to acquire additional evidence, and the intelligent judge desired detailed responses that only the perpetrator of the crime would know. If the accused offered a confession, the precision of information confirmed it. The uninformed confession was of little value. A clerk takes down the questions and answers, another document to be added to the dossier beside him on the desk. One element missing here, though present in the illustration of water torture, is two honorable men, usually local lawyers, who observed and assisted. The torturers drive wedges along the tightly bound "laced boot" (*brodequin*) and thereby increase pressure on the leg and ankle. They seem to be "doing their duty" with little evidence of enjoyment or antagonism. If anything, the man holding the defendant appears to express sympathy. The victim grits his teeth — as well he might. The burning candle, located on a small shelf in the upper left, may serve the practical need for illumination. On the other hand, it traditionally symbolized the all-seeing wisdom of God and was often associated with the taking of an oath and the act of torture. Pieter Bruegel the Elder, for example, places a lighted candle beside the torturer's rack in his "Justice" (1559).[36] The image seems appropriate; for the magistrate, after all, sought through torture precise, reliable, and otherwise unobtainable evidence.

The investigatory stages completed, the magistrate retires to ponder the evidence and consult with his associates. A decision must be rendered and judgment pronounced. The frontal orientation and symmetry of the condemnation scene (*Figura Condemnationis Reorum*, Figure 5)[37] call to mind popular Northern European Last Judgment imagery.[38] The judge, possessed of an almost sacerdotal quality, resides upon his throne flanked by four associate jurists. The hand gestures, however, differ from those previously noted. The right is foreshortened, extended toward the viewer and turned downward — a "concluding" gesture. Conversation has ended. The other, drawn across his breast, conveys the notion that he has consulted his "heart" and is about to render his disposition.[39] He no longer holds the scroll of the law, for it offers little further guidance. The ubiquitous clerk prepares the trial's

FIGVRA CONDEMNATIONIS REORVM

Figure 5. The magistrate's condemnation of the accused. Woodblock print from Jean Milles de Souvigny's *Praxis criminis persequendi* (1541).

final document. The presence of the executor of high justice and the burning torch correctly portray judicial practice. So, too, do the defendants' postures. Heads bared, hands bound, and legs shackled, they kneel with contrition and penitence, awaiting their fate. Indeed, justice seeks not revenge, but a recognition on the part of the criminal that he has erred and transgressed. The emphasis is upon repentance and emendation, even in the face of impending death.

A collage of the various modes of execution (*Figura Reorum Plecten-dorum*)[40] concludes the series. A huge crowd assembles on foot and horseback. Others watch the spectacle from high window vantage. The condemned die on gallows, the block, the wheel, and a variety of other deadly instruments. Justice may be compassionate, but it is also firm.

Throughout these trial scenes, two things are noteworthy by their absence: the figure of the public prosecutor and fully developed allegorical imagery. The royal attorney general (*procureur général du roi*) had since the fourteenth century assumed the role of public prosecutor for criminal litigation in France. He could initiate judicial action and his subsequent motions paced trial procedure. He recommended the initial gathering of depositions, motioned for the suspect's arrest or summons, consulted with the magistrate on the decision to use torture, and presented his final "conclusions" immediately prior to judgment and sentencing.[41] The omission of this crucial figure cannot be accidental. Would his presence not simply detract and distract from the visual encomium of the judge? A related interpretation explains the lack of extensive allegorical devices.

Nowhere does "Dame Justice" appear blindfolded with sword and balance. The officers of the court never hold the thorny stick or rod.[42] The symbols that do occur — clock and pillow, for example — seem informative rather than heavily admonitory, a matter of record rather than allegory. They remind the members of the court to be temperate and moderate. Another characteristic of the woodcuts that runs to a similar effect is the repeated and endearing presence of small children. On some occasions (the presentation of the murdered bodies or the release of the defendant), they add a compelling touch, standing at their mothers' skirts holding silly, irrelevant toys such as a miniature windmill or a bow and arrow. At other times, they furnish witty relief from the gravity of the subject matter. The tableau of arrests contains a streetpeddler whose tray is about to be upended by a mischievous urchin. And in the final woodcut, one youngster is about to vomit in response to the array of public executions being carried out in the town square. These childish details help deflate the solemn, even pompous legal proceedings described in de Souvigny's text, and they lend an altogether human perspective.

The one properly legal device that most frequently reappears is the scroll of the law held fast in the judge's hand. It is a learned attribute and contrasts, for instance, with the *Bambergische halsgerichtsordnung*, whose magistrate always clutches a rod symbolic of corrective power. Implicit in the *Praxis'* presentation of criminal procedure is a distinction between the law and executive force. The magistrate does not simply administer the sovereign law, that is to say, judge in the king's stead. He also commands the necessary royal executive and punitive power.[43] These two aspects of justice, however, are sharply separated in the woodcuts. Not unlike courtroom scenes from the imperial Roman world,[44] de Souvigny's magistrate is in every sense magisterial. He presides over scenes of interrogation, judgment, and condemnation. He serves the law, which is his infallible guide in the provision of justice. Lesser agents, often armed with swords, arrest and conduct the suspect; they torture and execute him. These deputies are executive power.

Through a variety of traditional imperial and Christian themes, now secularized in the service of the royal French state, a distinct impression emerges. The magistrate is a thoughtful person, steeped in the law. He investigates thoroughly and dispenses justice compassionately. The inquisitorial system, after all, places a special burden on a wise and impartial magistracy. Thus the harsher aspects of justice tend to be masked. The emphasis is on integrity and virtue.

Notes

The author wishes to thank the National Endowment for the Humanities and The Newberry Library, Chicago, for support of his research.

1. R. R. Palmer and Joel Colton, *A History of the Modern World*, 4th ed. (New York, 1971), 329.

2. Jean Milles de Souvigny, *Praxis criminalis persequendi, elegantibus aliquot figuris illustrata, Ioanne Millaeo Boio Sylvigniaco. . . authore* (Paris, 1541). All references are to this initial edition. Subsequent editions appeared at Lyons, Paris, and Venice during the late-1540s and 1550s. The illustrations reproduced here were graciously provided through the Reuel Drinkwater and Saditha McCullough Robbins Fund of the Law Library, University of California, Berkeley.

3. The *table du marbre*, seated in the *palais* on the Ile de la Cité, included the courts of the admiralty, the constableship, and the waters and forests. The waters and forests administered the royal fisheries and forests along with the revenues derived from them. Roger Doucet, *Les institutions de la France au XVIe siècle* (Paris, 1948), 1:124–25 and 2:519–20. J. M. H. Salmon, *Society in Crisis: France in the Sixteenth Century* (New York, 1975), 73. Gaston Zeller, *Les institutions de la France au XVIe siècle* (Paris, 1948), 193–95.

4. Attributed to Johann von Schwarzenberg, the modern critical edition, containing reproductions of the original woodcuts, is *Die Bambergische halsgerichtsordnung*, (eds. J. Kohler and W. Scheel) (Halle, 1902). Joost Damhouder, *Practique*

iudiciaire ès causes criminelles (Antwerp, 1564).

5.   The adoption of Roman-canon inquisitorial procedure is described in R. Howard Bloch, *Medieval French Literature and Law* (Berkeley and Los Angeles, 1977); Adhemar Esmein, *Histoire de la procédure criminelle en France et spécialement de la procédure inquisitoire depuis le XIIIe jusqu'à nos jours* (Paris, 1882); John H. Langbein, *Prosecuting Crime in the Renaissance: England, Germany, France* (Cambridge, Mass., 1974); Bruce Lenman and Geoffrey Parker, "The State, the Community and the Criminal Law in Early Modern Europe," in *Crime and the Law: The Social History of Crime in Western Europe since 1500*, eds. V. A. C. Gatrell, Bruce Lenman, and Geoffrey Parker, (London, 1980); and for its specific application in heresy trials, Raymond A. Mentzer, Jr., *Heresy Proceedings in Languedoc, 1500–1560* (Philadelphia, 1984).

Alfred Soman, "Deviance and Criminal Justice in Western Europe, 1300–1800: An Essay in Structure," *Criminal Justice History: An International Annual* 1 (1980): 1–28, offers fresh and useful insights on questions of criminal justice and treatment of judicial documents. In addition, Soman's "Criminal Jurisprudence in Ancien-Régime France: The Parlement of Paris in the Sixteenth and Seventeenth Centuries," *Crime and Criminal Justice in Europe and Canada*, ed. Louis A. Knafla (Waterloo, 1981), 43–75, raises some of the very issues discussed in the present essay.

6.   Milles de Souvigny, *Praxis*, fol. 3.

7.   Bloch, *Literature and Law*, 34–35. Langbein, *Prosecuting Crime*, 4–5.

8.   Jean Bouteiller, *Somme rurale, ou le grand coustumier general de practique civil et canon* (Paris, 1603), 221. Doucet, *Institutions*, 2:536. Esmein, *La procédure criminelle*, 108–12. Annik Porteau-Bitker, "L'emprisonnement dans le droit laïque du moyen-âge," *Revue historique de droit français et étranger* 46 (1968): 225–26.

9.   Milles de Souvigny, *Praxis*, fol. 8. Though not especially well developed in this instance, a certain parallel exists between legal inquest and early depictions of anatomical dissection. Compare the frontispiece of Andreas Vesalius, *De Humani Corporis Fabrica* (Basel, 1543).

10. The formula generally employed was "inquisitions faites d'authorité de la cour à la requête de. . . ." Archives départementales de la Haute-Garonne (hereafter ADHG), B, Chambre de l'Edit, criminel, registre 1 (17 janvier 1597), (23 janvier 1597), (6 février 1597), (12 février 1597). This and other examples of judicial practice are drawn from the records of the Parlement of Toulouse, the tribunal with which the author is most familiar.

11. Katharine Fremantle, "The Open *Vierschaar* of Amsterdam's Seventeenth-century Town Hall as a Setting for the City's Justice," *Oud Holland* 77 (1962): 209–11.

12. Esmein, *La procédure criminelle*, 136–41. Jean Imbert, *La practique judiciaire, tant civile que criminelle, receue et observée par tout le royaume de France, enrichie. . .par M. Pierre Guenois. . .et B. Automne* (Cologny, 1615), 574–76. François Isambert (ed.) et al., *Recueil général des anciennes lois françaises depuis l'an 420 jusqu'à la révolution de 1789* (Paris, 1821–33), 11:362, 367; 12:630. Langbein, *Prosecuting Crime*, 224–28.

13. Milles de Souvigny, *Praxis*, fol. 11v⁰.

14. Esmein, *La procédure criminelle*, 141–42. Imbert, *La practique judiciaire*, 646–47.

15. Jane Aptekar, *Icons of Justice: Iconography and Thematic Imagery in Book V of "The Faerie Queene"* (New York and London, 1969), 57 and 251, n. 7. Erwin Panofsky, "Jan van Eyck's Arnolfini Portrait," *The Burlington Magazine* 64 (1934), reprinted in *Renaissance Art*, ed. Creighton Gilbert (New York, 1973), 4, 7. Erwin Panofsky, *Early Netherlandish Painting, its Origins and Character* (Cambridge, Mass., 1966), 1:202.

16. Ilene H. Forsyth, *The Throne of Wisdom* (Princeton, 1972), 90. Ralph E. Giesey, *The Royal Funeral Ceremony in Renaissance France* (Geneva, 1960), 118–19. André Grabar, *Christian Iconography: A Study of its Origins* (Princeton, 1968), 49, 79. Robert R. Harding, *Anatomy of a Power Elite: The Provincial Governors of Early Modern France* (New Haven and London, 1978), 12–13.

17. Esmein, *L procédure criminelle*, 140–42, 155–56. Imbert, *La practique judiciaire*, 574–81, 594. Langbein, *Prosecuting Crime*, 228.

18. Milles de Souvigny, *Praxis*, fol. 34.

19. Ibid., fol. 37.

20. Ibid., fol. 37v⁰.

21. A defendant was commonly "ouy sur la sellete" (heard on the interrogation stool). ADHG, B, Chambre de l'Edit, criminel, registre 5 (13 décembre 1600). "Être sur la sellette" still means to be under cross-examination or, figuratively, to be in the hot seat.

22. ADHG, B, Chambre de l'Edit, audience, registre 1 (7 août 1579) and (11 août 1579), criminel, registre 5 (15 juin 1600), (28 juillet 1600), (12 août 1600), (7 septembre 1600).

23. Esmein, *La procédure criminelle*, 142–43. Imbert, *La practique judiciaire*, 627–28. Isambert, *Recueil général*, 11:364; 12:630, 633. Langbein, *Prosecuting Crime*, 227–28.

24. Cf. the emblem of Dame Kindness (*Benignité*) in Jean Baudoin, *Iconologie, ou nouvelle explication . . . tirée des recherches et des figures de Cesar Ripa* (Paris, 1677), 1:35, 39. She stands erect and to her right is a chair with a large cushion. Fremantle, "The Open *Vierschaar*," *Oud Holland* 77 (1962): 212–13, 230, reports that cushions were integral to the ceremony of condemnation at Amsterdam during the seventeenth century. On the images of clock and pillow, see also: Charles De Tolnay, *The Drawings of Pieter Bruegel the Elder* (New York, 1952), 27; Rosemond Tuve, *Allegorical Imagery, Some Medieval Books and their Posterity* (Princeton, 1966), 74; Raimond Van Marle, *Iconographie de l'art profane au moyen-âge et à la Renaissance*, (The Hague, 1931), 2:52 (fig. 57).

25. Milles de Souvigny, *Praxis*, fol. 48v⁰.

26. Esmein, *La procédure criminelle*, 144–45. Imbert, *La practique judiciaire*, 638–41. Langbein, *Prosecuting Crime*, 231–32.

27. Esmein, *La procédure criminelle*, 152–53. Imbert, *La practique judiciaire*, 658–60. Jean Papon, *Recueil d'arrests notables des cours souveraines de France* (Pont-à-Mousson, 1608), 1314. Annik Porteau-Bitker, "Le système de l'élargissement sous caution en droit criminel français aux XIIIe et XIVe siècles," *Recueil de la Société Jean Bodin* 29 (1971): 79–80. For the release of aged or ailing defendant: ADHG, B, Tournelle, registre 38 (3 novembre 1551), registre 40 (10 février 1552), registre 44 (7 janvier 1553).

28. Esmein, *La procédure criminelle*, 142–48. Imbert, *La practique judiciaire*,

647–49. Langbein, *Prosecuting Crime*, 234–39.

29. Milles de Souvigny, *Praxis*, fol. 56.

30. Bernard Schnapper, "La répression pénale au XVIe siécle: l'example du Parlement de Bordeaux (1510–1565)," *Recueil de mémoires et travaux publié par la société d'histoire du droit et des institutions des anciens pays de droit écrit* 8 (1971): 13–20; and "La justice criminelle rendue par le Parlement de Paris sous le règne de François Ier," *Revue historique de doit français et étranger* 52 (1974): 260–62.

31. Carlo Cecchelli, "Christianity and Iconography," *Encyclopedia of World Art* (New York, 1959–68), 3:598. Forsyth, *The Throne of Wisdom*, 1, 86. J. J. M. Timmers, *Symboleik en Iconographie der Christelijke Kunst* (Roermond-Maaseik, 1946), 113–14.

32. For a general discussion of judicial torture, see: Piero Fiorelli, *La tortura giudiziaria nel diritto comune* (Milan, 1953–54); and John H. Langbein, *Torture and the Law of Proof: Europe and England in the Ancien Régime* (Chicago and London, 1977).

33. For the appeal of a decision to torture: ADHG, B, Chambre de l'Edit, civil, registre 6 (3 juillet 1595), criminel, registre 1 (16 septembre 1597), registre 3 (4 mars 1599), registre 5 (23 décembre 1600); when the "question sera seulement exhibée": civil, registre 6 (4 novembre 1595), (13 novembre 1595), criminel, registre 1 (20 juin 1597), registre 2 (14 février 1598) and (14 avril 1598); when the "question sera modérée à un bouton" or "à un tour": civil, registre 6 (10 juin 1596) and (4 novembre 1596), criminel, registre 2 (17 février 1598) and (29 avril 1598), registre 5 (23 décembre 1600).

34. Schnapper, "Le Parlement de Paris," *Revue historique de droit français et étranger* 52 (1974): 258–65.

35. Milles de Souvigny, *Praxis*, fols. 61, 61v⁰, and 62.

36. De Tolnay, *Drawings of Bruegel*, fig. 61. The characters of Knowledge (*Cognoissance*) and Doctrine (*Doctrine*) in Baudoin, *Iconologie*, 1:48 and 2:152, carry lighted candles to illuminate truth and make things intelligible. Panofsky, "Arnolfini Portrait," *Renaissance Art*, 17, and *Early Netherlandish Painting*, 1:202, discusses the significance of the lighted candle in Flemish art. The *Praxis'* torturers, incidentally, bear little resemblance to the tormentors in traditional depictions of Christ's passion. Cf. James H. Marrow, *Passion Iconography in Northern European Art of the Late Middle Ages and Early Renaissance* (Kortrijk, 1979).

37. Milles de Souvigny, *Praxis*, fol. 83.

38. The frontality can be contrasted with the "Seizure of Sisamnes" in Gerard David's "Judgment of Cambyses" (1498). The chair of the "evil" judge is placed at an oblique angle to the frontal plane. Charles D. Cuttler, *Northern Painting from Pucelle to Bruegel* (New York, 1973), 103, fig. 240.

39. The positioning of the hands is similar for the figures of "Justice" illustrated in Baudoin, *Iconologia*, 2:66 and Cesare Ripa, *Della novissima iconologia* (Padua, 1642), 278–80.

40. Milles de Souvigny, *Praxis*, fol. 85. While less grandiose, this particular illustration is not unlike Jacques Callot's "Les Supplices" (1634). Cf. Georges Sadoul, *Jacques Callot, miroir de son temps* (Paris, 1969), 312–15.

41. Doucet, *Institutions de la France*, 1:172–73. Isambert, *Recueil général*, 12:630. Langbein, *Prosecuting Crime*, 217, 249–50.

42. Emblems of this nature abound. Damhouder, *Practique iudiciaire*, fol. 120v⁰, depicts "Justice" as a Janus-like, two-faced woman seated upon a throne. One face is blindfolded. She grasps a sword with her right hand and a balance in the left. For other examples, see: De Tolnay, *Drawings of Bruegel*, fig. 61; Craig Harbison, *The Last Judgment in Sixteenth Century Northern Europe* (New York and London, 1976), fig. 23; Tuve, *Allegorical Imagery*, 17; Van Marle, *Iconographie*, 12, 14, 25, 35, 45, 46, 48, 55, 61, 62, 64, 100. A poetic rendition with identical characteristics can be found in Ronsard, "Hymne de la Justice," *Hymnes*, ed. Albert Py (Geneva, 1978), especially page 142.

43. An elaborate seventeenth-century depiction of this duality exists in Otto van Veen, *Q. Horati Flacci emblemata* (Antwerp, 1607), 79, and is explained by Aptekar, *Icons of Justice*, 21–24.

44. Grabar, *Christian Iconography*, 49.

Penal Practices in Early Modern Spain

Ruth Pike
Hunter College,
City University of New York

In this article assessing the theory and practice of the penological system of early modern Spain, special emphasis will be placed on the last years of the eighteenth century, when the traditional system underwent a transformation under the impact of changing conditions and the criticism of the enlightened penal reformers. Even though the old system continued into the nineteenth century, its spirit and practice were significantly altered. The last quarter of the eighteenth century marked a turning point in the history of punishment in early modern Spain.

The theory that the European penal system became progressively less severe in the last two hundred years has gained general acceptance in modern times. According to this view, first expressed by the sociologist Emile Durkheim, punitive penal practices prevailed in medieval and early modern times, while the nineteenth century saw the adoption of restrictive codes. To Durkheim and his modern-day followers like Michel Foucault, the ritualized violence and terror of public executions and mutilations exemplified the justice of the early modern period.[1]

The model of European criminal law and its evolution constructed by Durkheim has its origins in the writings of the eighteenth-century enlightened thinkers. They described the system of their day as arbitrary, cruel, and unjust, and held that there had been no progress in punishment since the end of the Roman Empire and the beginning of the Middle Ages. In many respects, things had become worse. They also were convinced of the universality of the system, that is to say, the same unjust laws and abuses existed throughout Europe.[2]

The eighteenth-century vision of early modern penal practices is still the basis of modern historical interpretation, despite the fact that it is widely recognized that the enlightened penal reformers exaggerated the evils of the system in order to gain support for their reforms. European criminal legislation was based on similar principles and derived from common sources, i.e. Roman law and Germanic custom, but there were important differences depending on the country.[3] At the same time, there was a wide gap between the laws and everyday penal practice. While the severity of the system cannot be denied, such penalties were used only for certain categories of offenses and types of criminals.[4] The early modern penal system was a multifaceted one with a wide range of penological options, and there was no standard pattern of incidence. The oversimplified model of European penal law and its evolution needs to be modified.

Criminal justice in early modern Spain was governed by laws contained in the *Nueva Recopilación*, a collection of edicts that comprised elements of earlier Visigothic and medieval Castilian codes, and which remained the law of the land until 1805. During the Habsburg period, the *Nueva Recopilación* was given its final form in a revision of 1567. In subsequent years it went through ten new editions (between 1567 and 1777) and was gradually augmented with the incorporation of new royal decrees, but there was no attempt to bring about any consistency or uniformity in the law by eliminating obsolete and contradictory legislation.[5] Furthermore, the laws of the earlier codes, such as the *Fuero Real*, remained in effect in so far as they had not been repealed by later legislation, and the thirteenth-century code of the *Siete Partidas* was valid as supplementary law. The lack of unity and clearness in the law created confusion. No one could be certain whether or not a law was still in effect, but it became the practice of the legal writers of the period to cite the *Nueva Recopilación* and the *Siete Partidas* as well as any additional royal decrees not included in the *Nueva Recopilación*.[6]

The theory of punishment expressed in the *Nueva Recopilación* and the supplementary codes like the *Siete Partidas* was based on the principles of retribution and vengeance. Punishments were not inflicted to reform the offender, but rather to secure the communities' revenge and, most of all, to intimidate potential evildoers.[7] The repressive and vindictive objectives of early modern justice could best be accomplished by harsh capital and corporal penalties carried out in public. Imprisonment as a punishment was almost unknown, and jails were primarily places of detention for persons awaiting trial.[8]

While there was a strong commitment to capital punishment, this penalty was imposed regularly only for certain categories of crimes and criminals. Those executed were either persistent or blatant offenders (such as bandits) who were a public menace. In addition the death penalty was almost always exacted for certain particularly serious offenses. They included premeditated murder, parricide, infanticide, sodomy, treason, and counterfeiting (conceived in the period as equivalent to treason since it undermined the majesty of the state as expressed in its coinage).[9]

Loss of records makes it impossible to determine the frequency of capital punishment in early modern Spain. For Madrid, extant documents from the Archivo de Villa indicate that at the end of the seventeenth century and during the first half of the eighteenth century, there were years in which there were executions every two or three months. Often two or more persons (members of the same gang) were executed together. In the 1770s the ratio began to decline, and the downward trend continued in the 1780s. In the 1780s and 1790s no more than a few executions took place annually, and in some years there were none. The condemned persons in all the cases studied were either counterfeiters, bandits, or murderers.[10]

The death penalty could be inflicted in various ways. Since the laws did not always specify the means of execution, judges could use their discretionary powers to determine the form of death. Certain methods common to the rest of Europe in this period were not used in Spain, namely, breaking on the wheel and boiling in oil.[11] The preferred forms in Spain were hanging and the *garrote* (strangulation with an iron collar affixed to a post and tightened with a screw). Death by hanging (*la muerte ordinaria*) was used throughout the period until its abolition by Joseph Bonaparte in 1809. The *garrote* began to be employed in the seventeenth century, but it was not in general use until the eighteenth century. Since it was considered a less degrading death than the gallows, it was applied usually to persons of higher social status. In the eighteenth century sentences for hanging were sometimes changed on appeal to death by *garrote* as a kind of modification of the penalty. Other forms of capital punishment prescribed by the laws, e.g., beheading and burning alive, had fallen into disuse by the eighteenth century.[12]

Capital punishments were either simple or aggravated. The ordinary forms of simple executions were hanging or the *garrote*, but for particularly heinous crimes further sufferings and humiliations were introduced. In the sixteenth and seventeenth centuries this could mean torture and mutilations before death, but in the eighteenth century additional corporal penalties were almost always carried out after death. It was standard procedure in the eighteenth century to subject the bodies of executed bandits to quartering with the exposition of the severed parts (heads and sections) at the scene of their crimes.[13] Likewise the remains of counterfeiters were burnt, while murderers often had their right hands cut off and displayed after execution.[14]

For minor crimes, flogging was a common punishment for both men and women. It could be employed as a penalty by itself or accompanying public shame and banishment. The ritual of public shame and flogging remained unchanged through the eighteenth century. The only modification occurred in 1792, when public indignation forced the *Sala de Alcaldes de Casa y Corte* (the principal court of Madrid) to order that women sentenced to be flogged and exposed to public shame be provided with a tunic to cover their nakedness. Up to that time, women like men were required to appear naked from the waist up.[15]

Public punishment was considered essential to the early modern penal system. It was felt that a public execution served to edify the observers as well as to demonstrate the rewards of crime and the power of the state. Foucault has described it as a ritual to restore an injured sovereignty as well as a punishment of an individual offense. The aim was to make an example, that is, to let the people know that all offenses were punished and to inspire terror through the spectacle of the king's power being applied to those who had offended society. The whole ceremonial surrounding the public execution was devised to create collective fear. The gallows and scaffolds were erected in public squares. The condemned persons were brought there in procession while being humiliated and subjected to insults and sometimes attacks by spectators. The corpses of executed persons were displayed for days near the scenes of their crimes.[16] In addition, those executed for treason suffered confiscation of property and infamy, which was extended to their descendants, making them ineligible to hold public office. Partial or complete confiscation of goods also was a frequent penalty accompanying death in cases of counterfeiting and aggravated homicide.[17]

The memory of the executed person's deeds and punishment was further perpetuated in a form of popular literature known as the *literatura de cordel*. In Madrid, the Confraternity of Blindmen (*la hermandad de ciegos*) solicited from the *Sala de Alcaldes* official accounts of the details of crimes and executions, which they put into verse as ballads and sang in the streets. In order to deepen the impression of the example, the ballads were printed as broadsheets (*pliegos de cordel*) and allowed to circulate.[18] The posthumous proclamation of crimes and punishments justified the system, but they also glorified the criminals by the sheer extent of their widely advertised crimes. For this reason, Manuel de Lardizábal and other Spanish penal reformers of the eighteenth century objected to the ballads and wanted them suppressed, although they continued to believe in the need for a similar kind of publicity for the edification of the populace. Lardizábal suggested that the judicial texts of the sentences be printed and sold to spectators at executions, as was done in France. In his opinion, this would have more effect than "the ballads of the blindmen with their exaggerations and distortions that converted the condemned criminals into heroes."[19]

While the system of harsh capital and corporal penalties continued to be used throughout the period, the idea arose that the state could utilize the labor of prisoners for its own interests. Thus, for those guilty of capital offenses, penal servitude at hard labor on the galleys was introduced in the early sixteenth century as an alternative form of corporal punishment more useful to the state. A series of laws beginning in 1530 gradually extended galley service to all kinds of offenders (both major and minor), as well as to those whose deviant behavior was defined by the laws of the period as criminal.[20] As the years passed, the continuing need to fill the galley benches made the galleys the most common form of sentence. When the galleys were abolished in 1748, their place was taken by the naval arsenals and overseas presidios in North Africa and the Caribbean, where convicts were used to construct and maintain fortifications and other facilities. Public works presidios were established for petty offenders in the same period to provide the large labor force at minimum cost necessary for the public works program undertaken by the Bourbon rulers, especially Charles III (1759–1788). By the last quarter of the eighteenth century the presidio sentence was the usual punishment for all offenders.[21]

The state's pursuit of the utilitarian objective of the penalty had the effect of modifying the penal system. It is likely that the decrees of Charles V and Philip II in the mid-sixteenth century commuting the penalty of mutilations for that of the galleys facilitated the disappearance of the former.[22] Similarly, royal pressure on magistrates to condemn as many men as possible to the galleys and presidios worked against the death penalty and was an important factor in its reduction.

Another element mitigating the early modern penological system was discretionary judgment. In this period judges had vast discretionary powers in assigning penalties. Fines alone were often left entirely to their determination. Even where a punishment was prescribed by law, it could be modified or aggravated by the judge. The only real restriction was that magistrates not invent a completely new penalty. The admission of extenuating circumstances allowed judges to change or modify penalties.[23] A good example of the way the discretionary element could change the law can be seen in the implementation of the laws establishing penal servitude on the galleys. This legislation substituted the galleys for capital and corporal penalties, and left the decision to commute to the discretion of the judges. Regardless of the fact that flogging and public shame were among the afflictive penalties included in these laws, they continued to be used. This meant that men sentenced to the galleys were customarily flogged and subjected to public shame before being sent to their destination.[24]

The judges, utilizing their discretionary powers, could also impose lighter penalties than those required by law. This was done on a regular basis by the judges of the higher tribunals when they visited the jails. In Madrid, two judges were required to visit the jails once a week and to interrogate the inmates as to the causes of their detention. Prisoners whose cases were on appeal, and those sentenced to the galleys, presidios, or military service, were excluded from the *visita*.[25] If, after examining a case, the judges determined that further detainment was unnecessary, they could free the prisoner. The *libros de acuerdos*, recording the decisions of the judges of the *Sala de Alcaldes* and the *visita* lists, bear testimony to the frequency of the practice. For minor offenses such as licentious behavior, drunkenness, mistreatment of wives, or vagrancy, prisoners often were released and reprimanded; and if they were not natives of Madrid, they were freed on the condition that they leave the city and not return. Occasionally the judges altered or reduced sentences, for example, when they involved banishment or the payment of fines.[26]

Another method by which the magistrates could change penalties and substitute others was through the appeals system. The extant records of the *Sala de Alcaldes* show that the judges regularly altered the punishments imposed by the lesser courts when cases were appealed to them. In general, reductions seemed to have been more numerous than the reverse.[27]

The penal system was further tempered by the use of royal clemency, one of the most important prerogatives of the monarchy. In Spain, there were two categories of royal pardons, general and individual. General amnesties were granted by the king on the occasion of an important event, i.e., the birth of an heir, a succession to the throne, a royal marriage, or an important military victory. They could be full pardons in which offenders were free from all blame and penalty, or they could involve a commutation of the penalty. General amnesties also were issued annually in commemoration of Christ's passion on Good Friday (*Perdones del Viernes Santo*), but these pardons were restricted to unpremeditated homicides and limited to twenty offenders a year.[28]

While the royal prerogative to grant pardons was unquestioned in the early modern era, it was expected that the king would use this power judiciously. In the seventeenth century the system was abused, and general amnesties were issued for many unimportant events. In the eighteenth century they were less frequent, particularly in the second half of the century.[29]

In contrast to general amnesties, individual pardons were very common throughout the period. They were issued by the king at the request of individuals in return for some service rendered, or on account of the nobility, character, knowledge, or ability of the culprit. In practice, persons who did not have any of the necessary requirements often obtained these pardons. One of the main reasons was that individual pardons involved monetary compensation (*al sacar*) while the general amnesties were granted gratis (*al gratis*). The amounts varied depending on the social status and economic position of the offender, and they were a good means to replenish the royal treasury.[30]

The royal right to pardon was an essential part of early modern justice because it served as a corrective to the system. The harshness of the law was balanced by the frequency of pardons. While royal clemency was a palliative for the early modern judicial system, it also had a political objective. The royal right to pardon and commute sentences helped to strengthen the foundations of the state. It was conceived as an act of grace emanating from a merciful monarch and was part of the fabric of paternalism that upheld the monarchy.[31]

In the sixteenth and seventeenth centuries public opinion was not hostile to the criminal system of the time. Its cruelty, its arbitrariness, its inequality were all deemed necessary to the proper functioning of society. Furthermore, the generous use of royal clemency and judicial discretion combined with the utilitarian policies of the state served to mitigate the severity of the system and to lessen the need for a revision of the penal law. In the eighteenth century this point of view began to change, and eventually all aspects of the criminal justice system came under attack. This change in mind was due in large part to the intellectual movement that marked the second half of the eighteenth century and rested on two ideas: reason and humanity.

The writings of Montesquieu and Beccaria entered Spain in the 1760s and 1770s and were espoused with great enthusiasm by a group of Spanish enlightened thinkers.[32] While the penal reform movement attracted all sectors of the Spanish educated elite, its most outstanding supporters were members of the bar and judiciary. Manuel de Lardizábal, Gaspar Melchor de Jovellanos, Juan Meléndez Valdés, Juan Pablo Forner, and Juan Sempere y Guarinos were practitioners of the law as well as theorists. Principal among them was Manuel de Lardizábal, who published his *Discurso de las penas* in 1782. This work constituted the basis for the Spanish reform movement. Like Beccaria, Lardizábal rejected torture and harsh penalties and advocated the principle that the penalty must fit the crime. While accepting the utilitarian and intimidatory purpose of the penalty, he emphasized the correction of the offender as the ultimate objective. As for the death penalty, Lardizábal and the other Spanish reformers rejected Beccaria's argument for its abolition. They accepted its necessity for certain crimes, but argued against its indiscriminate use. They also disagreed with Beccaria on the question of royal clemency. They believed that royal pardons should continue to exist, but in the case of serious offenses, they should be limited to a reduction of the penalty so as to "allow for the correction of the offender."[33]

The main objectives of the Spanish reformers were the acceptance of the principle of proportionality of penalties, the abolition of torture, and the adoption of a revised criminal code embodying the new ideas. Three reformers, namely Lardizábal, Jovellanos, and Meléndez Valdés, were closely associated, at one time or another, with the powerful court of the *Sala de Alcaldes* in Madrid. Jovellanos was a judge on the *Sala* in 1778, while Lardizábal and Meléndez Valdés served as prosecuting attorneys (*fiscales*) for that same tribunal in the 1780s and 1790s. Given its enlightened membership, the *Sala de Alcaldes* played an important role in the transformation of Spanish criminal justice in the last quarter of the eighteenth century. In the late 1760s the judges of the *Sala* succeeded in establishing the principle that the penalty must be commensurate with the crime, and this concept was incorporated into Spanish law by the reform legislation of 1771 that reorganized the presidios.[34] The *Sala* also took the lead in discontinuing the judicial use of torture in the late 1770s, precisely the period during which Jovellanos served on the court. Other Spanish tribunals soon followed the example of the *Sala*, and torture fell into disuse in the last quarter of the eighteenth century, although it was not formally abolished until the nineteenth century.[35]

The sentencing practices of the judges of the *Sala de Alcaldes* in the last decades of the eighteenth century reflect the changing attitudes toward the objectives and methods of punishment. The *libros de acuerdos* show how the judges were altering procedures and penalties in accord with the new penal ideas. An examination of the *libros de acuerdos* for the years 1780–1799 indicates a rapid decline in capital punishment and corporal penalties like flogging, and a parallel rise in sentences to penal labor. Serious crimes were punished by long sentences to the naval arsenals and overseas presidios, while the public works presidios were used for lesser offenders. For minor delicts and misdemeanors, the majority of sentences involved fines, or warnings and reprimands.[36]

Statistics from the one remaining yearly account of penalties imposed by the *Sala* corresponding to the year 1802 confirm the sentencing trends of the 1780s and 1790s. Of a total of 1,939 sentences passed by the *Sala* in that year, twenty-six percent involved forced labor either in the presidios, arsenals, or houses of correction, while five percent imposed service in the armed forces. The largest number of sentences (fifty-six percent) belonged to those who were fined, warned, or reprimanded, and seven percent were acquitted. There were no death sentences, and only one person was sentenced to be flogged.[37]

The *Sala* also took the initiative in the attempts to revise the criminal law and to compile a new code. In 1776 Manuel de Roda, an enlightened minister of Justice under Charles III, persuaded the king to ask the *Sala* to prepare a new compilation of the penal law in which antiquated and contradictory legislation would be eliminated and new and existing laws included. The task was entrusted to Lardizábal, who completed the work and submitted it to the *Sala*, but the "new criminal code," as the reformers optimistically called it, was somehow lost in the bureaucratic labyrinth of government and never became a reality.[38]

The failure of the enlightened reformers to bring into existence a new code of penal law shows clearly that the king had retreated in face of what appeared to be the destabilizing effects of a new criminal code. Enlightened penal reform was incompatible with absolute monarchy and the hierarchical social order. Despite the efforts of Lardizábal and other Spanish reformers to reconcile absolutism and penal reform, any fundamental alteration in the system had to wait until after the fall of the Old Regime. On the other hand, the traditional system had already been in the process of change for several decades. The ideas of the penal reformers had so changed the spirit of the courts in the last years of the eighteenth century that their decisions were more in accord with enlightened thought than with existing laws, but the triumph of the new penal ideology was delayed until the nineteenth century. It was left to the nineteenth-century liberals to overthrow the traditional system in 1822 and to fulfill the aspirations of the eighteenth-century enlightened penal reformers.

Notes

AHN and AVM, cited below, refer to the Archivo Histórico National, Madrid, and the Archivo de Villa, Madrid, respectively.

1. Emile Durkheim, *The Division of Labor in Society*, trans. George Simpson (Glencoe, Ill., 1947); and Michel Foucault, *Discipline and Punish*, trans. Alan Sheridan (New York, 1979).
2. Leon Radzinowicz, *Ideology and Crime* (New York, 1966), 4; Carl Ludwig von Bar, *A History of Continental Criminal Law*, trans. Thomas S. Bell (Boston, 1916), 315.
3. Joaquín Pacheco, *El código civil* (Madrid, 1888), L; Cesare Beccaria, *On Crimes and Punishments* (Indianapolis, Indiana, 1977), Introduction, xxii–xxiii.
4. Bruce Lenman and Geoffrey Parker, "The State, the Community and the Criminal Law in Early Modern Europe" in *Crime in Western Europe since 1500*, ed. V. A. C. Gatrell, Bruce Lenman, and Geoffrey Parker (London, 1980), 14.
5. John Vance, *The Background of Hispanic-American Law* (New York, 1943), 121, 126.
6. Eugenio Cuello Calón, *Derecho penal* (Barcelona, 1926), 96.
7. *Las Siete Partidas*, trans. Samuel Parsons Scott (New York, 1931), Partida VII, title XXXI, law 1.
8. The dominant principle from the Middle Ages to the eighteenth century was that prisons exist only in order to keep men, not to punish them. See *Las Siete Partidas*, Partida VII, title XXXI, law 2. For a history of penal servitude, see Ruth Pike, *Penal Servitude in Early Modern Spain* (Madison, 1983).
9. See *Las Siete Partidas*, Partida VII for a discussion of these crimes and their

penalties. Also Cuello Calón, *Derecho penal*, 84–86; Francisco Tomás y Valiente, *El derecho penal en la monarquía absoluta (siglos XVI–XVIII)* (Madrid, 1969), chap. 4.

10. Conclusions are based on an examination of documents in AVM, Secretaría, sec. 2, leg. 414, no. 8 and sec. 2, leg. 454, no. 66. This collection is too fragmented to permit systematic, quantitative analysis. It consists mainly of official notices of death sentences for condemned criminals and bills submitted by the public executioners to the municipality to cover the costs of executions. See also AHN, Consejos 1039–98.

11. Pacheco, *El código penal*, L. Branding in the face, cutting the nostrils, plucking out the eyes, stoning to death, crucifixion, and throwing over a precipice were forbidden in the *Siete Partidas*. See Partida VII, title XXXI, law 6.

12. *Las Siete Partidas*, Partida VII, title XXXI, law 6; title VII, law 10; AHN, Consejos, libro 1039, Feb. 18, 1751; ibid., March 3, 1751; Tomás y Valiente, *El derecho penal*, 382–85.

13. AVM, Secretaría, sec. 2, leg. 414, no. 8; sec. 2, leg. 454, no. 66. It is not clear whether or not the penalty of drawing and quartering alive was ever actually employed in Spain. The only reference that I have found to it is in Pellicer, when he states that in 1641 Philip IV commuted the penalty of the traitor Miguel de Molina from drawing and quartering by four horses to hanging and quartering of the body because "he did not want to introduce into Spain methods of execution that had not been used by his predecessors." José de Pellicer, *Avisos históricos* (Madrid, 1965), 274–75.

14. AHN, Consejos, libro 1173, *Noticias para el gobierno de la Sala*, ch. 33; libro 1069, year 1781 (hanging, quartering and the right hands cut off and displayed for two bandits who committed a vicious murder and robbery); AVM, Secretaría, sec. 2, leg. 454, no. 6, June 1751 (hanging a murderer and cutting off his right hand and displaying it).

15. AHN, Alcaldes de Casa y Corte, year 1792, ff. 277–82; Manuel de Lardizábal, *Discurso de las penas*, in José Antón Oneca, "Estudio preliminar: El derecho penal de la Ilustración," *Revista de la Escuela de Estudios Penitenciarios* 10 (1966): 708–10; *Las Siete Partidas*, Partida VII, title XXXI, law 11. The Asociación de Señoras, a charitable organization founded in 1787 to help women prisoners, made the tunics.

16. AHN, Consejos, libro 1173, *Noticias*, 51–52; Foucault, *Discipline and Punish*, 47–54; *Las Siete Partidas*, Partida VII, title XXXI, law 11.

17. *Las Siete Partidas*, Partida VII, title II; *Nueva Recopilación* in *Códigos españoles concordados y anotados* (Madrid, 1850), Book VIII, title 18, law 2; title 23, laws 5, 10; title III, law 5.

18. J. Gavira, "La hermandad de ciegos de Madrid," *Revista de la biblioteca, archivo y museo* 4 (1927): 482–84; Vicente Vizcaíno Pérez, *Código y práctica criminal arreglado a las leyes de España* (Madrid, 1797), 3:355. For the *literatura de cordel*, see Julián Caro Baroja, *Ensayo sobre la literatura de cordel* (Madrid, 1969).

19. Lardizábal, *Discurso*, 655. See also Juan Meléndez Valdés, *Discursos forenses* (Madrid, 1821), 131.

20. Félix Sevilla y Solanas, *Historia penitenciaria española (la galera), apuntes de archivo* (Segovia, 1917), 30–32, lists this legislation.

21. See Pike, *Penal Servitude*, especially Part 2.

22. Tomás y Valiente, *El derecho penal*, 381; *Nueva Recopilación*, Book VIII, title 4, laws 4, 5 (cutting off the tongue); title 17, law 7 (pulling out the teeth); title 24, law 4 (cutting off the hand).

23. *Las Siete Partidas*, Partida VII, title XXXI, law 8; Tomás y Valiente, *El derecho penal*, 375–80; Lardizábal, *Discurso*, 662, 680–90.

24. Tomás y Valiente, *El derecho penal*, 387; *Nueva Recopilación*, Book XIII, title 24, law 4.

25. AHN, Consejos, libro 1173, *Noticias*, ch. 3; Vizcaíno Pérez, *Código*, III, 383–407. The weekly visits took place on Saturday. There also were three annual visits corresponding to the principal religious holidays (Christmas, Easter, and Pentecost).

26. See the *libros de acuerdos* and *visita* lists in AHN, Consejos, libros 1039–89 (years 1751–99). This collection begins in 1751 and ends in 1834.

27. AHN, Consejos, libros 1039–89; Vizcaíno Pérez, *Codigo*, III, 234–35.

28. Vizcaíno Pérez, *Código*, II, 367–82; *Las Siete Partidas*, Partida VII, title XXII, law 1. See the collection of Good Friday pardons in AHN, Consejos, legajos 5575–5769.

29. AHN, Alcaldes de Casa y Corte, year 1793, ff. 731–763; AHN, Consejos, libro 1048, year 1760; Gaspar Melchor de Jovellanos, *Informe de la Real Sala de Alcaldes al Consejo de Castilla, sobre indultos generales*, in *Biblioteca de autores españoles* (Madrid, 1858), pp. 451–54.

30. Tomás y Valiente, *El derecho penal*, 403–4; *Las Siete Partidas*, Partida VII, title XXXII, law 1; Jovellanos, *Informe*, 452–53.

31. Lardizábal, *Discurso*, 657–88; Vizcaíno Pérez, *Código*, II, 368; Jovellanos, *Informe*, 451–54.

32. Beccaria's essay *Dei Delitti e delle Pene* (1764) was not translated into Spanish until 1774, but Spanish reformers could read it in the French edition of 1766.

33. Lardizábal, *Discurso*, 637–718.

34. Pike, *Penal Servitude*, 70–71.

35. The practice of judicial torture has been studied by Francisco Tomás y Valiente, *La tortura en España* (Barcelona, 1973).

36. Conclusion based on data from the *libros de acuerdos* to be used in a larger study of crime and punishment in early modern Spain.

37. AHN, Alcaldes de Casa y Corte, year 1803, fol. 1141.

38. Juan Sempre y Guarinos, *Ensayo de una biblioteca española de los mejores escritores del reinado de Carlos IV* (Madrid, 1786), 3:173–75; Tomás y Valiente, *La tortura*, 203. In the meantime, a new edition of the *Nueva Recopilación* was necessary, and in 1805 the *Novísima Recopilación* was promulgated, but it suffered from the same defects as the earlier ones. See Vance, *Hispanic-American Law*, 123.

Crime and Punishment in the Tupacamaru Rebellion in Peru

Leon G. Campbell
University of California, Riverside

The Trial of Tupac Amaru

Shortly after dawn on the morning of May 18, 1781, a small group of prisoners entered the *plaza mayor*, or main square, of Cuzco, Peru, the former capital of the Inca Empire and one of the major urban centers of Spanish Peru. A large gallows dominated the center of the plaza, an extensive open area around which the primary symbols of Spanish authority—the Cathedral and the *Ayuntamiento* (city hall)—were situated. On this day the plaza was jammed with *vecinos* (townspeople) who awaited the spectacle of a public execution. The event was the solemn creation of the Spanish Visitor-General José Antonio de Areche, who hoped to "create public terror" through the execution of José Gabriel Tupac Amaru Inca, a hereditary *cacique* (chief) of southern Peru and a direct descendant of the Inca royal line. Tupac Amaru had staged a massive revolt against royal authority in November 1780, and with his senior commanders had been convicted of sedition three days earlier.[1]

Following mass and communion, the nine Tupacamaru defendants were brought into the plaza bound hand and foot, and were placed ignominiously in leather sacks of the kind used to bring *yerba mate* from Paraguay. These sacks were tied to the tails of horses drafted for service of this sort. The group was dragged to the foot of the gallows. The plaza was surrounded by militias of Cuzco, but, interestingly, the four sides of the gallows were encircled by militiamen from the companies of mulattoes and those from Huamanga, armed with muskets and fixed bayonets. These companies had distinguished themselves for loyalty in a rebellion that had severely divided the provincial forces of the entire region.

An observer of the spectacle unfolding in the plaza noted the physical location of the various social classes of Cuzco in attendance. Members of the Spanish and creole nobility, royal officials, and representatives of the civil,

57

military, and clerical bureaucracies sat behind richly carved balconies or in reserved areas atop galleries built especially for the event; below them, on the stairs of the public buildings, were arranged minor civic officials, soldiers, and clergy, according to their rank within their respective corporations. Beyond these corporate representatives, farthest from the center of the square, were vast numbers of *plebeyos* (commoners), persons of indefinite race and apparent social status who formed the majority of the city's workforce, as well as *lepéros* (underemployed or vagrants who were always under surveillance by authorities). The voice of the crier announced that this was the form of justice that the king owed to such perfidious delinquents. In many ways the event was similar to many public spectacles in Cuzco where noisy crowds thronged to celebrate a feast day or royal birthday. Yet in other ways the event differed markedly from other more festive activities. For one thing, the square fell absolutely silent as Commandant of Militias Simón Gutierrez at the head of a picket of grenadiers led the procession into the plaza. For another, the witness noticed that there were no Indians to be seen despite the overwhelmingly indigenous social composition of the diocese.[2] The execution of the Tupacamarus was a Spanish event that apparently went unrecognized by these native people.

As he later confided to Minister of the Indies José de Gálvez, the harsh sentences Areche visited upon the Tupacamaru defendants were for the specific purpose of invoking "all the forms of terror necessary to produce fear and caution" among any persons considering an act of *lesa majestad* (sedition) against the King as Tupac Amaru had done.[3] On November 4, 1780, José Gabriel Tupac Amaru Inca, a young *mestizo* (of Spanish-Indian extraction) cacique from the province of Tinta, located south of Cuzco, had taken prisoner the Spanish *corregidor* (local official) Antonio de Arriaga. Tupac Amaru and his followers subsequently tried and executed the corregidor for a variety of crimes, notably his excessive administration of the *repartimiento de mercancias* (forced sale of goods to Amerind communities), which not only snared the Indians in a cycle of debt and depression but weakened as well the family unit and the Indian township.[4] The rebellion caught hold in the southern highlands region and spread well beyond its original confines in southern Cuzco. The southern sierra region between Huamanga and Potosí had suffered over sixty revolts, many of which were directed at venal royal functionaries; yet, these events hardly seemed to justify the extraordinary measures taken by the Spanish to dispatch these defendants.

A stronger reason for the ferocity with which the Spanish legal system moved against this group of defendants lay in the fact that, in the opinion of the trial court, this aristocratic chieftain had, after considerable planning, put together a large and effective military and civil command that included numerous creoles and mestizos. Tupac Amaru had appealed to these groups in the name of the King and promised to lower sales taxes and invoke other fiscal reforms. On the other hand, he had also demonstrated a clear intention to "dispossess the King of his Realm" by invoking the name of Tupac Amaru Inca (a name replete with connotations of kingship), collecting tribute for his own purposes, appointing judges and other local officials, and often behaving as a virtual sovereign. Areche stated that Tupac Amaru maintained until his death his "right of rule over those dominions" and refused to confess the commission of any crimes, thus threatening the preservation of royal authority, considered by Spanish authorities to be the highest attribute of sovereignty and the cornerstone of the colonial system.[5]

The sentences levied against the initial group of Tupacamaru defendants including Tupac Amaru, his wife Micaela Bastidas, and seven of his closest confederates, indicated that the authorities regarded the crimes of this group as threatening to the social fabric of the entire viceroyalty. In rapid succession the court ordered hanged four of Tupac's captains, including his brother-in-law Antonio Bastidas. Then his uncle Francisco Tupac Amaru, and his oldest son Hipólito, had their tongues cut out before being hanged. Next, Tupac's highest-ranking female associate, Tomasa Titu Condemaita, the *cacica* of Acos, Quispicanchis, was executed by means of a *garrote* (an iron collar containing a screw), which produced death by asphyxiation. Micaela Bastidas, regarded by the natives as *La Coya* (Inca Queen), had her tongue cut out; but apparently her neck was either too small for the garrote or the machine malfunctioned, making it necessary for the two executioners to dispatch the woman by strangulation using a lasso around her neck. Finally, after witnessing this terrible scene, Tupac Amaru was brought foward. The cacique's tongue was cut out, after which he was thrown to the ground by the two executioners who bound him hand and foot to the haunches of four horses. On a given signal these were driven in four different directions by four mestizo attendants, a spectacle not seen in Cuzco since a similar sentence directed by the Viceroy Francisco de Toledo against Tupac Amaru I in 1572 for a similar crime of sedition.[6]

As the horses strained, but failed, to dismember the Inca, one observer noted that the rebel seemed to control the horses, either because "the Indian was in reality made of iron," or because the horses were too weak to perform their duty. Tupac remained suspended in space "like a spider." Probably annoyed at the inadvertent show of strength by the rebel chief, Areche signalled from his seat on the balcony of the former Jesuit *Colegio San Borja* for the executioner to terminate the execution by beheading the defendant. Then a sudden wind arose, followed by a driving rain that sent the crowd running for cover. A witness held that the Indians interpreted this as the mourning of Heaven for the barbarous death the Spaniards had visited on the Inca.

That day, only the rebel's youngest son, Fernando, a boy of nine, was exempted from capital punishment. Instead, the boy was required to watch the execution while bound in chains and was passed under the gallows, which rendered him hysterical. Later, the forty remaining Tupacamaru defendants were sentenced according to their rank.[7] That afternoon, the bodies of the nine defendants were dismembered and taken away to various provinces that had supported the rebellion, to be placed on pikes along the roadways and in other public places. The trunks of Tupac Amaru and Micaela were taken to the hill of Picchu overlooking Cuzco, the site from which the Inca had earlier directed the siege of the city. There they were burned and a flat stone set in place enumerating their many crimes, including treason and sedition against the crown.[8]

The severity of the sentences levied against the Tupacamarus prompted inquiries on the part of creole liberals and even senior ministers of King Charles III, although the sentences ultimately were confirmed. Nineteenth-century historians unsympathetic to the cause of Spanish colonialism pointed to the cries of Fernando Tupac Amaru as "the death knell of Spanish domination in America," which of course it was not, while Peruvian historians have emphasized the anti-Incaic provisions of the sentence that ordered the destruction of all vestiges of the Inca past: Printed works such as the *Comentarios Reales* of the Inca Garcilaso de la Vega, art forms such as native dramas like *Ollantaytambo* (a play celebrating Inca life), music, native dress, the Quechua language, hereditary caciqueships, and other public displays were destroyed in a "cultural genocide" against these native peoples.[9]

Further analysis of the Tupacamaru trial records is of interest to social historians and legal scholars because of the light these trials shed on the Spanish system of criminal justice and the relationship between crime and punishment in late colonial Spanish America. Recent studies for sixteenth-century Mexico and Peru by Woodrow Borah and Steve Stern, for example, approach the subject from quite different perspectives, yet both suggest the ability of Spanish institutions and Spanish legal systems to control the problem of domestic rebellion either by dividing Indian communities on the basis of *ayllu* (kin group), class, or ethnic lines to avert violence, or to channel discontent into alternate forms of protest to protect public safety.[10] Ruth Pike's work on penal practices traces their evolution throughout the seventeenth and eighteenth centuries, noting that the discretionary power of courts under the Hapsburgs was reduced under the successor Bourbons, with full penal reform being achieved in Spain only in the nineteenth century. In criminal cases of a serious nature, however, Pike contends that public displays of justice were always considered essential to the preservation of royal authority.[11] Far less is known about eighteenth-century standards of justice in Spanish America apart from particular studies of the Inquisition and military tribunals, both of limited applicability to civil court systems.[12]

One of the few books to consider the subject—William Taylor's penetrating regional study of deviance, crime, punishment, and rebellion in certain colonial Mexican villages—demonstrates that in criminal cases involving revolt the authorities proceeded summarily against conspirators but leniently against the community, taking into account the miserable condition of the natives, and the local, spontaneous nature of most revolts, which were usually defused by withdrawing offensive officials or suspending certain ordinances affecting Indian communities. The limited research that has been done for both Peru and Mexico indicates that only a fraction of these incidents were litigated.[13]

Yet these judicial standards hardly applied to major rebellions that questioned Spanish colonial policy or royal authority. Not only was the Great Rebellion pan-Andean in scope, it was viewed by Spanish authorities as an effort to create an alternative legal system that would systematically deprive whites of their rights and status. Thus, in these judicial proceedings, historians are afforded an opportunity to examine the workings of the Spanish legal system in a major viceroyalty at a critical stage in its colonial development. In addition, insights are provided about Incaic social organization and the nature of indigenous legal systems.

Comparative studies about native and Spanish legal systems in the colonial period of Spanish Americn history are entirely lacking. Surviving accounts of Aztec or Incaic legal systems as draconian but eminently fair in their willingness to mete out severe punishments to nobles and plebians alike, in comparison with the more elitist and uneven standards upheld by Spanish American courts, which favored members of the Spanish authority at the expense of commoners, may be overdrawn.[14] The difficulty is compounded somewhat because a conceptual basis for Spanish law and society remains, allowing us to interpret judicial decisions, whereas for the Aztec and Incaic systems we lack both a theoretical norm and a corpus of legal opinion necessary to frame a discussion. The present article thus addresses a series of questions concerning the theoretical and practical bases of the Spanish system of criminal law as it operated during one major trial of the eighteenth century where the principles of Spanish colonialism were defended against the threat of Inca nationalism.

Colonial Rebellions

A brief survey of native separatist movements directed against the representatives of the Crown in colonial Peru during the sixteenth and seventeenth centuries indicates that the courts were quite disposed to act publicly and

severely against native chiefs who questioned royal authority. The public execution in Cuzco of the Inca Tupac Amaru I in 1572 and that of Gabriel Manco
Capac in Lima in 1667 are, according to John Rowe, two rather notable
exceptions to the rule that Peruvian authorities were able to maintain royal
sovereignty and restrict the recurrence of Inca nationalism at a reasonable
level.[15] This can be seen by the Viceroy Martín Enriquez's promulgation in
1583 of the *Informaciones sobre el origen y gobernación de los Incas*, an
order that placed restrictions on Inca overlords to assure their fidelity. The
privileges were largely restored in the *Ordenanzas del Perú* issued in 1685,
which reestablished community celebrations, dances, games, the wearing of
distinctive dress, and other customs revered by the Inca nation.[16]

Despite the relative infrequency of rebellions, however, the Spanish were
aware of the persistence of resurrection myths that presumed the
reconstitution of Tahuantinsuyo and the resurrection of *Inkarrí* (Inca King),
the prototypical Indian savior-leader. This millenarian hero was, in Andean
cosmology, to return on Judgment Day to reverse the existing world order
and free the Indians from the Spaniards' yoke of domination and exploitation.
The death of Tupac Amaru I, for example, was regarded by the Indians as
"the second death of the Inca," the first having been the death of Atahuallpa
at the hands of Francisco Pizarro during the Conquest. Decapitation, or "la
separación de cuerpo y tronco," permitted reunification of the Inca beneath
ground; hence, the appearance of another Inca messiah was eternally repeat-
able in Andean culture. The important aspect of Andean resurrection myths,
which have existed in world history from the time of the Egyptian God Osiris
and earlier, was that the Indians viewed them as reality rather than historic
fact.[17]

It is important in assessing the severity of colonial rebellions to recognize
the distinction—drawn by both the rebels and the royal courts—between these
epic events, which were seen as part of a larger ritual, a *pachacuti* (a
cataclysmic upheaval designed to reverse the world order), and those lesser
revolts that sought only to supplant a venal corregidor or frustrate tax
collection. In recent years scholars investigating the subject of native rebellion
in colonial Peru have made it clear that the Great Rebellion of 1780 was
situated within a larger context of domestic protest, and that the Tupac
Amaru Rebellion simply forms the largest and most obvious manifestation
of a cycle of revolt that seemed to intensify between the legalization of the
repartimiento de mercancias in 1765 and the conclusion of the visitation
headed by José Antonio de Areche in 1783.[18] On the other hand, for the
purposes of examining the responses of Spanish courts to these millenarial
movements, or those which seem to exhibit strong Inca nationalist tendencies,
it is necessary to consider these separately from the more regular occurrence

of revolts (led by native elites with undefined or misunderstood objectives) that resulted in the punishment of the principal leaders but not of the natives as a group.

Two rebellions occurring in Peru during the eighteenth century demonstrate the conventional model of crime and punishment in this latter form of domestic rebellion. In January 1783, for example, the cacique Andrés Ignacio Cacma Condori of Azángaro, along with seventeen other caciques including José Orco Huaranca, chief of the prestigious San Blas parish of the city of Cuzco, were tried and convicted for sedition. The thirty-eight principals received capital sentences of death by hanging while another eighty-nine adherents were sentenced to hard labor in the *obrajes* (workshops) of Cuzco. Although no fewer than seventeen provinces were implicated in the rebellion, no effort was made to punish these communities.[19] In 1750, the authorities uncovered another rebellion (led by Francisco Inca of Huarochirí and Pedro de los Santos in Lima) that involved a more diverse social following, allegedly including Indian nobles, mestizos, and creoles. The trial court, hoping not to make matters worse, sentenced and hanged the principals but did not convict the 193 persons implicated in the rebellion. As was relatively common in Spanish law, which was based on recognition of society as a series of *estamentos* (estates), caciques other than Francisco Inca were exiled to Juan Fernandez Island off the Chilean coast, while female adherents were dispatched to nunneries out of consideration for their sex.[20]

During the 1740s messianic leaders such as the shadowy Juan Santos Atahuallpa appeared in frontier regions such as Tarma, although most were never brought to trial.[21] After 1750, however, deteriorating economic conditions and a reform administration devoted to both efficiency and fiscal improvement may have helped to create a climate propitious for the appearance of these social types. Attacks by native communities against corregidors intensified in the provinces of Urubamba, Sicasica, Pacajes, Huamachuco, and Chumbivilcas during the turbulent decade 1770–1780. Fully 61 or 44 percent of the total of 137 recorded revolts taking place in Peru prior to 1780 occurred during this period.[22] In geographic terms, native revolt was most pronounced in the southern sierra region between Huamanga and Potosí, with the regions of Arequipa, Cuzco, Apurimac, and Ayacucho being most active. Revolts also occurred, however, in Charcas along the northern coast, and even in Lima.[23] Magnus Morner has demonstrated for Cuzco that no correlation with economic oppression exists. Revolts were common in areas where repartimiento levels were relatively low, such as Chumbivilcas and Cotabambas, and were less pronounced in areas of higher per capita exaction, such as Tarma and Huarochirí.[24] On the other hand, economic factors—such as Areche's 1777 decision to erect customs houses in Cochabamba, La Paz, Arequipa, and Cuzco, as well as his enforcement of royal orders forbidding the exchange of hard currency between Cuzco and La Paz—undoubtedly weakened the economy of the region and the status of its artisans by reducing demand levels for cloth, sugar, cocoa, and grain.[25]

Between Areche's arrival in Peru in 1777 and the outbreak of the Tupac Amaru rebellion in November 1780, a perceptible shift in sentencing by Peruvian courts hearing cases of sedition can be observed. The ethno-historical research of Jorge Hidalgo confirms that as early as the 1760s Indian communities of Peru in correspondence with Spanish authorities had begun to make it clear that they were voicing opposition to the Spanish colonial system on the essentially moral grounds of unfairness.[26] Yet, to cite one example, an urban revolt by a group including eight creoles, nine Indians, six persons of undetermined social status (probably mestizos), and a Spaniard, which broke out in Maras, Urubamba, in 1777 and was directed towards the reduction of the *alcabala* (sales tax), resulted in the levying of modest sentences against the twenty-four defendants. The trial was held in Lima in 1778, and the court limited the sentences to hard labor at the Presidio *Real Felipe* in Callao but released many of the men the following year. On the other hand, in the 1780 "Revolt of the Silversmiths" in Cuzco, a group of eleven creoles led by Lorenzo Farfán de los Godos and the noble Indian cacique of Pisaj, Bernardo Pucaylli Tambohaucso (who had plotted a revolt for essentially the same reasons), received capital punishments from the judges of the trial court despite the fact that the plot had been broken up before it materialized.[27]

Several reasons may help to explain the court's apparent willingness to extend more severe punishments to convicted defendants in cases of domestic rebellion. In 1777, in the town of Macha, in the province of Chayanta in Upper Peru, a charismatic cacique named Tomás Catari demonstrated how proper leadership could change the nature of domestic protest. After a long series of efforts to correct inequities in the system of tribute collection in his communities, Catari discovered a law that authorized Indians able to prove malfeasance against their corregidors to assume the position of cacique, a post which had increasingly become the preserve of mestizos. During his struggle with the authorities he was able briefly to restore the spirit of the laws, and when he was jailed by the authorities an angry mob of supporters secured his release. Catari, in order to dramatize his struggle, undertook an arduous journey on foot to visit the new viceroy in Buenos Aires (Upper Peru having been separated from Lima's jurisdiction the year previously). Although Catari was able to wring some concessions out of the viceroy, these were overturned by the Audiencia judges in Charcas, who probably also had a hand in the eventual assassination of Catari. The apparent lesson of the fruitless Catari revolt was that it helped convince the Indians that corruption and immorality could be overcome; the Indians need not wait for the redemption of Heaven as the Bishop of Cuzco had maintained. On the other hand, the revolt undoubtedly alerted authorities, even though its appeal prompted independent responses by the people.[28]

Although no Inca messiah appeared in Cuzco prior to 1780, there were tentative movements in this direction indicating the vitality of Inca nationalism. Spanish authorities had information, for example, that the Indians regarded the year 1777, "The Year of the Three Sevens," as having unusual significance—one in which it was prophesied that the old social order would be restored and the wrongs inflicted by the Spanish righted. So tense was the city during this period that when individuals such as Josef Gran Quispe Inca appeared in the *chicherias* (public houses) as self-proclaimed heirs to the Inca throne and messiahs, they were warmly received by communities that had apparently nurtured this belief for some time. Quispe was accordingly tried for sedition and jailed for his utterances. Even more serious was the news that Indian communities apparently took seriously the rumors of a cataclysm preceding the millennium, storing grain to withstand the famine and pestilence they anticipated and awaiting further orders from Cuzco whenever these events took place. Again, while native protests to royal officials were conventional in that they were directed toward specific abuses and individuals, the rationale for such protests was the breakdown of the moral and legal order that had traditionally existed between the king and his native subjects.[29] Although there is no firm evidence on the point, it appears that news of events in Maras and Cuzco convinced the courts that the phenomenon of messianism, which had formerly been confined to the frontier, had reached the confines of Cuzco, the citadel of Inca culture and cultural nationalism, a phenomenon which, if allowed to proceed unchecked, could allow local protests to transcend local limitations.

Just as importantly, by the time the Silversmith defendants went on trial in Cuzco late in 1780, the serious revolt in Arequipa in January 1780 directed against the customs house had been succeeded by the more extensive Tupac Amaru rebellion in Cuzco, raising fears that these movements were somehow connected. Although there are no explicit linkages between the urban riot in Arequipa directed against the corregidor Baltasar de Semanat and the customs, *pasquines* (lampoons) making references to the North American Revolution and hailing the return of the *Inca Casimiro* (considered to be a legitimate king who was both "Reasonable and of the Law") appeared both in Arequipa and Cuzco. The lampoons in Cuzco spoke of *Nuestro Gabriel Inca*, a legitimate king "who all *Indianos* felt would protect their rights."[30] In this climate the trial court in Cuzco litigating the Silversmith's Conspiracy received evidence that Indians had approached Farfán to lead them as their Inca. Thus despite the fact that Farfán was the scion of a *Cuzqueño* (of Cuzco) family prominent in the government of that city, the judges hanged all the creole conspirators as well as the cacique Tambohuacso who was vaguely linked to Tupac Amaru by one witness. Boleslao Lewin contends this trial represents a break with earlier judicial policy of leniency toward defendants of higher social status, yet this leniency was only permitted as a means of offsetting the lack of a strong centralized government and seems to have diminished as a defense throughout the Bourbon century.[31] By 1780, at least, in Peru trial courts seemed determined to suppress movements that threatened the regional order and those that admitted social alliances, both of which were present in the Silversmith case. The sentences correlate with Jacobus Ten Broeck's thesis that legal sentences are generally more severe in times of stress when institutions are perceived to be under attack.[32]

Thus by the eighteenth century the ability of Spanish institutions to divide Indian society on the basis of *ayllus* (communities), or to preside over ethnic and class conflict, placed greater pressure on its judicial mechanisms and courts of law. First, with the outbreak of the Tupacamaru rebellion in Cuzco in November 1780, following closely on the heels of smaller revolts in Maras, Cuzco, Jujuy, and Arequipa, the volume of criminal cases brought to trial increased significantly. Second, beginning with the Catari revolt in Chayanta and continuing with the subsequent movements led by Tupac Amaru in southern Cuzco and by his counterpart, Julian Apasa Tupac Catari in La Paz, the courts were forced to deal with charismatic leaders whom they accused of fostering the crime of *lesa majestad* (sedition) against royal authority — a crime based on proven "intent to dispossess the king of his realm, or procure the unauthorized revolt of any lands, or peoples, against their sovereign." The usual penalty for such a crime was death and the confiscation of the defendant's goods.[33]

The Tupacamaru Rebellion and Royal Authority

The purpose of this article is to review the trial testimony and sentencing procedures involved in the Great Rebellion of 1780 as a means of obtaining additional insights into this phenomenon. As stated above, although the Great Rebellion was set within a larger cycle of domestic protest, the exceptional nature of its leader and his efforts to create an alternative, Incaic legal system demanded that sentencing be not only rigorous but also effective. By evaluating the sentencing procedures used in 1781 and 1782 it is possible to learn more about the legal alternatives proposed by the rebels, as well as to determine through them whether the judges in charge of the cases held the same views as to the meaning of the rebellions as did other viceregal officials. Put another way, it is possible to determine whether the court was proceeding in an attempt to obliterate Inca nationalism, or whether its true intention was to prosecute the creoles and mestizos whose machinations were suspected to be at the heart of the protest. Thus differential sentences, defense pleas, and trial evidence provide valuable keys to the ideology and social basis of this rebellion and allow for a closer examination of changes taking place in Spanish judicial policy at the close of the colonial period. Finally, the article makes a case for the use of trial records as a key to understanding penal institutions and practices in colonial Spanish America, a subject understudied for the eighteenth century.[34]

Before proceeding to the trial records of the Great Rebellion, it should be reaffirmed that although the Tupacamaru rebellion occurred hard on the heels of numerous smaller revolts in which jails were destroyed and archives containing tribute rolls and other evidence were destroyed, or even more serious attacks against local corregidors, the events of 1780 were nonetheless exceptional both in terms of their scope and for the deep significance the natives accorded them. Concomitantly, they required unusual responses on the part of the crown. A vivid, iconographic approach to the question of meaning in the rebellion—that is, the "messages" conveyed by the rebel to his native followers—has been taken by art historian Teresa Gisbert, who has drawn from artworks of the period and references to painted likenesses of the Tupacamarus, in an effort to uncover the deeper, inner meaning of the rebellion through symbolic evidence. It is striking, for example, that following an important victory the Inca had a likeness of him and his family painted that depicted the group in full Inca regalia in an effort to memoralize the rebellion not only in Cuzco but beyond, even to Spain. There is circumstantial evidence that the trial court had copies of this art, which circulated as far as Upper Peru, and that it influenced Visitor Areche's decision to expunge the Incas from human memory.[35] It is entirely likely therefore that the trial court was aware that the natives regarded Tupac Amaru as *Inkarrí* and that they viewed his movement as a *pachacuti* or "world reversal," a complete inversion of a legal and ideological order based on Spanish domination and authority in spite of conflicting evidence that the Inca himself never may have considered such an event.[36] Despite this declaration, the court considered that the Inca's assumption of royal prerogatives such as tax collection and appointment of officials was sufficient to uphold their judgment that the rebellion was seditious and separatist. For example, Tupac's appointment of two chiefs in Tungasuca, a colonel and a captain, adhered much more closely to the Incaic practice of selecting representatives from the *hanan saya* (superior) and *urin saya* (inferior) jurisdictions than it did to the traditional

Spanish designation of the subordinant as an adjutant.[37] The court viewed the rebellion in its larger meaning as an effort to create an alternative legal and administrative system, an objective that demanded appropriate retribution. As the judge Benito de la Mata Linares wrote to Minister of the Indies José de Gálvez, those defendants who dared "to violate [such] sacred respect for the Crown" ought to die, since they had not only usurped royal prerogatives, but their actions also robbed the kingdoms of the four pillars of royal sovereignty: humanity, fidelity, vassalage, and religion.[38]

In an insightful article dealing with Tupac Amaru's genealogy and his prolonged struggle to validate his hereditary claim to direct descent from the Royal Inca line (a matter never fully validated by the judges of the Audiencia of Lima), John Rowe presents the figure of Tupac Amaru as a proud cacique-attorney who spent over a decade fruitlessly litigating his case in the confines of the Spanish legal system.[39] Despite the fact that the cacique's conflict with Antonio de Arriaga, the corregidor of Tinta who threatened him with harm and dishonor over the alleged non-payment of a debt, may have acted to catalyze the rebellion that resulted in Arriaga's capture and death, other perhaps more significant legal meanings within the rebellion also are evident. First, the very assumption of the rights and prerogatives of Inca royalty betrayed Tupac's belief that Inca hereditary rights could be maintained intact despite the existence of contravening Spanish laws. In this sense Tupac's actions in apprehending Arriaga can also be viewed as an attack on the Spanish legal system and a rejection of a decade of effort within the system.

In a provocative article with far-reaching implications, Jan Szeminski has analyzed the Tupacamaru rebellion in terms of an essentially "Incaic" administrative and legal system that had become manifest prior to 1780 with the adoption of the title *Inga* (Inca) to their surnames, the creation among other things of Incaic forms of administrative appointments correlated to ancient moieties and kinship groups (*ayllus*), and the revival of familial relationships between leadership (*madre* and *padre*) and subordinates (*hijos* and *hijas*). Although the rebellion can be interpreted in a variety of ways, the author finds particularly critical its illumination of what he calls an "Andean conception of history." This conception drew its inspiration from the Inca past and an essentially cyclical view of history presupposing the cataclysmic end of immoral regimes (*pachacuti*) and the appearance of messianic leadership capable of prefiguring these events.[40] Using this frame of reference, one might point to Tupac Amaru's choice of November 4, 1780, the birthday of King Charles III, to ask whether this was simply a convenient date to apprehend the nefarious Arriaga, or whether it was selected as a possible anniversary to mark the advent of a new *Incario*. Similarly, Tupac's subsequent behavior in not only removing officials such as Arriaga but also replacing them with his own officers and tax collectors, his practice of addressing supporters either in Spanish on the steps of churches (to reinforce the loyalist, proclerical nature of the movement), or alternatively in Quechua, in or near *cemetarios* (Indian burial grounds) to remind them of their responsibilities toward their forefathers, indicates the existence of an ideological and administrative system quite distinct from the traditional Spanish model. It is notable, for example, that only five of the nineteen edicts to provinces of southern Cuzco make any reference to the Crown despite the fact that Tupac initiated his revolt under the pretext of acting under secret orders from the King, and that with increasing frequency these directives were signed by Tupac as the Inca.[41] In the Edict to the Province of Chumbivilcas of November 29, for example, Tupac made a number of references to an Incaic form of social organization that prohibited banditry as punishable by death under Incaic law.[42] According to Bishop Moscoso some six hundred mestizos of Chumbivilcas interpreted the meaning of the edict as a call for a revival of Inca nationalism and chose to ask for absolution and protection by the Church.[43]

In recent years it has been customary for social historians to use extensively the trial records produced by prominent institutions such as the Tribunal of the Inquisition in order to obtain an improved picture of the internal dynamics of this body. In the case of the Great Rebellion, studies produced by Scarlett O'Phelan and myself, utilizing record groups of the Tupacamaru defendants taken prisoner in Lagui in April 1781, and those of the remaining Tupacamaru and Catari defendants placed on trial in Cuzco and La Paz during the period 1782–1783, provide a more precise social definition of the Great Rebellion and have allowed some tentative judgments about rebel motivation.[44] While these works have shed considerable light on the social structure of rebel leadership, we must be sanguine about attaching precise meaning to rebel behavior since the inferences are drawn from a relatively small group of defendants on trial for their lives where evasion and subterfuge can be anticipated. More important, perhaps, the perspectives offered by rebel elites as to the goals and objectives of the rebellion may be quite distinct from those of the rebel mass, which perceived of Tupac Amaru and his wife Micaela as *Inkarrí* (Inca King) and *La Coya* (Inca Queen). In certain parts of Tinta and Quispicanchis, for example, communities referred to Tupac Amaru as "the Liberator of the Kingdom," "a Restorer of Priveleges [sic]," and "the common father of those who endure the yoke of repartimiento," while still others viewed him as "a Moses come to break his brothers' chains," carrying likenesses of "José I" into battle with them. The interpretive works of Gisbert and Jan Szeminski, which seek to uncover the meaning of these Inca rebellions on the basis of surviving pictorial representations that provide symbolic evidence of the rebellions' "meaning" from a rebel perspective more reflective of the rebel mass, leave little doubt that Tupac was regarded as a messiah by many of his followers.[45] According to Bishop Moscoso of Cuzco, Tupac Amaru allegedly promised groups of women that he would restore to life any of their husbands who died in battle within three days of his coronation in the city.[46]

Thus, within the context of a pan-Andean social rebellion and the threat posed by the charismatic leadership of Tupac Amaru, I interpret the public trials of the defendants which took place during April and May of 1781 in Cuzco as examples of the history of criminal justice in late colonial Peru. Jurgen Golte, for example, making reference to the brutal sentences described above, states that the only way to explain their harshness is in terms of the court's belief that the Tupacamaru rebels proposed a new form of government based on a restructuring of society in which Spaniards and creoles would be denied their privileges. The anti-Inca nature of the sentences, Golte feels, demonstrates how effectively the rebel cacique had challenged the prevailing Spanish legal system.[47] On the other hand, if one places this sensational trial in a broader judicial context, we are also able to determine whether or not it represents a successful effort by the Spanish wing of the Peruvian judicial system — in the persons of Visitor General Areche and the Spanish judge (and later Intendant of Cuzco) Benito de la Mata Linares — to invoke a new and stricter standard of justice; and thus whether in judicial terms the Great Rebellion also initiated a new era in penal reform in colonial Peru.

In a previous book I dealt briefly with the efforts of Viceroy Manuel de Amat y Junient to crack down on civil and criminal offenders in Peru after 1762, and in a related article with the rivalries existing between the Spanish and creole wings of the Audiencia of Lima (Peru's supreme court) during the period before and after the Great Rebellion.[48] Prior to the rebellion, Areche frequently manifested his frustration over the fact that in urban revolts such as that which took place in Arequipa in January 1780, a combination of slender evidence and a militia whose loyalty was suspect apparently had convinced local justices to limit sentencing to five convicted Indian and one mestizo defendants, although the participants far exceeded this number. The combination of fearful, or even sympathetic, creole judges and a creolist Viceroy, Manuel de Guirior, who made concessions of suspending the sales tax and other measures designed to avert a revolution in Arequipa, caused Bourbon reformers such as the zealous Areche to chafe at the laxity of the Peruvian judicial system.[49] Moreover, the trials of the Tupacamaru defendants must be considered within the context of other trials prosecuted against prominent creole sympathizers such as Bishop José Manuel de Moscoso y Peralta of Cuzco, the Ugarte brothers of the same city, the scribe José Palacios, and the lawyer Julian Capetillo. These men were absolved from any complicity in the rebellion, largely through the efforts of able defense lawyers such as Drs. Miguel Iturrizara and Gregorio Murillo, who were provided by the Audiencia of Lima. The context makes it clear that the Great Rebellion trials also constituted a debate between the Spanish and creole wings of the Peruvian judicial system over the culpability of the Indians and standards of punishment in the colonial order.[50]

The Trials of the Great Rebellion

Although there is no firm evidence to connect the Tomás Catari revolt that broke out in Chayanta in 1777 with the Tupacamaru rebellion of Tinta, and only circumstantial evidence links these with the other, smaller revolts erupting in the interim, a comparison of sentencing procedures prior to and after the apprehension of the Inca Tupac Amaru seems to indicate that his rebellion provoked a more stringent response from penal authorities. For example, in the trial of Dámaso Catari (one of two brothers of Tomás Catari who had continued his revolt in Chayanta), the accused were captured and sentenced in March 1781, while Tupac Amaru was still at large, and only six of the fifty-five defendants placed on trial were executed. A month later, following the capture of the Inca in April, Dámaso's brother Nicolas was placed on trial by the same tribunal in La Plata (Sucre or Chuquisaca), and all the defendants received capital punishments either by hanging or a firing squad. Since the two groups were accused of identical crimes, it appears that the court acted more decisively in the latter case once the Inca Tupac Amaru was in chains because it was then unafraid of provoking further revolution in an effort to eradicate this social cancer.[51]

In the trials of the seventy-three persons who were apprehended earlier or were prejudged to have been involved in the Tupacamaru rebellion, the trial court in Cuzco, which began its interrogatories on April 19, was faced with problems quite dissimilar to those the Peruvian courts had faced earlier in adjudicating criminal cases of this sort. The apprehension of Tupac Amaru in Langui in April had not occurred due to any failure of the people to respond to the rebellion, but resulted instead from traitors in the rebel organization. Indeed, the rebel had recruited broadly in the provinces of Tinta and Quispicanchis and had destroyed an urban militia sent out from Cuzco in the neighboring pueblo of Sangarará before sweeping into the Collao provinces adjacent to Lake Titicaca, where the rebels decimated properties belonging to the royalist Choqueguancas, a rival native family. The rebellion seemed to gather momentum as it proceeded towards the city of Cuzco. Nevertheless, the Inca never seems to have considered a direct attack against the city, which contained numerous Indians and mestizos as well as a number of important creole families thought to be sympathetic to the revolt. This may have been because the Inca dealt with Cuzco as a separate Spanish legal-adminstrative complex rather than as a military objective. When the Cuzqueños failed to welcome the rebels and instead conscripted a native militia drawn from Indians of the twelve royal ayllus as well as those commanded by corregidors who had fled from neighboring provinces, the rebels retreated to the Inca's native province of Tinta where he and his followers were ultimately apprehended. However, Tupac's prestige and that of his family remained high in spite of their capture. Thus it was crucial that the subsequent judicial process not only end the rebellion, but also that it secure the desired goal of demonstrating to those remaining that sedition against the Crown was not permissible and would be punished vigorously.

Visitor Areche charged seventy-three out of perhaps two hundred persons who had been implicated in the rebellion. The accused included two Spaniards, twenty-one creoles, twenty-six mestizos, a mulatto, a *zambo* (Black-Indian mixture), three Negroes and nineteen Indians, a socially diverse group that by dint of its diversity posed additional problems for the trial court.[52] The group included artisans, shopkeepers, muleteers, clerks and *jornaleros* (urban wage earners), a group that traditionally functioned as a conservative buffer between the privileged elites and impoverished masses, but that had now chosen to serve the cause of the rebellion.[53] This shift in attitude underscored the gravity of conditions in southern Peru and probably determined the court's decision to focus on the Tupacamaru defendants, perhaps in an effort to draw attention away from the fact that the rebellion had had the support of all social sectors. Unlike earlier urban riots in Cuzco and Arequipa, where the courts had seen the hand of the privileged but had lacked sufficient evidence to convict, the social complexity of the rebel defendants made it clear that different social classes had formed linkages in support of the rebellion, a far more dangerous situation than before since they represented potential class alliances.

In this sentence, handed down on May 15, 1781, Areche stated that the Inca (whom the court always pointedly referred to as "the vile traitor José Gabriel Condorcanqui," his Christian surname) was being put to death,

> for the various ideas which he has spread among almost all the Indian nation, which is full of superstitions, and which is inclined to believe the impossibility of imposing capital punishment on one of such elevated character, being of the principal *tronco* (line) of the Incas, as he refers to himself, and therefore as the absolute and natural owner of these dominions and his vassals.[54]

Benito de la Mata Linares, the young Spanish jurist of Lima whom the viceroy had sent to Cuzco in his stead, noted in his report on the trial that of the over two hundred persons involved in the rebellion only eighteen had been executed for their crimes.[55] Both statements emphasized the unavoidable.

No fewer than forty-nine of the seventy-three defendants were branded as principals, with a total of seventeen being horribly executed, twenty-one receiving jail sentences of varying lengths, twenty-one being whipped or exiled from Peru according to the severity of their crimes, and only fourteen unconditionally freed.[56] Quietly overlooked was the fact that unlike past trials that favored defendants from the higher social classes, social status did not seem to act as a factor in sentencing. Leniency seems only to have been granted to informers, persons acting under duress, or those who aided in the prosecution; notably the six creole and mestizo scribes who had served the rebels and were released after testifying on behalf of the prosecution.

As Mata was to aver in subsequent trials against the Tupacamarus, "strong political reasons" demanded that convictions be secured against these prestigious rebels.[57] These reasons were clarified in later trials as will be explained below. Yet while the court proceeded publicly against the leading exponents of Inca nationalism, it was also quietly and effectively litigating against prominent creoles such as the Ugartes and Bishop Moscoso, against whom the zealous Mata won prolonged exiles. Thus the court further reduced the opportunity for these suspected conspirators to operate in the viceroyalty.

Two other aspects of the trial were unusual for the time. The first was Areche's sentence, which listed eleven separate charges of lesa majestad, beginning with Tupac's presentation of himself to the people as the liberator of the miserable and his intention to crown himself as king of the territories of Peru and Buenos Aires. Nowhere was the defendant accused of killing corregidor Arriaga, of sacking haciendas and other properties, or for having put to death thousands of royal subjects. Because these things were verifiable, the failure of the trial court to include them further underscores the fact that the justices saw the rebellion as a political and legal challenge and responded to it accordingly. A second distinctive feature of the trial was its treatment of female defendants. Despite the fact that the *Siete Partidas* made no provision for women in Section 7–2–2, which dealt with the crime of sedition (since it was not assumed that they were capable of committing such a crime), the court convicted no fewer than thirty women during the Great Rebellion and sentenced several of them to death, one more indication of the rigid judicial policy stemming from the rebellion.[58]

In the case of Tupac's wife, Micaela Bastidas, testimony from participants called the Coya "more cruel, rebellious, arrogant, and despotic" than Tupac Amaru himself, while others swore that she had commanded five thousand troops in battle.[59] Although the elevation of Micaela as a strategist and warrior was part of the court's subtle strategy to discredit her husband, the judges also believed that the Tupacamarus intended to reign as the leaders of an independent Inca monarchy, which they may have envisioned as some form of protectorate within the confines of the viceroyalty.[60] By convicting and executing these charismatic and powerful women the court also extended their infamy to their male heirs, thus denying them the right of ever holding a hereditary caciqueship and reducing the chances of future commotions. The only concession made to these females was that they were to be garroted rather than hanged "because of the decorum of their sex." In general, the sentences levied against the defendants (i.e. dismemberment, garroting) seem not to have been unprecedented.[61]

With the close of the first trial phase of the Great Rebellion, several emergent aspects of the Peruvian penal system were clarified. First, the trial appeared to be a victory for the "Spanish" wing of the Peruvian bureaucracy headed by the zealous Visitor-General Areche, the personal representative of Charles III, and his Minister of the Indies José de Gálvez. Both were dedicated to the task of reforming and cleansing of corruption the viceregal bureaucratic administrations according to the precepts of enlightened absolutism then prevalent in Europe.[62] By strongly punishing the rebel leadership and extending the law to include even women, the court seemingly achieved its goal of executing or jailing all the principals. This was a far cry from previous revolts, such as that led by Francisco Inca in Lima in 1750, when only a handful of defendants were tried and convicted although a cohort of 193 persons was identified.[63] While the court had stopped short of accepting the plea of Pablo Figueroa, the *fiscal* (prosecutor) of the Audiencia of Lima who served as the royal prosecutor in Micaela's case, that the Tupaca-marus be extinguished by executing all family members to the fourth degree of consanguinity, the judges seemed satisfied that the major leaders had been dispatched and that subsequent litigation had led to at least the exile of several creole sympathizers. By May 1781 the "Creolist group," which included the Viceroy Agustín de Jáuergui (who had offered the rebels a pardon early in the rebellion), Inspector-General José del Valle (who had failed ignominiously to capture the important city of Puno, thus allowing the proliferation of the rebellion in Upper Peru), and the discredited Bishop of Cuzco, José de Moscoso y Peralta, were on the defensive. In this state of mind the court forwarded the trial documents to Madrid for final approval.

The death of Tupac Amaru, however, did not return the Viceroyalties of Peru and the Río de la Plata to peace. Tupac's cousin, Diego Cristobal Tupac Amaru Inca, had earlier established headquarters in the province of Azángaro, where this group continued to wage war in tandem with Julian Apasa — a tributary Indian of Sicasica in Upper Peru who had appropriated the name of Tupac Catari in an effort to secure the backing of both Quechua and Aymara peoples and foment a rebellion in La Paz. Relationships between the aristocratic, Quechua-speaking Tupacamarus and the Aymara commoner

Cataris were never cordial and often deteriorated into serious hostilities.[64] Following the failure of two protracted sieges of the city of La Paz in which the Tupacamarus and Cataris nominally cooperated, the former group sued for peace with the royalists in exchange for full pardons, while the more radical Cataris were soon hunted down and captured. Thus began the second trial phase of the Great Rebellion.

In November 1781 authorities brought to a rapid trial thirty more defendants, twenty of whom were members of the radical Catari faction of La Paz who had publicly urged the killing of all whites, and an additional ten who were adherents of Miguel Bastidas Tupac Amaru Inca, José Gabriel's brother-in-law, and his nephew Andrés Tupac Amaru Inca. The nine Indian and two mestizo Catari defendants, including their wives, were sentenced to death in a manner similar to that practiced on the Tupacamaru defendants earlier, while an additional thirty-six Indians where whipped. Andrés and Miguel Tupac Amaru, on the other hand, were given generous pensions because, as one official noted, "Miguel was a Tupacamaru." Miguel was subsequently sent into comfortable exile with his family to Zaragosa, Spain. The trial record commended him for reducing "the brutal Catari to the role of viceroy," raising some suspicion that the Tupacamarus may have assisted in their apprehension.[65]

In the interim following the execution of José Gabriel in November 1781 and the surrender of his successor Diego Cristobal in January 1782, Viceroy Jáuregui forwarded the trial records to Madrid along with an annotation indicating his disapproval of the brutality evinced by the trial court. He probably hoped to discredit the Spanish judges and perhaps avoid recall to Spain. Meanwhile, the royalists crushed smaller revolts in Tupiza, Santiago de Cotagita, and Jujuy, and sentenced their leaders to death.[66] Authorities in Madrid quickly approved the sentences in a royal order issued on January 8, while on January 27 in Sicuani, months of negotiations and a pardon extended by Viceroy Jáuregui persuaded the sole remaining Tupacamaru chieftain, Diego Cristobal Tupac Amaru Inca, to lay down his arms with fifteen thousand of his followers.

With the surrender of Diego Cristobal, a second struggle began between the creolist Viceroy Jáuregui, who was persuaded that the danger in Peru had passed, and the more militant Spanish officers such as Areche and Mata Linares. Mata, along with Gabriel de Avilés, the new Inspector-General of the Army who had served as military commandant in Cuzco following the death in September 1782 of the discredited José del Valle (whose military incompetence was felt to have prolonged the war), both warned the court that without continued vigilance the Indian leaders remaining at large might rally their supporters in Cuzco and initiate another rebellion. Should Cuzco fall, Mata believed, it would result in the loss of the entire viceroyalty. Areche was firmly convinced that the rebellions had begun because of the policy of appeasement followed by the creolist Viceroys Guirior and Jáuregui and continued to press for the latter's removal.[67]

The Crown began accordingly to take steps to reform the Peruvian legal and administrative system. On June 21, 1781, Jáuregui forwarded to Madrid the sentences handed down by Mata and Areche against José Gabriel Tupac Amaru Inca and his confederates, adding his personal comment that the punishments were, in his opinion, unjustified on the basis of the available evidence. Since the Crown did not have the full trial record and was constrained to demonstrate its support of its ministers, the King issued a royal order of January 8, 1782, approving the sentences. In the interim, following receipt of the full trial transcripts, Galvez referred the issue of the trial to a three-judge *mesa* (board) of the Council of the Indies for complete review. The Crown began at the same time to initiate administrative changes to insure that the postwar legal system would be sufficiently strong to uphold the social and economic order of the viceroyalty, which depended upon it for survival. In September 1781, the King ordered Areche recalled and replaced by Jorge de Escobedo, who had served in the same office in the silver mining center of Potosí. Jáuregui was replaced in 1784 by Teodoro de Croix, a career military officer then serving as Commandant of the Interior Provinces of New Spain, and a man with substantial experience in Indian affairs. Gradually during the period after 1782, a nearly complete shift in the administrative structure of Peru was accomplished, with creole bureaucrats and militias being replaced by Spanish officers and Spanish regular forces. In September 1783 Brigadier Avilés was appointed as Commandant-General in Cuzco.

Gálvez had begun to use the trial process and the exercise of appointment policy largely at the urgings of Mata and Avilés, not only to end the threat of native rebellion, but also to more firmly implant in Peru the fiscal and administrative reform program that the viceroyalty desperately needed. Although the Crown recognized the basis of Indian grievances and was determined to reform the system to improve the situation of these natives, it had also determined to crush the rebellion militarily and punish its adherents publicly. As the Chilean judge Francisco Tadeo Diez de Medina, who had presided over the Catari trials in Chuquisaca, ventured: "[N]either the King nor State feel it fitting that a seed or branch of [the Tupac Amaru] family remain because of the passion which their name arouses among the natives."[68]

Punishment of the Rebels

During the balance of 1782 Peruvian authorities began to arrest those persons whom they believed to be conspiring to revive the rebellion. The case of

Melchor Laura in Chucuito, who stated that his affection for the Tupacamarus was so strong that he could not condone the pardon issued by Diego Cristobal since he believed that this ran counter to José Gabriel's wishes, offered substantiation of this fidelity. Suspected rebels were also apprehended in Marcapata and Lauramarca in the Cuzco province of Quispicanchis, and dispatched without trial by simply attaching their limbs to four horses and dismembering their bodies in the style of punishment by then commonplace for rebel leaders.[69] On February 15, on orders from Gálvez, authorities arrested Diego Cristobal Tupac Amaru Inca and 132 suspected accomplices on the grounds of violating their pardons, a pretext designed to remove the threat of this royal family in Peru. In April Viceroy Jáuregui, probably with some reluctance, announced the appointment of Mata Linares as chief justice along with Avilés as royal prosecutor. Since the viceroy was aware of the Crown's approval of the earlier sentences, and cognizant also of Royal displeasure with his earlier efforts at ending the rebellion through conciliation, including abolition of the repartimiento and the subsequent pardon extended to Diego Cristobal and his followers, he had every reason to support the orders.

The trial of the Diego Tupac Amaru defendants was far more of a political event than its predecessor. Unlike the cases drawn up against José Gabriel and his faction, Mata, in a letter to Gálvez of May 31, complained that he was hard-pressed to find "a substantial thing" to convict Diego of the charges against him other than the fact that the Indians considered him to be "the heir of their Liberator."[70] Nevertheless, Mata contended that by disposing of the last Tupacamarus, Spain might effect a "Reconquest" of the highlands and recover "the sacred respect" owed to the Crown. He pointed out to Gálvez that the swift justice practiced by the Catari trial court in Chuquisaca in the Viceroyalty of the Río de la Plata demonstrated that authorities there were unwilling to compromise with criminals.[71] Upon his arrival in Cuzco, Mata reviewed the charges against the defendants and dismissed them against fifty-seven persons who were not members of the Tupacamaru family and who had no proven connections with the rebellion. After conducting extensive interrogatories, Mata and Avilés pronounced sentences against Diego and his closest associates, including his wife Marcela de Castro and several others. Diego was tortured by being impaled on red-hot tenterhooks before being executed and dismembered. The balance of his supporters, including five children under twelve years of age, were sent to Lima for shipment to presidios in Spain and Africa.[72] The following year a court in Lima sentenced to death the cacique of Huarochirí Felipe Velasco Tupac Inca Yupanqui and eight fellow caciques who had risen there in rebellion. Yupanqui stated at the trial his belief that the Inca was still alive in the *Gran Paititi* (legendary native kingdom believed to exist in the interior of Peru), and that God had demanded that the Indians take up arms on his behalf.[73] With the execution of these sentences Peruvian authorities effectively completed the judicial *reconquista* of Peru. Apart from the small, sporadic, and usually fruitless local revolts that were a commonplace in colonial Peru, no extensive native rebellions occurred in the viceroyalty thereafter prior to independence.[74]

On November 8, 1783, the Council of the Indies completed its review of the trial record of the Great Rebellion and sent it to Minister of the Indies Gálvez.[75] In essence, the board confirmed the record, holding that it did not contain any substantial defects that might have allowed appeal or permitted the overturn of the judgments. But the Council also expressed several concerns about the nature of the sentences and pointed out irregularities on the parts of the trial judges that they felt might encourage a repetition of this dangerous situation.[76]

On November 28, 1783, the Crown expressed its opinions on the sentences and issued a series of orders to royal functionaries in cases of this sort. First, the King disapproved of Areche's ordering the tongues of Tupac and Micaela cut out while the prisoners were alive, stating that only the King could command such punishment. Second, although the mesa had disapproved of the public burning of the defendants' bodies, the Crown upheld this punishment on the grounds of invoking "public terror." Third, the Crown upheld the extension of the crime of infamy to all Tupacamaru family members, citing the fact that Viceroy Jáuregui had illegally pardoned Diego Cristobal, who subscribed to the Inca's "crazy ideas." In this way the Crown confirmed these later trials as well. Fourth, the King admonished the trial judges in Cuzco for apparently destroying Tupac's testimony before the Audiencia of Lima in which he had carefully explained his genealogy and claim to the Royal Inca line. The King ordered that all copies be sent to Madrid, considering them too dangerous to remain in Peru. Fifth, the Crown reaffirmed its exclusive right to determine the issue of royal descent among the Incas. Sixth, in the matter of abolishing hereditary caciqueships, the Crown agreed with the board's recommendation that disloyal chiefs be exiled and that the viceroys and audiencias alone be empowered to appoint chiefs on the basis of fidelity and probity rather than birth. Although the political persuasion of this group cannot be definitively determined, Gisbert's review of surviving Inca art forms from the period suggests the fidelity many of these chiefs exhibited toward their monarch after the rebellion and reaffirms the certainty of the Crown's decision.[77] Thus the Crown sanctioned mechanisms that insured the extinction of the royal Inca line, perhaps the most significant legal result of the rebellion. Seventh, the Crown dismissed the board's upholding of Areche's order to extinguish all Inca cultural forms such as dress, public displays, art works, and other memorials, stating only that Areche had exceeded his authority in this regard. Eighth, the Crown upheld the court's prohibitions against the use of the title Inca and the existence of royal Inca genealogies, leaving it to local officials to assure that these were not used as a pretext to manufacture cannons or gunpowder as had occurred in 1780. Ninth, the King urged prudence in enforcing the court's prohibition of the Quechua language. The Crown completed its review by certifying the sentences forwarded to it of the sixty-four defendants convicted during the first phase of the Great Rebellion, but admonished Peruvian authorities to proceed cautiously, with an awareness of the hysteria which had gripped Peru in 1781 and of the defendants who were still awaiting trial.

During the period after 1783 the authorities in Cuzco and Lima began to proceed against Tupac Amaru's suspected creole associates, including the creole Bishop of Cuzco Juan Manuel de Moscoso y Peralta, who was ultimately sent to Spain. Mata had also tried and failed to secure convictions agains the Ugarte brothers, the lawyer Julian Capetillo, and the clerk Palacios, all of whom were sent to Lima for trial. There, according to Mata, the creole judges on the *Sala del Crimen* (criminal court) of the Audiencia of Lima, absolved them of guilt and allowed them to return to Cuzco. The same occurred in the cases levied against Lucas Aparicio, a mestizo of Potosí, Mariano Barrera, the merchant Miguel Montiel, the priest Vicente Ceteno, Hermengildo Delgado of Acomayo, and the cacique of Santa Marta, all of whom Mata and Avilés hoped to convict as a deterrent to future creole involvement in native insurrections. What the officials could not accomplish by legal means, however, they secured through attrition. By 1787 several defendants had died in prison and another had disappeared. In 1787 four surviving creole defendants were sent to Spain for the ultimate disposition of their cases, thus removing them from Peru, as had been hoped.[78]

Conclusion

This study of crime and punishment during the Great Rebellion in colonial Peru demonstrates that the study of crime can serve as a vehicle both to better understand the dynamics of Spanish American legal systems and as a resource for the social history of colonial Peru. As Susan Socolow has pointed out in an article on women and crime in colonial Buenos Aires, research on crime and punishment in colonial Latin America lags far behind similar studies in Europe.[79] The several Peruvian trials that served to bring the rebellion to a close by bringing native elites, mestizos, creoles, women, blacks, and other social groups before the bar of justice, provide a unique glimpse into the attitudes of Peruvian governmental elites towards these specific groups. Through these records we are not only allowed some idea of how men and women actually behaved; the court's views of sex roles and other specific perceptions among the ruling elite are also illuminated. In addition, the study of crime and criminal laws illustrate how written statutes differed from actual practice, particularly in cases having political and social overtones. The relationship of specific classes, sexes, and races to the Peruvian legal system, as demonstrated through trial records, helps to clarify class and power relationships, and manifests the ways gender and ethnicity affect the application of laws to individuals.

Colonial Peru in 1780 was an area regarded as particularly corrupt by Spanish authorities. Although historians such as William Taylor have demonstrated that crime and criminal behavior among Indian peoples was commonplace in Mexico during the eighteenth century, Peru seems to have been a special legal case because graft and corruption were pervasive at the highest levels of government, helping to foster a climate of illegality. During his tenure as Visitor-General of Mexico, Gálvez had issued substantially harsher verdicts in criminal cases after 1767 in order to reform the criminal justice system, a fact not lost on Areche, who accompanied the visitation.[80] Thus it appeared that the arrival in Peru of the Areche visitation in 1777, coincidental with the appearance of several charismatic native leaders such as Tomás Catari, Tupac Amaru Inca, and Julian Apasa Tupac Catari, created a unique environment that dictated that any trial proceedings against these individuals and their followers would be designed both to punish sedition and to reaffirm the sanctity of the Peruvian legal system. As Taylor has observed for Mexico, in matters of justice, the Spanish Bourbons considered the preservation of royal authority to be the highest attribute of sovereignty.[81]

Thus the Great Rebellion constitutes a watershed in Peruvian colonial legal history. Authorities had successfully used negotiated settlements or eschewed litigation entirely in bringing numerous urban revolts to a conclusion. In the Great Rebellion, however, the striking social fact was that the rebellion was led by native elites who had gained the support of certain creoles and other non-Indian groups.[82] Although the number of these adherents was not large considering the total non-Indian population of Peru, the fact that these leaders also enjoyed the blind affection of larger numbers of Indians, who regarded them as messiahs and redeemers, raised the possibility of a mass rebellion of epic proportions and insured draconian punishment of the principals.

Tupac Amaru rebelled only after patiently working within the legal system, and he had gone on to implement major changes in the legal and administrative areas under his governance, including the suggested creation of a supreme court in Cuzco and the removal of certain Spanish *corregidores de indios*, or local justices and tax collectors. Evidence suggests that the Inca had developed an alternative Incaic legal system in areas under his control.

Thus the trial court had little recourse but to eradicate the Tupac Amaru family and end the threat of Inca nationalism. Once this was achieved, however, Peruvian legal authorities began to work toward the related goal of preventing future rebellions by securing the dismissal of permissive, "American" ministers such as Viceroy Jáuregui and his predecessor Guirior, and to place the central highlands under the control of Spanish officials, preferably regular military officers. By 1786 a complete administative reorganization of Peru had taken place as creole militia units were demobilized and their places taken by Spanish regular units. Even high-ranking European military officers such as Juan Manuel de Campero, the governor of Tucamán and commandant in Cuzco, were replaced by more rigid officials such as Avilés, in part because they were married to creole women of Cuzco—such as Doña Juana de Ugarte, Campero's wife—whose families were considered sympathetic to the plight of the natives.[83]

While the trials of the Great Rebellion have often been judged as a clumsy and counterproductive effort to rid Peru of the stain of Inca nationalism, they were also public efforts to reimpose the authority of the Bourbon monarchy, which had been severely challenged by the Tupacamaru reforms. It is by this standard that their effectiveness should be judged. Once the native defendants were dispatched, Mata and Avilés turned their full attention to the more difficult task of rooting out conspirators, particularly prominent creoles who were better able to defend themselves than the native elites placed on trial after 1780. Mata continued to seek authority to exercise summary justice when evidence of a plot was uncovered, arguing to Gálvez that the legal process was cumbersome and that the complicity of many Cuzqueños made it impossible for him to obtain sufficient numbers of witnesses to satisfy the liberal judges on the high court in Lima. Moreover, Mata complained that the formal legal process forced him to disclose his informants, making it even more difficult to obtain witnesses' testimony or secure convictions.[84] Despite these limitations, the courts were more effective than the army in bringing domestic rebellion in Peru to a close.

The trials of the Great Rebellion were not the major reason for the dampening of rebellion in Peru after 1780, despite their notoriety. Instead, social segmentation characteristic of every colonial society was accentuated in Peru after 1780, making it more difficult for Indians and whites to join forces against the Crown. Knowing this, the Crown was unwilling to grant to Mata the sweeping legal powers he sought in defense of royal authority. Instead, the Spanish Empire in America continued for two decades into the nineteenth century by maintaining practices and policies that divided its subjects on the bases of race, class, and sect, leaving the courts to demonstrate the unwisdom of challenging this primacy.

Notes

The present article is a revised version of the author's paper, "Crime and Punishment in the Tupacamaru Rebellion," delivered at a session on Immorality, Crime, and Rebellion in Spain and Colonial Spanish America, American Historical Association Meeting, San Francisco, December 29, 1983. The author wishes to thank Louis A. Knafla and Christon Archer, both of the University of Calgary, for their assistance in preparing the manuscript for publication.

1. The sentences and contemporary observations of the executions of the Tupacamaru defendants are set out in the *Colección Documental de la Independencia del Peru* (hereafter *CDIP*), 30 vols. (Lima, 1974–.), Tomo II, vol. 2:765–78.

2. "Relación de los hechos mas notables acaecidos en la sublevacion general. . ." in *Documentos históricos del Peru en las epocas del coliniaje después de la conquista y de la independencia hasta la presente*, ed. by Manuel de Odriozola, 10 vols. in 6 (Lima, 1863–1877), 1:211–13.

3. Archivo General de las Indias: Sección Audiencia de Lima, Legajo 1087 (hereafter AGI: AL), José Antonio de Areche to José de Gálvez, Lima, July 20, 1782. The best socio-economic history of the Cuzco region during the colonial era is Magnus Morner's *Perfil de la sociedad rural a fines de la colonía* (Lima, 1977). In 1780 the Diocese of Cuzco had a population estimated at 160,000, approximately 78 percent of which was considered to be indigenous.

4. The best economic interpretation of the rebellion is Jurgen Golte, *Repartos y rebeliones. Tupac Amaru y las contradicciones de la economía colonial* (Lima, 1980), who (at 141–47) also provides a preliminary tabulation of local revolts occurring during the decade preceding the Great Rebellion of 1780. Since research has only been carried out at the provincial level for the southern provinces, it is likely that the number of uprisings is, if anything, understated. The research of Murdo MacLeod and William Taylor for New Spain and Segundo Moreno Yañez for New Granada reaffirms the findings of historians investigating colonial Peru that native revolt was widespread.

5. AGI: AL 1085, Areche To Gálvez, Cuzco, May 18, 1871. I have surveyed the various interpretations of the rebellion in my article, "Recent Research on Andean Peasant Revolt, 1750–1820," *Latin American Research Review* (hereafter *LARR*), 14, no. 1 (1979): 3–49. Since the writing of this article, a number of revisionist interpretations have been published, many of which are referred to below.

6. "Relación de los hechos," *Documentos* 1:211–13. The death of Tupac Amaru I is described in Nathan Wachtel, *La visión de los vencidos* (Madrid, 1976), 291. According to this witness, Visitor Areche was angry enough to arrest the *corregidor* of Cuzco for his failure to provide stronger horses for the ceremony. Although other accounts of the executions do not mention these details, they agree with the sequence of events, preferring only to withhold judgment about the powerful Visitor's actions.

7. The complete trial testimony of the Tupacamaru defendants is located in AGI: Audiencia de Cuzco (hereafter AGI: AC), 32 and 33, and reprinted in the *Procesos a Tupac Amaru y sus compañeros*, published by the Comisión Nacional del Bicentenario de la Rebelión Emancipadora de Tupac Amaru (hereafter *CNBTA*), vols. 4 and 5 (Lima, 1980). Other trial testimony from the period of the Great Rebellion is reproduced in the *Colección documental de la indepen-*

dencia del Perú (CDIP), 2:2–3.

8. AGI: AC 33, Sentencia pronunciada por José Antonio de Areche contra José Gabriel Tupac Amaro, Cuzco, May 15, 1781, folios 253–66. Also see the record as reprinted in *CDIP* 2:2.

9. Contemporary reactions to the sentences are summarized in Campbell, *The Military and Society in Colonial Peru, 1750*–1810 (Philadelphia, 1978), 135–53. For a contemporary observation, see Alberto Flores Galindo, "Tupac Amaru y la sublevación de 1780," in Flores, *Tupac Amaru—1780. Antología* (Lima, 1976), 306–8.

10. Woodrow Borah, "The Spanish and Indian Law: New Spain," in *The Inca and Aztec States, 1400–1800: Anthropology and History* ed. George A. Collier, Renato I. Rosaldo, and John D. Wirth; Borah's recent work, *Justice by Insurance: The General Indian Court of Colonial Mexico and the Legal Aides of the Half-Real* (Berkeley, 1984); and Steve J. Stern, *Peru's Indian Peoples and the Challenge of Spanish Conquest: Huamanga to 1640* (Wisconsin, 1982), particularly Chapter 5, are efforts to treat legal issues in social terms. Borah's work demonstrates the Indians' mastery of complex legal procedures and the Spaniards' need for a constant labor source, which resulted in the commutation of capital sentences for homicide, robbery, and rape, in certain instances. Stern's analysis of Inca and Spanish legal institutions is summarized in his article in *Inca and Aztec States*, 289–320. While concluding that the Indians of Peru were able to use litigation to reduce labor exploitation, Stern finds that the long-term price paid was factionalism and conflict within the Indian world, the corollary being the perpetuation of colonialism.

11. Ruth Pike, "Penal Practices in Early Modern Spain" (Paper delivered at a session on Immorality, Crime, and Rebellion in Spain and Colonial Spanish America, American Historical Association Meeting, San Francisco, December 29, 1983, and published in this volume).

12. The work of Richard Greenleaf on the Mexican Inquisition comes to mind here. I have used cases invoking *fuero militar* in my book, *The Military and Society in Colonial Peru, 1750–1810* (Philadelphia, 1978), 189–209.

13. William Taylor, *Drinking, Homicide, and Rebellion in Colonial Mexican Villages* (Stanford, 1979), especially 119–20. See Golte, *Repartos y rebeliones*, 141–47, for a sample of local revolts and their judicial conclusions during the period after 1760 in Peru.

14. The unpublished paper of William L. Sherman, "Crime and Punishment in Early New Spain," and the comment delivered by Murdo MacLeod at the Rocky Mountain Council on Latin American Studies meeting, Tucson, Arizona, February 21, 1984, are illustrative of the contemporary debate over these two legal systems.

15. John H. Rowe, "El movimiento nacional inca del siglo xviii," *Revista Universitaria* 107 (Cuzco, 1954): 17–47.

16. Other treatments of Peruvian revolts in the post-Conquest include Rowe, "The Incas Under Spanish Colonial Institutions," *HAHR* 37, no. 2 (1957): 155–99, and Stern, *Peru's Indian Peoples*, 51–79. A related article, describing the shift from the Incaic legal system to a Spanish one, is Carlos J. Díaz Rementería, "La costumbre indígena en el Perú hispánico," *Anuario de Estudios Americanos* 33 (1976): 189–215.

17. Franklin Pease, *Los ultimos Incas del Cuzco* (Lima, 1972), 117; Pease, "El mito

de Inkarrí y la visión de los vencidos," in *Ideología mesiánica del Mundo Andino*, ed. Juan M. Ossio (Lima, 1973), 444. I have also benefited from the insights in Rosalind Gow's "Inkarrí and Revolutionary Leadership in the Southern Andes," *Journal of Latin American Lore* 8, no. 2 (1982): 197–223.

18. Golte, *Repartos y rebeliones*, 141–47.

19. Diego de Esquivel y Navía, *Anales del Cuzco, 1600 a 1750* (Lima, 1901), 291; Rowe, "Movimiento nacional Inca," 32.

20. Lewin, *La rebelión de Tupac Amaru*, 124–25; Karen Spalding, "Indian Rural Society in Colonial Peru: The Example of Huarochirí," (Ph.D. diss., University of California, Berkeley, 1968), 232–34, 243. A fuller account of the 1750 rebellion is Hildebrando Sotelo, *Las insurrecciones y levantimientos en Huarochirí y sus factores determinantes* (Lima, 1942).

21. There is little firm evidence on Juan Santos, and some are doubtful of his very existence. The standard work on the subject is Stefano Varese, *El sal de los cerros* (Lima, 1968), which is as important for its exposition of Andean mythology as it is for its discussion of the rebellion.

22. Golte, *Repartos y rebeliones*, 141–47.

23. Scarlett O'Phelan, "Tupac Amaru y las sublevaciones del siglo xviii," in *Tupac Amaru 1780. Sociedad colonial y sublevaciones populares*, ed. Flores Galindo (Lima, 1976), 67–81.

24. Magnus Morner, *Perfil de la sociedad rural del Cuzco a fines de la colonia* (Lima, 1977), 31–58. This interpretation is questioned in Golte, *Repartos y rebeliones*, which hardly considers noneconomic causal factors.

25. Vincente Palacio Atard, *Areche y Guirior. Observaciones sobre el fracaso de una visita al Perú* (Lima, 1946).

26. Jorge Hidalgo, "Amarus y Cataris: aspectos mesiánicos de la rebelión indígena en Cuzco, Chayanta, La Paz, y Arica," *Bibliotheca Americana*, forthcoming. I am indebted to the author for providing me with an advance copy of this work.

27. Scarlett O'Phelan, "The Urubamba Rebellion (1777), The Silversmith's Conspiracy (1780), and the Great Rebellion of Cuzco (1780)," *Bibliotheca Americana*, forthcoming.

28. María Eugenia Valle del Siles, "Tupac Katari y la rebelión de 1781. Radiografía de un caudillo aymara, " *Anuario de Estudios Americanos* 34 (1977), 633–64, provides background on this revolt; and my own, "The Great Rebellion, 1777–1783: A Comparison of the Tupac Amaru and Catari Rebellions," *Bibliotheca Americana*, forthcoming.

29. Hidalgo, "Amarus y Cataris," *passim*.

30. Guillermo Galdos Rodriquez, "Vinculcaciones de la subversiones de Tupac Amaru y Arequipa en 1780," *Actas del Coloquio Internacional "Tupac Amaru y su tiempo"* (Lima, 1982), 271–78.

31. Lewin, *La rebelión de Tupac Amaru*, 161.

32. See, for example, Jacobus Ten Broeck's study of Japanese resettlement during World War II, *Prejudice, War, and the Constitution* (Berkeley, 1954).

33. Pertinent sections of the *Siete Partidas* and the *Recopilación* dealing with the crime of *Lese majesté* as they were applied to the Tupac Amaru defendants are explained in Carlos J. Díaz Rementería, "El delito de lesa majestad humana en las Indias. Un estudio basado en la sublevación de Tupac Amaru (1780–1781)," *Anuario de Estudios Americanos* 31 (1974): 229–42.

34. Besides the brilliant study of Taylor, there is only Colin Maclachlan's *Criminal*

Justice in Eighteenth-Century Mexico: A Study of the Hibunal of the Acordada (Berkeley, 1974), a work based more on statutes than trial records, and one which thus lacks the proof this sort of documentation can provide for theories about penal practices. Peru has no comparable studies.

35. Teresa Gisbert, *Iconografía y mitos indigenas en el arte* (La Paz, 1980), 208–11. The work of Robert Darnton, *The Great Cat Massacre and Other Episodes in French Cultural History* (New York, 1984), which investigates, through an anthropological perspective, ways of looking at "alien" cultures such as the Aymara and Quechua were to eighteenth-century Spaniards, is another promising approach to these issues. The Indians of Peru also "said" things with things as well as words. Their uses of cultural objects—paintings, flags, attire, etc.—can thus serve as keys to the meaning of these rebellions.

36. *CDIP*, II, vol. 2: 767.

37. *CDIP*, II, vol. 2: 352. Magnus Morner and Efrain Trelles are actively investigating this subject.

38. Benito de la Mata Linares to José de Gálvez, Lima, December 1, 1782, cited in María del Carmen Cortes Salinas, "Benito de la Mata Linares: juez y testigo en la rebelión de Tupac Amaru," *V Congreso Internacional de Historia de América*, 1 (Lima, 1971): 455.

39. John H. Rowe, "Genealogía y rebelión en el s. XVIII: antecedentes de la sublevación de José Gabriel Thopa Amaro," *Histórica* 6, no. 1 (1982): 65–85. Anthropologist Rowe also uses the example of the proper orthography of "Tupac Amaru" or "Thopa Amaro" to demonstrate changes in the rebel's attitude towards the Spanish system of government. Symbolic language, as is explained below, is increasingly important for the examination of native attitudes toward dominant forms of government.

40. Jan Szeminski, "La concepción andina de Historia: su influencia en el Movimiento Tupamarista," *Actas del Coloquio Internacional*, 563–98. I have drawn heavily on this work in my analysis of rebel organizational behavior, "Organization and Factionalism in the Great Rebellion, 1780–1783" (Paper delivered at a conference on the subject of "Resistance and Rebellion in the Andean World, 18th–20th Centuries," sponsored by the Social Science Research Council and the University of Wisconsin, Madison, April 27, 1984). In a separate study, "Banditry and the Tupac Amaru Rebellion in Cuzco, 1780–1784," *Bibliotheca Americana* 1, no. 2 (1982): 131–62, I emphasize the messianic nature of the rebellion in applying to it the theories of E. J. Hobsbawn concerning primitive rebels.

41. Juan José Vega, *Tupac Amaru* (Lima, 1969), 90–99, raises the issue of the rebellion as a legal challenge. Luis Durand Florez, "La formulación nacional en los bandos de Tupac Amaru," *La rebelión de Tupac Amaru Antología* (Lima, 1981): 29–49, examines these edicts. Durand and Szeminski reach different conclusions about the integrative, nationalist orientation of the rebellion, revolving around the question of whites and their position within the rebel social organization.

42. Edict to the province of Chumbivilcas, November 29, 1780, *CDIP* II, vol. 2: 332–33.

43. "Relación de los hechos," *Documentos*, Bishop Juan Manuel de Moscoso to Dr. Gregorio Francisco de Campos, Huayllabamba, July 20, 1782, at 1:255.

44. Scarlett O'Phelan, "La rebelión de Tupac Amaru: organización interna,

dirigencia, y alianzas," *Histórica* 3, no. 2 (1979): 89–121; Leon G. Campbell, "The Army of Peru and the Tupac Amaru Revolt, 1780–1783," *Hispanic American Historical Review* (hereafter *HAHR*) 56, no. 1 (1976): 31–57; Leon G. Campbell, "Social Structure of the Tupac Amaru Army in Cuzco, 1780–1781," *HAHR* 61, no. 4 (1981): 675–93; Scarlett O'Phelan, "El movimiento tupacamarista: fases, coyuntura económica, y perfil de la composición social de su dirigencia," *Actas del Coloquio Internacional*, 461–86. A forthcoming edition of *Bibliotheca Americana* is devoted to the subject of native rebellion in colonial Spanish America and covers the phenomenon of eighteenth-century rebellion in Peru, Upper Peru, northern Chile, and New Granada, providing further information about social structure and interrelationships. There is still little consensus about the meaning of the rebellions.

45.   Gisbert, *Iconografía*, 208–9 and *passim*. A letter dated Cochabamba, February 26, 1781, *CDIP* II, vol. 2: 509, noted that the Indians there "referred to Tupac as their King and Redemptor without any reference to King Charles III."

46.   Cited in "Relación de los hechos," *Documentos*, 252, 257.

47.   Golte, *Repartos y rebeliones*, 469.

48.   Leon G. Campbell, *The Military and Society in Colonial Peru, 1750–1810* (Philadelphia, 1978), 94–95. Leon G. Campbell, "A Colonial Establishment: Creole Domination of the Audiencia of Lima During the Late Eighteenth Century," *HAHR* 52 (1972): 1–25. Further information on Mata and Areche is provided in J. R. Fisher, *Government and Society in Colonial Peru: The Intendant System, 1784–1814* (London, 1970).

49.   The Arequipa revolt is covered in Atilo Sivirichi Tapía, "Bicentenario de la rebelión de Arequipa (1780–1980)," *La Revolución de los Tupac Amaru. Antología*, at 26–27. The revolt had some Inca nationalist features, although it was a mestizo tax protest. See the *pasquín* (lampoon) alluding to the Inca Casimiro, December 31, 1779, in *CDIP* II, vol. 2: 125.

50.   There is no study of these creole trials. See my article, "Church and State in Colonial Peru: The Bishop of Cuzco and the Tupac Amaru Rebellion," *Journal of Church and State* 22, no. 2 (1980): 252–70. Luís Durand Florez, "El Caso Moscoso," *Actas del Coloquio Internacional*, 490–520, avoids the question of Moscoso's complicity in the rebellion. See note 77 below.

51.   Trial records of Nicolas and Dámaso Catari, La Plata, March 17–April 7, 1981, in "Relación de los hechos," *Documentos*, 301–3, 333–35. All of the defendants here were Indians or acculturated Indians passing as mestizos.

52.   See note 44 above.

53.   Torcuato S. Di Tella, "The Dangerous Classes in Early Nineteenth Century Mexico," *Journal of Latin American Studies* 5, no. 1 (1973): 79–105.

54.   Sentence handed down against the Tupacamaru defendants by Visitor Areche, Cuzco, May 15, 1781, *CDIP* II, vol. 2: 766–67.

55.   María del Carmen Cortes Salinas, "Benito de la Mata Linares: Juez y téstigo en la rebelión de Tupac Amaru," *V Congreso Internacional de la Historia de América*, I (Lima, 1971), 434.

56.   Four of 14 (28.6 percent) of all creole or Spanish defendants received capital punishments out of the 38 defendants who were part of the army, while 4 of 15 mestizos (26.7 percent) and 2 of 9 Indians (22 percent) received capital punishments. I am grateful of Professor John M. Gates of the College of Wooster, Ohio, who first brought this correlation to my attention.

57. Mata to José de Gálvez, Lima, December 1, 1782, cited in Carmen Cortés, "Mata Linares," 454.
58. Leon G. Campbell, "Women and the Great Rebellion in Peru" (Paper delivered at the Pacific Coast Branch meeting of the American Historical Association, San Diego, August 21, 1983), forthcoming in *The Americas* (1985).
59. AGI: AC, Testimony of Francisco de Molina, Cuzco, April 21, 1781.
60. Tupac Amaru to the Ecclesiastical Cabildo of Cuzco, Ococoro, January 3, 1781, *CNBTA* 1: 328–30.
61. Ruth Pike notes that the garrote was used for women and persons of higher social status in criminal cases since it was considered more humane. Apparently, the machine malfunctioned in this case, requiring the executioners to strangle Micaela with a noose to produce death.
62. The best study of Bourbon administrative reformism in Peru is J. R. Fisher, cited in note 48.
63. Lewin, *La rebelión de Tupac Amaru*, 121–25.
64. For background, see Valle del Siles and Campbell, cited in note 28. My forthcoming article, "The Great Rebellion, 1777–1783: A Comparative Study of the Tupac Amaru and Tupac Catari Rebellions," *Bibliotheca Americana*, forthcoming, describes in more detail the divisions in the Indian world, a subject also studied in Karen Spalding's *Huarochirí: An Andean Society Under Inca and Spanish Rule* (Stanford, 1984). Another examination of these rivalries and their influence on the course of the rebellion in Puno is Augusto Ramos Zambrano, "Vilca Apaza y aspectos de la revolución Tupamarista en Puno," *La Revolución de los Tupac Amaru. Antología*, 149–202. The Catari's rejection of the separate peace signed by the Tupacamarus is discussed in Campbell, "The Great Rebellion," 172–74. The Spaniards' skillful use of differential rewards and punishments kept these social divisions alive and reduced pressures on the Spanish penal system by preventing ethnic alliances.
65. The Catari trial records are reproduced in *CDIP* II, vol. 3 163–86. Miguel's treaty of November 3, 1781, is reproduced at 143–46.
66. These trials are set out in Pedro de Angelis, compiler, *Documentos para la história de la sublevación de José Gabriel Tupac Amaru* (Buenos Aires, 1836), 270, 285, 755–66.
67. Mata Linares to José de Gálvez, Cuzco, June 30, 1783, in Carmen Cortés, "Mata Linares," 465; AGI: AL 640, Gálvez to Marqués Teodoro de Croix, Madrid, March 28, 1783.
68. Cited in Lewin, *La rebelión de Tupac Amaru,* 697. Areche's battle to avoid censure after 1783 is outlined in Eunice Joiner Gates, "Don José Antonio de Areche: His Own Defense," *HAHR* 8, no. 1 (1928): 14–42.
69. Cited in L. E. Fisher, *The Last Inca Revolt, 1780–1783* (Norman, 1966), 369, 375.
70. Mata to Gálvez, Lima, May 31, 1783, in Carmen Cortés, "Mata Linares," 437–38.
71. Mata to Gálvez, Lima, December 1, 1782, in Carmen Cortés, 456.
72. The *procesos* of these trials are located in Archivo General de las Indias, Audiencia de Lima, Legajo 1045, and in Charcas 598. The description of the sentence and execution of Diego Cristobal is set out in AGI: AL 1046, cuaderno 6. The opposition of the *Protector de Naturales* of Lima to this sentence is reproduced in *CDIP* II, vol. 4: 222–24. Most of the Tupacamarus sent to Lima

in chains apparently died en route, although twenty reached the capital. One version of this Indian odyssey is Juan Bautista Tupac Amaru's *Memoria*. Carmen Cortés' research in the Colección Mata Linares in the Real Academía de História in Madrid has uncovered a similar sentence to that levied against Diego issued by a French court in 1757 against one Francisco Roberto Damien for the crime of sedition. From this and other evidence she has concluded that these sentences were more the work of Avilés than Mata. The evidence, in my opinion, is not conclusive on this point. Mata wanted to end what he felt was a policy of appeasement encouraged by Jáuregui and fostered by Avilés, and del Valle lionized Diego Tupac Amaru after Diego's surrender. Jáuregui's *Relación de Gobierno*, ed. by Remedios Contreras (Madrid, 1982), 189–94, describes the sentence without comment. Another Spanish defense of Peruvian judicial policy is Eulogio Zudaire Huarte, "Analisís de la rebelión de Tupac Amaru en su bicentenario (1780–1980)" *Revista de Indias* 40 (1980): 68–76.

73. Oscar Santiesteban Tello, "La insurección de Tupac Inca Yupanqui," *Anales del IV Congreso Histórico del Perú* (Lima, 1967), 4: 354–55.

74. Early nineteenth-century rebellions tended to be the work of creoles who used native leaders to broaden their base of support and lay claim to the Tupac Amarist heritage. See J. R. Fisher, "Regionalism and Rebellion in Late Colonial Peru," *Bibliotheca Americana* 1, no. 1 (1982): 45–60, a study of the Aguilar-Ubalde conspiracy of 1805 in Cuzco. More extensive research on domestic violence in Peru after 1780 would inform us about the impact of the rebellion on the formation of social coalitions.

75. These findings are set out in AGI: AC 32. See the *Extenso Informe que hacen en Madrid, Romero, Porlier, y Muñoz de la Torre*, Madrid, November 8, 1793, reprinted in *Los procesos a Tupac Amaru*, 5: 612–16. The Crown's annotated responses of November 28 are glossed on the copy of the report, reprinted at 633–40. The order informing the new viceroy and visitor general of these inadmissions, dated Madrid, November 10, 1784, is printed at 617–19.

76. For example, the iconography of Diego Mateo Pumacahua, the royalist cacique of Chincheros, portrays the chief as a *puma*, or leopard, attacking an *amaru*, or serpent (Tupac Amaru translates as "shining serpent" in Quechua), above the legend "Vini, Vidi, Vinci." Pumacahua and his wife, Doña Juliana Cori Huaman, dressed in Spanish garb, were to the side, admiring the *Virgen de Monserrat* as an example of their Christianity. Gisbert, *Iconografía*, 214 ff.

77. Correspondence concerning these defendants is reprinted in the *Procesos*, 5: 621–32, 5: 640–42. It is likely that the Council of the Indies took these cases under submission because they were skeptical of the impartiality of the creolist judges of the Sala del Crimen: Mansilla, Corpa, and Arredondo. Cf. Campbell, "A Creole Establishment"; Fisher, *Government and Society*, 44–45.

78. Taylor, *Drinking, Homicide, and Rebellion*; Susan M. Socolow, "Women and Crime: Buenos Aires, 1757–1797," *Journal of Latin American Studies* 12 (1980): 39–54.

79. Taylor, *Drinking, Homicide, and Rebellion*, 168–69; Fisher, *Government and Society*, 12.

80. Taylor, *Drinking, Homicide, and Rebellion*, 122.

81. See note 44. Gustavo Vergara Arias, "Los criollos y la inquietud revolucionaria en el Cuzco," *La rebelión de los Tupac Amaru. Antología*, 374–79, pieces together some of the evidence developed against these creole conspirators.

83. Campbell, *Military and Society*, 154–88.
84. AGI: AC 35 Mata to Gálvez, No. 10, Cuzco, August 4, 1785, cited in Fisher, *Government and Society*, 45.

State Versus County: Prison Policy and Conflicts of Interest in North Carolina

Darnell F. Hawkins
University of North Carolina,
Chapel Hill

A central feature of modern prison practice in the United States has been the shift from local to state control of criminal punishment. Like other aspects of the administration of justice, the scope and pace of this change varied from state to state and by regions.[1] States of the northeast were quick to move to establish state-controlled prisons, while southern and western states did so more slowly.[2] Regional and state differences in the movement toward state-controlled prisons have been generally attributed to ideological and cultural differences among regions. For example, most prison researchers such as Harry Barnes, Blake McKelvey, and Hilda Zimmerman stress the importance of prison reform sentiments.[3] Despite the importance of the shift from local to state control of prisons, previous investigations, whether comparative or within a single locality, have failed to fully examine this aspect of criminal justice development.[4] American municipalities and counties were legally created by state governments and represented in various ways in them. Yet criminal justice researchers have ignored the interplay among these governmental units and its relevance for understanding the operation of state criminal justice systems today and in the past.

Furthermore, studies of intergovernmental relations by non-criminal justice researchers, such as those described by Deil Wright, have seldom been conducted at the state-county level.[5] Barnes provided no detailed information on the response of local officials to the pioneering development of state-operated prisons in Pennsylvania.[6] Thus we cannot determine whether these officials generally acquiesced to state authorities, or whether their reactions were not considered important for his analysis. It appears that the latter is more likely. Friedman and Percival, in their study of a California county (1870 to 1910), noted that the operation of that county's criminal justice system was affected minimally by state or federal authorities.[7] Because their study was not designed specifically to examine the interface between county and non-county criminal justice operations, many questions remain unanswered.

This study combines aspects of legal history, organization analysis, and intergovernment relations in an investigation of one state's prison operations. Historical data for North Carolina suggest that both state and county governments at first evaded responsibility for the custody of the state's prisoners. Later, they cooperated in devising a system of shared responsibility. This was followed by a period of protracted struggle for control of the prison population. The political-economic conflict centered around the use of convict labor as a source of revenue. Finally, as the state penal system grew, its supporters succeeded in abolishing the elaborate system of county-operated prisons and established a centralized, state-controlled operation. North Carolina's history displays many elements in common with other states, especially in the south, but also has some unique elements. Their detailed consideration reveals the existence of deep problems in the political economy of the state and region and also adds to our knowledge of the development of prisons in the United States during the last two hundred years.

Of the pre-Civil War states, only North Carolina, Florida, and South Carolina had not built a state-controlled prison. North Carolina opened its first state-operated prison in 1870. After the war, North Carolina, like all the other southern states, adopted an elaborate system of convict leasing, chain gangs, and prison farms. Hard labor, not idle confinement, was the principal form of punishment, and variants of these practices lasted until the 1960s. However, to a greater extent than other states, North Carolina developed a dual, county-state system of imprisonment. Some convicts who would otherwise have been sent to the state prison were kept by counties (sometimes cities) and worked on local public works projects such as highway construction. Others were sentenced to state supervision and were leased by the state to railroads and other contractors, or were worked in prison industries, state public works projects, or prison farms. This dual penal system was not consolidated until 1933, long after state consolidation elsewhere, north and south.[8] As in other southern states, racial factors greatly influenced the development of the North Carolina criminal justice system. I do not consider these factors in the present paper, except insofar as they bear upon specific prison labor practices.[9] So too did the work of penal reformers, but their efforts down through the 1860s were not successful.

The penal reform movement in the south in the decades just before the Civil War had much more impact on other southern states than on North Carolina, if impact is measured by the establishment of state correctional facilities and the adoption of criminal law reforms such as the restriction of the death penalty. In the years between 1828 and 1849 most of the southern states saw a number of changes in penal practices, many of which had already been implemented in states of the northeast.[10] Zimmerman speculates that a part of the reluctance of North Carolina to build a prison may have been due to its perception that prisons in other southern states were not faring well.[11] Attempts to assure that prisons were self-supporting characterized the development of state prison systems, and prison industries were a part of prison operations. Nevertheless, prisons in nearby Virginia and Georgia were not self-supporting. The fear that prisons might become a drain on the state treasury was cited by opponents of the state prison in North Carolina during many debates in the legislature between 1791 and 1850.

After the Civil War the Reconstructionist state government was ready to proceed with plans to build a prison. The North Carolina constitution of 1868 provided the legal basis for the development of the modern state-controlled criminal justice system.[12] It established only three forms of punishment: death, imprisonment with or without hard labor, and fines. The state was permitted to use the death penalty for four crimes only: murder, rape, arson, and burglary. It was limited to two, murder and rape, by the first legislature that met after the constitution was approved. Prison and fines became, therefore, the principal forms of punishment. Prison terms ranged from six months to ten years and fines from one hundred to ten thousand dollars.[13] Ironically, many of the prison reformers of this era advocated longer terms in order to assure that prisoners were rehabilitated.[14] The Constitution also authorized the state to build a prison. That institution, first referred to as the State's Prison or Penitentiary and later as Central Prison, was modeled after a noted prison in Pittsburgh (the Auburn plan) and designed by an Ohio architect. Construction began in 1870. Almost all of the labor needed to build the prison was provided by the inmates themselves. After some debate over where it should be located, the state capital, Raleigh, was chosen as a compromise site. The goal from the beginning was to make the prison self-sustaining.[15]

One of the notable features of county-state relations from 1741 to 1868 was the effort by both state and local government to avoid the financial burden of caring for the state's prison population. Although penal reformers were active in the struggle to improve conditions in local jails and to secure the passage of legislation authorizing a state prison, purely reformist ideals did not significantly affect the legal and political developments in North Carolina as they had in northern, and some southern, states. Counties successfully evaded responsibility for the building of permanent, fully functioning houses of correction, while the state legislature repeatedly voted down efforts to authorize a state prison. Final approval for a state prison came only after the state government had been significantly altered during Reconstruction.

The movement toward a state-operated prison system was accompanied in North Carolina by a series of major changes in the county prison system — changes that were not always anticipated. The constitutional mandate for a state prison was preceded and accompanied by the passage of legislation that strengthened the county penal system and led to an elaborate system of county chain gangs. North Carolina gradually developed a state penal system along with a number of individual county systems. In 1866 the legislature passed a law providing for the establishment of county houses of correction or workhouses.[16] Unlike jails, these facilities would be used to rehabilitate criminals. As had been done in 1741, the counties were required to take responsibility for the administration of criminal justice. This legislative action was partly in response to the mounting political pressure to improve the conditions of county jails. Much of this pressure came from the continuing efforts of penal reformers who had tried unsuccessfully to establish a state prison. The 1866 law also gave judges the responsibility of supervising county efforts. This pleased the reformers who saw the law as a way of insuring penal reforms despite county control of prisoners. Because many counties had extreme financial difficulties, the next session of the legislature provided in 1867 that two or more counties could unite and establish a common house of correction.[17] This eased the burden somewhat but failed to satisfy many county officials who thought that the responsibility for the care of prisoners should be that of the state.[18] Since many of the counties could not or preferred not to make large investments in correctional facilities, they began to explore ways to avoid or minimize the expenses of housing prisoners. These efforts led to significant changes in sentencing practices and the increasing use of prison labor in public works projects, primarily road construction and maintenance.

There were already many statutory and judicial precedents to support the use of convict labor in public works projects; however, most of these precedents had involved the sentencing of free blacks to public works or lease during slavery.[19] Although the use of convict labor on public works projects was a common practice in most states of the north, it had not yet gained widespread acceptance in the south, especially for white prisoners.[20] Therefore, changes in the legal code or reinterpretation of existing law were needed to institute such practices in North Carolina. Most of these changes did not occur until after the plans were made to establish a state prison; meanwhile, the issue of prisoner custody was pressing. Before the Civil War, counties with the help of judicial officials merely avoided sentencing convicts to prison terms; instead, other forms of punishment were used.[21] Thus, although counties had been required since 1741 to operate jails, these were seldom used to detain prisoners for long periods of time or to house convict laborers. The post-Civil War changes of law and policy set the stage for a six-decade struggle between state and county for the control of the prison population. In contrast to the pre-Civil War era, after 1870 both county and state wanted custody of convicts, although somewhat reluctantly at first. The 1866 legislation offered counties a way to avoid the costs of imprisoning convicts, and indeed had given them a way to make such imprisonment profitable. On the other hand, the state was mandated to use convict labor to make the state prison system self-supporting. Economic self-interest was at the center of the forthcoming legal and political struggles.

With the beginning of construction of the state prison in 1870, the expressed goal of state officials and penal reformers was ultimately to bring all inmates in the state into state-operated institutions. The major obstacle was the lack of facilities to house the prisoners. The first convicts sentenced to the prison were apparently kept in hastily assembled temporary quarters. Because of this, and perhaps also in recognition of the counties' need to avoid the costs of housing prisoners until state facilities were built, the legislature passed a series of laws that further strengthened the counties' ability to obtain and retain custody of North Carolina's prison population. The 1870–71 session of the legislature provided that inmates sentenced for two years or more would be sentenced to the state prison.[22] Those with lesser sentences or those specifically sentenced to imprisonment with hard labor could be employed on county and state roads or at other useful labor under the supervision of the counties.[23] This law did not give the counties control over inmates permanently. Since the state could only house a few inmates, inmates serving two years or more were to be sent immediately to the state prison, while those with lesser sentences were to be sent later when facilities were available.[24] In the interim, counties would house the other prisoners and could at their discretion use them on public works projects or at other useful labor. This latter provision would later be interpreted to allow the leasing of convicts to private individuals and businesses.[25]

The legislature sought in 1870 to reserve to itself the ultimate authority to determine which public works projects were appropriate under the provisions of the law, while leaving the courts and counties to determine which convicts would be assigned and to provide supervision. Thus counties were required to petition the legislature to obtain approval for each project. In another act during the same session, the legislature permitted the use of convict labor to help construct an intercounty turnpike.[26] It may have been the desire of the legislature to restrict the use of convict labor to projects that would benefit more than one county; however, individual county petitions were soon approved. Between 1870 and 1887 a number of these marked the beginnings of a state-wide county chain gang system.

The County Chain Gang System

The counties, with the approval and encouragement of the state's General Assembly after 1870, appear to have realized fully the economic potential of convict labor projects. Prisoners could be used to build the increasingly important network of county and state roads. Some counties permitted the leasing of convict labor for use on private farms. The counties also were aware that such use of convict labor was a way of circumventing the 1866 requirement for county houses of correction. Most prisoners working on public works projects were provided with only temporary, and usually inadequate shelter. In addition, the economic returns from their labor more than made up for the meager costs of food and supervision. Much of the guarding of convicts was left to other convicts. Later there would be some evidence that chain gangs were not always financial assets,[27] but during the late 1800s they were productive.

The expansion of the county public works projects led to (or was aided by) changes in the legal code that made it easier to obtain a larger labor supply. In 1873 the legislature increased the authority of the counties to use convict labor.[28] Counties without chain gangs could hire out convicts to other counties, corporations, or individuals engaged in work of a public nature.[29] The 1875 legislature broadened the categories of persons who could be sentenced to chain gangs. Judicial interpretations of existing statutory law up to this point had restricted the hiring out of persons who could not pay court costs.[30] The 1875 legislature extended the 1870 convict leasing law to cover those who were liable for costs and provided further that persons convicted of a criminal offense in any court might be sentenced to public works projects.[31] Thus, even persons tried in municipal courts for violation of municipal ordinances could be sentenced to work projects.[32]

The 1875 legislature also amended the 1868 constitution to add compulsory public works projects to the list of punishments approved by the state, i.e., death, imprisonment with or without hard labor, and fines. In 1876-77 the Assembly gave cities and towns the power to operate chain gangs.[33] Such power had already been exercised by municipalities in the past, but now they were given explicit statutory approval. In subsequent years a number of the larger cities in the state would set up their own public works projects to exploit this opportunity.[34]

Between 1876 and 1885 the legislature, on the basis of the 1870-71 and later laws, approved statutes granting individual counties the right to use prisoners sentenced to houses of correction for less than two years as convict laborers on public works projects that were under direct county control, that is, operated by the county government.[35] Previous public works projects had involved private companies with whom the counties had contracted to build public facilities. In 1887, with amendment in 1889, the need for individual county petitions was replaced by legislation that permitted any county to set up its own chain gang system without prior state approval, although some guidelines were set out and county governmental supervision of all convict laborers was required. This law was incorporated into the Consolidated Statutes of 1919.[36] It was after the passage of this (1887) legislation that county chain gangs began to develop most rapidly in the state. It was also during the years after 1887 that the struggle between the state and county prison systems became more public and obvious. Much of the initial opposition to the county system came from the State Board of Charities; later opposition came from state prison officials.

The State Board of Charities had the responsibility to monitor county jail conditions. North Carolina was the first state in the south to establish such a board in 1868.[37] After the state prison was established in 1870, the Board was used by the state government to supervise its operations. The Board had become a forum for penal reform advocates who had lobbied for the state prison and now wished to bring all prisoners under state supervision. It used its annual reports and other official statements to criticize the operations of county chain gangs. The first report of the Board in 1870 decried the poor conditions of the county jails and also provided the first comprehensive census of the state's jail population. The Board's reports in 1889, 1893, 1894, and 1897–98 attacked the county chain gangs. Not only were there attacks on the conditions under which county prisoners labored, but the Board also suggested that the intermingling of hard-core and minor offenders on the chain gangs prevented rehabilitation and led to increased criminality. The Board further complained that the county units lacked discipline and adequate supervision, and therefore might potentially threaten the security of the public. For example, it was noted that some convicts were allowed to spend nights at home in order to save money.[38]

By 1896, nine years after the passage of comprehensive county chain gang legislation, the county prison system had begun to reduce the number of able-bodied inmates sent to the state prison. It was then that state prison officials, who were also required to issue reports on prison conditions, began to criticize the county chain gang system. In that year the warden of the prison complained that the counties were sending only their feeble and disabled men and women to the state prison, and were keeping healthier convicts to work on the local public works projects.[39] Both the number of counties employing prison labor and the number of convict laborers per chain gang unit had increased between 1887 and 1896.

The impact of the county chain gangs on the state prison is best illustrated through an examination of changes in the size of the state's convict population after 1870. Figures 1 and 2 provide admission and end-of-year population data for the state prison between 1870 and 1934. The source of these data are the state prison reports. As the data show, the size of the prison population under state control grew rapidly despite some fluctuations from 1870 through 1898.

Between 1899 and 1920 there was a slight downturn. Only 286 prisoners were admitted to the state prison during 1905–6, a record low for any biennium except the years immediately after the prison was opened. By 1928 the population had again increased substantially.

A number of legal and social factors may explain these trends. The substantive and procedural criminal law changed considerably during this period. The population of the state also increased. Court sentencing policies varied. Nevertheless, it is also true that these statistics partly reflect the ongoing struggle between state and counties for control of the prisoner population. Unfortunately, comparable convict data are not available for the one hundred counties of North Carolina during this period, but some limited data for selected years (and by inference for 1933) are available.

Table 1 shows the number of prisoners in county-operated prison units at various points from 1868 through 1933. The Board of Charities census of county jails in 1868 showed 433 prisoners in custody throughout the state. Those remaining and sentenced to more than two years were sent to the state prison in 1870. In 1901, just four years after the state-wide chain gang law was passed, there were 25 counties using convict labor on road work. The average daily number of convicts employed was 675.[40] By 1907–8 there were 40 counties and 1,200 prisoners. This led the superintendent of the state prison to complain in 1908 that North Carolina had forty separate, independent state prisons and to call for discontinuance of the county chain gang system.

The superintendent went on to note that most felons were sent to the state prison while most misdemeanants were sentenced to county chain gangs where they received harsher punishment than the felons. He argued that the civilization of the age demanded the abolition of chain gangs.[41] This was to be the first of many direct calls between 1908 and 1930 for the abolition of the county prison system. These humanitarian concerns were important, but the real concern of state officials was the decreasing (or not sufficiently increasing) number of convicts available to offset the costs of operating the state prison. The state itself had begun an extensive system of convict leasing,

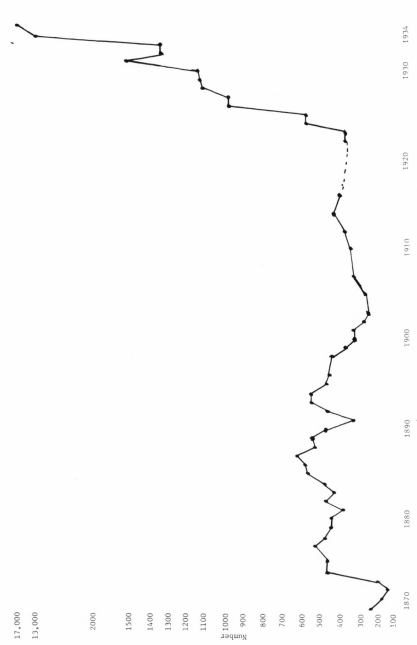

Figure 1. Number of prisoners admitted to the North Carolina state prison during the fiscal year, 1870–1934.

Table 1

Prisoners Under County Control: North Carolina, 1868-1933

YEAR	NUMBER OF PRISONERS	SITE OF CUSTODY/SOURCE
1868[a]	433	county jails
1901[b]	675	chain gangs
1908[c]	1200	chain gangs
1912[d]	2000	chain gangs
1926[e]	2500	chain gangs
1932[f]	4445	chain gangs
1933[g]	13,000 (est.)	chain gangs, jails, courts

[a] First Annual Report of the Board of Charities of North Carolina, 1870.

[b] Steiner (1927, p. 37)

[c] Steiner (1927, p. 39)

[d] *Biennial Report*, 1911–12, State Prison, p. 7.

[e] Steiner (1927, p. 5)

[f] Zimmerman (1947, p. 418)

[g] *Biennial Report*, 1932–34, State Highways and Public Works Commission — Prison Department. This is an estimate based upon the number of convicts officially transferred from the counties to the state in 1933. Many of these convicts were newly sentenced or were in jails rather than chain gangs.

chain gangs, and prison farms after 1870. That system was threatened by the practices of the counties.

Steiner and Brown report that by 1926 county chain gangs were operated in 48 out of the 100 counties, covering more than one-half the area of the state and more than two-thirds the population.[42] In 1930, 51 counties operated chain gangs.[43] Further, since counties could be assigned prisoners from other counties, convicts from almost every county in the state could possibly be sentenced by a court to county public works projects rather than to the state prison. When Steiner and Brown studied the chain gangs in 1926, the population of the road camps operated by the counties was almost double that of the prison population held by the state (1,400), numbering about 2,500.[44] This number had increased to 4,445 by 1932 (see Table 1).

A major factor contributing to the counties' increasing share of the prison population was the sentencing practice of presiding judges. Steiner and Brown report that during 1924–25, 48 percent of those convicted in Superior Courts were committed to the county chain gangs and only 8 percent to the state prison.[45] Under existing law the presiding judge could use his discretion to decide where to send a prisoner. The earlier hard and fast rules regarding

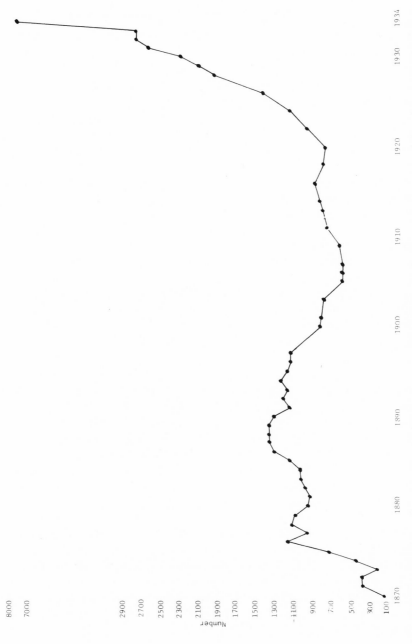

Figure 2. Number of prisoners under state supervision in North Carolina at end of fiscal year, 1870–1934.

where convicts should be sent were never really followed and were now abandoned. With the aid of this and other legal changes, the counties had now become a major competitor of the state for control of the prison population.

In addition to judicial discretion, a major legal change after 1887 which led to the increased size of the county prison population was the counties' use of local laws, or special petitions, to expand the counties' ability to work prisoners on the roads and other projects. Long before the earlier provision that all prisoners sentenced for more than two-year terms be sent to the state prison was completely voided by law and practice, most of the larger county operations had received exemptions. By the early 1920s these counties had obtained permission to work on the roads prisoners sentenced to as many as twenty years.[46] There is also evidence that persons convicted of rape and manslaughter were often kept in the county system, although most murderers (but not all) appear to have been sent to the state prison. The public's fear of such offenders was used by opponents of the chain gang system to encourage its abolition.[47]

Therefore, with the aid of a number of legal innovations, as well as by selective disobedience of the law, the counties were able to gain control over an increasing share of the state's prison population. The state legislature was, of course, primarily an assemblage of representatives of the counties and was quite sympathetic to the efforts of individual counties to initiate and maintain public works projects. Since judges were primarily local officials, they were also likely to be willing to aid the efforts of the counties by using their discretion to send most convicts to work on county roads. On the other hand, the state's prison department was not at first influential. It took many years of growth and continuing political pressure before the state prison department began to influence the state legislative body and the governor. In fact, for most years during this period it was not an official department within the state government. The existence of dual, even tripartite (state, county, city), system of corrections raised a number of legal, political, and economic questions, many of which would not be resolved for several decades.

State-Operated Chain Gangs

As earlier noted, the efforts of the state to abolish the county chain gang system were rooted in more than a conviction that state custody of prisoners was better for the convicts or that the state could do a better job of administering justice. County and state prison practices were virtually identical in many respects. Nor did the efforts appear to reflect sentiments favoring centralization as opposed to local control. Much of the motivation was economic, especially after 1887. At the inception of the state prison in

1870, the state legislature had insisted through a constitutional amendment that the prison be self-supporting. Such a requirement was needed to silence opponents of the state prison and was common in most states during the nineteenth century. Most penal reformers also saw the prison as an institution in which criminals would be engaged in productive work that would rehabilitate them and make it unnecessary to spend state funds on their care and supervision. As a result of these expectations, state prison officials in 1870 immediately began to make plans to provide employment for the prisoners.

At first most of the prisoners were assigned to build the new prison and work on various projects around the state capitol. This proved unsatisfactory. The prison population had grown considerably by 1874, and work on prison construction provided no cash payments for the state to help cover the costs of caring for and supervising the prisoners. In anticipation of the need to have the prisoners employed gainfully, the state legislature as early as 1872 authorized the leasing out of able-bodied convicts who could not be used productively at the site of the state penitentiary.[48] These were to be leased to railroads and other corporations. This law did not allow the state to hire out major felons, that is, those convicted of murder, manslaughter, rape, attempted rape, and arson.

No railroads or other large corporations had requested convict laborers by 1874. Because there were now too many prisoners to be fully employed at the prison construction site, the directors brought this matter to the attention of the legislature. Since, as Zimmerman reports, both major political parties supported the use of convict labor to build railroads, the legislature was quick to take action.[49] In 1875 the General Assembly expanded substantially the hiring options of the prison directors.[50] Private individuals were added to the list of entities that could hire convicts. During this year the first permanent prison structure, containing sixty-four cells, was completed by the convicts.[51] Two hundred fifty convicts were to be retained at the state penitentiary to continue work on the building and do road work. All other able-bodied prisoners could be hired out for food and clothing costs, or less.[52]

The 1875 legislative act further provided that a railroad recently acquired by the state, the Western North Carolina Railroad, would be given the first opportunity to hire convicts. This railroad became a major purchaser of convict labor after 1875. When the state sold its financial interest in the railroad to private entrepreneurs in 1880, what had been essentially a public works project now involved private corporate interests. Several other privately owned railroad companies were also provided with convict labor after 1875. Table 2 gives data on the number of convicts hired out to railroads and others

Table 2

Site of Custody, State Prisoners: End of Fiscal Year

YEAR	STATE PRISON[a]	RAILROADS	STATE USE[b]	FARMS[c]	TOTAL
1870–74[d]	NA	NA	NA	NA	—
1875	647	34	54	—	735
1876	794	456	9	—	1,259
1877	309	690	—	—	999
1878	365	737	—	—	1,102
1879	285	815	—	—	1,100
1880	301	667	25	—	993
1881	357	604	—	—	961
1882	412	584	—	—	996
1883	389	588	36	—	1,013
1884	409	635	41	—	1,085
1885	375	691	138	—	1,204
1886	393	860	62	—	1,315
1887	136	1,002	110	171	1,409
1888	173	992	93	189	1,377
1889	234	909	46	188	1,377
1890	173	748	147	234	1,302
1891	196	510	112	304	1,122
1892	116	—	353	749	1,218
1894	124	—	397	661	1,182
1895	152	—	52	1,061	1,265
1896	271	NA	75	NA	1,246
1896–97	195	—	—	940	1,145
1897–98	112	—	—	1,005	1,117
1899	NA	NA	NA	NA	1,091
1898–1900	294	NA	NA	NA	878
1901	NA	NA	NA	NA	860
1903	NA	NA	NA	NA	816
1905	NA	NA	NA	NA	658
1906	NA	NA	NA	NA	658
1907	NA	NA	NA	NA	662
1908–09	NA	300[e]	NA	300	677
1910	NA	NA	NA	NA	775
1912	NA	NA	NA	NA	806
1914	NA	323	92	NA	873
1916	138	NA[f]	300	462	900
1918	130	—	266	364	760
1920	136	—	391	226	753
1922	180	—	609	208	997
1924	239	—	361	545	1,145
1926	282	—	615	589	1,486
1928	308	—	882	778	1,968
1929	392	—	864	922	2,178
1930	452	—	992	873	2,317
1931	NA	—	NA	NA	2,685
1932	NA	—	NA	NA	2,808
1933(1)	624	—	1,031	1,167	2,822
1934	570	—	6,140	1,246	7,650

[a] Convicts at the state prison were working in a number of prison industries that are not enumerated here. This was especially true before 1900. Some prisoners housed in the state prison were also contracted out during only a part of the year.

[b] State use includes highway construction, public building construction, quarries, mining, excavation of canals and a number of similar public works enterprises. Most of these projects were by private companies.

[c] Does not include convicts housed at the prison who worked on smaller farms.

[d] During 1870–74 most convicts worked on construction of the prison building. A few worked under outside contracts or on miscellaneous state use projects.

[e] Average yearly figure.

[f] No evidence of railroad contracts exists after 1914 in the Prison Reports. However, during several years up to 1930, there was limited use of convict labor on one or two projects.

---

from 1870 to 1932. It also reports the location of custody of all state convicts during this period.

The 1875 law and the Constitution of 1876 required that leased out convicts remain under state supervision. The state, not the lessor, remained responsible for discipline and care of the convicts. In this respect, North Carolina's leasing system was unlike that of any other state. The cost of such supervision at scattered locations around the state was to become a concern of prison officials during the next fifteen years. There is some question as to whether the state always respected the requirement of state supervision. There were many exceptions. For example, in a contract made with one of the private railroad companies, the state agreed to permit the company to feed, clothe, guard, and provide medical care for the convicts. The company also agreed to pay the state $31.20 per year per convict. The state still had the responsibility of transporting and providing shelter for the convicts, but these obligations were also contracted away at times.[53]

The many abuses of the leasing system in North Carolina and other southern states have been chronicled by a number of studies.[54] Prisoners were physically abused, inadequately housed and fed, and often overworked. The result of such practices was an extremely large number of deaths resulting from abuse by guards and from disease. Similarly bad conditions existed at the county chain gang camps even as late as 1926, when Steiner and Brown conducted their study.

But because of the financial benefit of such labor for both the state and the railroad companies, the practice of hiring out convicts continued in North Carolina for many years. Despite increasing efforts by penal reformers to end the convict lease system, North Carolina and most states of the south abandoned the practice only after agricultural work on state farms was introduced. In North Carolina the profitability of convict leasing also became an issue. From the beginning, the use of convict labor on the railroads benefited railroad companies and allowed state legislators to satisfy constituents more than it benefited the state prison system. The practice also conflicted with the needs and plans of prison officials.

The state legislature passed eighteen laws in 1879 authorizing the leasing of 2,325 convicts to various railroad companies. Legislators, working for the support of their local constituents and business interests in their areas, were eager to use convict labor for the railroads. This pleased both law-and-order advocates and business-minded constituents.[55] However, the administrative needs of state prison officials were seldom considered, and, of course, the interests of the convicts were never considered. Of the over two thousand convicts contracted for in 1879, many of the assignments could not be carried out because the number of able-bodied convicts in state custody was never as large as the number assigned by the legislature. Yet these laws were passed each session.[56]

Railroad work may have served as a form of retribution for crime and as a public service for citizens of the state, but cash revenue from this type of leasing was limited. Under some leasing arrangements the state was forced to provide funds for guards, food, clothing, shelter, and other necessities. Although the costs were minimal in most instances, they required the expenditure of cash which the state prison authorities had to obtain from other prison or state operations. Even when the state avoided these expenses, the amounts the railroads paid for convict labor were meager. The state also had to pay the expenses of caring for the convicts who could not be sent to work on the railroads. Between 1870 and 1884 there was also the continuing need to provide some funds for the building of the state prison.[57]

When railroad leasing operations did turn a substantial profit after 1875, much of the surplus went to cover the costs of buying supplies to build the state prison, care for prisoners in custody, and for many other expenses. (Table 3 provides data on prison expenditures and receipts for most of the period between 1870 and 1933.) Before the expansion of railroad and other leasing operations in 1875, the prison depended on state appropriations. The maximum for these appropriations was set by law. That maximum varied over the years and often became a major problem for prison officials. For example, under an act passed by the Assembly in 1889, the prison was limited in its expense to $230,000 per year; in 1890, prison officials successfully recommended an amendment of this act.[58]

While the prison was being built, convict labor for the project yielded a substantial saving for the state. However, these indirect sources of revenue often could not be adequately represented in prison department annual and biennial budget reports. Prison officials attempted to estimate the value of prison labor (see Table 3), and using both direct and indirect sources of

Table 3

State Prison Operating Costs, 1874–1904

YEAR	APPROPRIATION	ALL RECEIPTS	EXPENDITURES	BALANCE[*]
1874	$ 91,000	$ 95,039	$ 90,346	$ 4,693
1875–76	205,165	216,506	235,872	– 21,678
1876–78	261,397	275,522	274,360	1,162
1878–80	100,000(est.)	291,329	290,650	679
1880–82	NA	331,523	346,733	– 15,211
1882–84	–	363,998	368,297	– 4,298
1883	75,000	–	–	–
1884	75,000	–	–	–
1884–86	–	339,681	386,816	– 47,136
1885	135,233	–	–	–
1886	121,900	–	–	–
1886–88	–	429,316	469,724	– 40,409
1887	100,000	–	–	–
1888	100,000	–	–	–
1858–89	–	190,388	216,887	– 26,499
1889–90	–	236,722	238,427	– 1,705
1889	75,000	–	–	–
1890	75,000	–	–	–
1890–92	–	400,000	373,617	26,991
1891	9,000[a]	–	–	–
1892	9,000	–	–	–
1893	12,500	213,479	163,061	50,418
1894	12,500[b]	–	–	44,208
1895	30,000	255,720	186,494	69,225[c]
1896	30,000	285,728	194,034	91,694[c]
	(5,000 used)			
1899	55,414	NA	NA	34,457
1900–1901	50,000	139,871	17,191	122,680[c]
1901	None	147,301	146,651	649[d]
1902	None	187,760	163,765	23,994
				(40,284)[e]
1903	None	153,266	124,884	28,355
1904	None	191,155	187,610	3,555
				(132,867)

[*] The "balance" column gives the amount of surplus or loss for the period. Because of inconsistencies in the record keeping practices, this figure may represent (1) actual liquid assets (generally cash or bank deposits on hand), (2) value of farm goods and similar inventories *plus* liquid assets, or (3) liquid assets, inventories *and* value of all real property, including land. See the following footnotes for more detail.

[a] Estimated appropriation. The average yearly appropriation for 1889–92 was $37,500 per year.

[b] Prison officials requested a special appropriation and an increase in the regular appropriation in this year's report.

[c] These balances generally contain small liquid assets. They represent mostly marketable farm products on hand at end of year.

[d] Liquid assets only.

[e] The figures in parentheses are *total* assets—basically farm products and cash.

Continued on next page

Table 3 (continued)
State Prison Operating Costs, 1905–1932

YEAR	APPROPRIATION	ALL RECEIPTS	EXPENDITURES	BALANCE*
1905	None	$ 174,472	$ 166,259	$ 8,213
1906	None	141,678	137,300	4,378
				(242,132)
1907	None	363,013	334,622	28,392
1908	None	284,415	143,059	141,357
				(154,676)
1909	$68,357	220,515	182,647	37,867
1910	None	273,246	184,897	88,349
				(218,929)
1911	None	330,851	198,500	132,350
1912	None	385,495	181,498	203,997
				(292,330)
1913	None	254,550	238,365	16,184
1914	None	208,293	188,193	20,100
1915–16	None	486,910	384,599	102,311
				(276,577)[f]
1916–17	None	121,559	23,226	98,332
1917–18	None	599,432	593,794	5,638
1919–20	None	1,087,221	1,094,941	– 7,720
1920–21	None	200,818	175,162	20,398
1921–22	None	191,003	228,939	– 37,936
				(100,939)
1922–23	None	372,770	517,712	– 144,942
1923–24	183,500[j]	631,093	694,123	– 63,030
				(1,904,114)[g]
1924–25	304,000	480,170	408,131	18,093[h]
1925–26	–	NA	NA	24,615[h]
				2,871,721[g]
1926–27	NA	655,293	600,601	54,692
1927–28	NA	859,909	788,229	71,680
1928–29	None	740,632	635,010	105,622
1929–30	None	683,227	839,800	– 156,573
1930–31	160,987	735,911	734,910	1,000
1931–32	555,911	556,911	555,911	1,000[i]
				(13,243,958)[g]

* The "balance" column gives the amount of surplus or loss for the period. Because of inconsistencies in the record keeping practices, this figure may represent (1) actual liquid assets (generally cash or bank deposits on hand), (2) value of farm goods and similar inventories *plus* liquid assets, or (3) liquid assets, inventories *and* value of all real property, including land. See the following footnotes for more detail.

[f] Convicts worked on several income producing projects from 1915–20 for which the state received no credit.

[g] These figures represent all assets, including the value of land, buildings, and inventions.

[h] Payments to convicts were required. This figure represents cash assets after payments.

[i] More than $229,000 were deposited in the state's general fund from prison operations during 1932.

[j] This appropriation was primarily for building renovation and construction.

revenue, the prison showed small surpluses from 1870 through 1874. But by the end of 1876, before railroad leasing had fully begun, a major deficit was reported.[59]

Railroad leasing increased earnings for a short time, but by 1882 the prison was again spending more than it earned. The railroad operations were not capable of offsetting both the expenses incurred by the prison's other operations and the costs of supervising and caring for the leased convicts at the railroad sites. In addition, as initial construction was completed after 1885, the railroads needed fewer laborers.[60] Thus, even before the counties began to take larger numbers of prisoners from the state, it was forced to explore other means of increasing the self-sufficiency of the prison system. The state explored three major alternatives: the creation of new and expansion of existing industries at the state prison, the establishment of state-operated convict farms, and the use of convict labor to build state roads. The convict farms proved to be the most profitable.

State Farming Operations

Given the essentially agricultural economy of North Carolina during the late 1800s and early 1900s, state officials were quick to recognize the financial benefits to be derived from the use of convict farm labor. Farm operations had several distinct advantages over railroad leasing. First, farm labor was less strenuous than railroad and road labor. This meant that the less able-bodied males, younger prisoners, and females could be gainfully employed. Second, farm operations were easier to monitor and supervise. Prisoners did not have to travel from place to place; instead large numbers could be kept at one site. In addition, field work at isolated farm sites minimized the possibility of escape. Third, farm operations had the fiscal advantage of producing both cash and goods needed by the prison population. The state could minimize its need to buy food and similar supplies on the open market. Finally, many prison officials believed that farm labor, like the chain gang, was better suited to southern convicts, in contrast to northern convicts who came from urban areas and who often were required to work in skilled prison industries.[61] For these reasons the state began to experiment with farm operations at the same time that it was leasing prisoners to private industry, railroads, and road units. A small garden at the prison site had provided food for convicts as early as 1874. These farming operations were later to become the major penal institution in the state and most of the south.

The 1878–80 biennial report of the prison administration pointed out that, of the prisoners then remaining inside the prison, 200 of the 285 were too old and decrepit for railroad work.[62] It advised that vacant land adjoining and near the prison be used as a farm that inmates might cultivate. The officials also included a general request for more appropriations for the prison, especially for completion of the building. The land was finally bought in 1882. It became known as Cooke Farm and showed a small profit during its first year of operation.[63]

North Carolina was the first southern state to use convict labor extensively in farming operations.[64] North Carolina's leadership in establishing convict farms may be attributable in part to the inability of the state prison officials to gain control over the inmate population from the counties. With a somewhat larger population of convicts the state might have been able to operate a self-sufficient prison system through leasing. Whatever the reasons for its beginnings, prison farm operations proved so successful in the state during the 1880s that by 1888 the state had leased, with an option to purchase, a large tract of land some distance from the state prison on which to operate a large farm. This tract, and other land acquired later by the state, became the Caledonia and Halifax farms of several thousand acres, which operated far into the twentieth century.

During the late 1880s some non-farm prison industries also provided revenue for the state prison. The brickmakers who were making bricks for the state prison appear to have provided surplus bricks for sale. In 1888–90, the prison brickyard earned a profit of $10,000.[65] However, the principal non-leasing enterprise during this time was the prison farm. Between 1888 and 1890, Roanoke, a smaller farm at the site of the large land purchase, reported a cash profit of over $13,000.[66] The state's expansion of farming activities required more convict labor and capital investment in buildings, land improvements, and so forth. These efforts began in earnest during the early 1890s. In their 1890–92 report prison officials noted that in order to continue the state prison on a self-sustaining basis,

> . . . [I]t is absolutely necessary to work at least forty-six percent of our prison population on farms, and inasmuch as we are now paying the sum of eight thousand two hundred and twelve dollars and seventy cents ($8,212.70) for the rent of farms we now have leased, and in order to make them available have placed large and valuable improvements on the same, we do most respectfully recommend that these farms be purchased at the option prices, and for that purpose that there be issued four percent bonds in amount sufficient to pay for them, and that said bonds be charged to the Penitentiary, and this Institution be required to set apart sufficient sums from its earnings to pay the semi-annual interest as it shall fall due.[67]

The state had leased large farm tracts after legislative approval in 1888 and 1889. Prison administrators now encouraged the state to purchase these tracts. Despite the advice of prison officials, the Assembly did not proceed immediately to purchase the land; leasing continued. Later the state also authorized the sale of bonds, which provided funds for prison operation and expansion after 1900.

North Carolina was leasing 8,090 acres of land for farming use in 1892. During 1893, three of the four large farms located away from the prison building site showed profits. The following acreages were reported for these farms in 1894: Halifax, 1,350 acres; Northhampton, 2,150 acres; Caledonia, 4,500 acres; and Castle Hayne, 600 acres.[68] The smaller farms located near the prison appear to have continued and were worked by prisoners who were not allowed or were unable to leave the prison. In 1895 and in 1898 the state purchased the three smallest farms.[69] Thus, between 1889 and 1898 the state's prison farm system expanded rapidly. Ironically, the success of the farms caused financial problems for prison administrators. After observing that the prison system was not losing money, the state legislature cut its appropriation (see Table 3). This would not have been a serious problem if the prison surpluses during this period had been cash surpluses. With the advent of farming the state began to conduct inventories of farm goods left at the end of the year. The value of these goods (at current market value) was used to compensate for actual cash deficits. As a result of this practice, and the drastic cuts in state appropriations, prison officials were forced to request additional funds from the state in 1894. In that year's annual report the superintendent asked for a $15,000 special appropriation plus a $35,000 regular one. Of the $44,207 surplus shown for the prison during that year, $44,000 was the value of surplus crops on hand at the end of the year. The state prison showed by 1896 an increase in its cash surplus (see Table 3).

The state's farming operations produced the sometimes large operating surpluses observed between 1900 and 1923. In fact, prison operations were so successful that the prison not only became self-sustaining but was also able to contribute large sums to the state's general fund for use in other areas of state government. The General Assembly passed an act in 1907 directing the Board of Prison Directors to pay the state Treasurer $175,000 out of its earnings.[70] Similar payments were required in other years when the prison showed large surpluses. In addition, the prison Board was forced to contribute to the operation of the Criminal Insane unit, a quasi-independent part of the state prison supported through state appropriations. The Prison Department even had enough money to invest in various private enterprise ventures between 1907 and the middle 1920s.

As the state prison began to be self-sustaining, the struggle with the counties gradually intensified. Around 1902 prison officials began to mount a campaign against the county chain gang system that would result in complete state control of the prison population by 1933. The state prison's fight against the counties was prompted by its need for farm labor; but the state had also begun its own public works chain gang system after 1870. These operations were separate and distinct from the earlier railroad leasing practice, and consisted primarily of highway construction and repair.

State Public Works Projects

Other states of the south, which had not developed so extensive a system of convict farming as had North Carolina, often used convict labor on state public works projects (often called state use or public account projects).[71] Because of penal reformers' opposition (and labor interests to a lesser degree) to convict leasing, especially to purely private corporations and individuals, states had turned to these more acceptable uses of convict labor. They often entailed the use of prisoners to build and repair roads, public buildings, levees, drainage ditches, and canals. As detailed above, in North Carolina this use of convict labor was encouraged for the counties. However, after the end of large-scale railroad leasing in the late 1880s, the state's prison officials began to use larger numbers of state convicts in state projects. Convicts were used to mine state-owned coal, work in rock quarries, and build canals. But because of the influence of the good roads movement, road building and maintenance was the major type of public works project operated by the state (and counties) during the late 1800s and into the twentieth century. Observing the success of such projects in other states and in its own counties, and as a result of public pressure, the state government began to take more interest in using convict labor to improve state roads. This concern, along with the state's growing prison farm system, helped to provide impetus for the attack by state prison officials on the county chain gangs.

The use of convict labor for state projects (county or private supervision) actually preceded the establishment of the state prison as in most other states. There are reports of such projects during the half century before the Civil War.[72] Like convict farming, state public works projects existed at the same time that the state was leasing convicts to the railroads. For example, during 1879 the smaller railroad companies received convict laborers only after the major companies had been assigned convicts and after the quota of prisoners assigned to help build state roads was filled.[73] Legislation sanctioned these allocation arrangements. Most of the state road work and other public works projects were performed by private companies that were allowed to lease state convicts. This arrangement benefited both the state and the private companies. In fact, North Carolina's leasing operations during this time have been described by Herbert McKay as combining elements of state controlled non-public and public use leasing.[74] Many states during this time opted for one or the other exclusively.

As railroad leasing began to diminish or to come more directly into conflict with the state's use of convicts for state road work, many people began to suggest that more convicts be used for work on highways. In 1887 the state's major newspaper, the *Raleigh News and Observer*, advocated such a policy.[75] Thus, while prison officials were finding prison farm labor to be financially rewarding, there was a growing lobby in the state to use convict labor to improve state roads. Both of these interests brought the state prison system into direct conflict with the counties for control of the North Carolina prison population.

The use of convict labor for road construction appears to have been at the hub of the pattern of conflicting interests, evasion of responsibility, and competition between county and state during this period. Even after the passage of enabling legislation, counties were reluctant to take on the responsibility of managing chain gangs. At first only the most populous and financially sound counties did so. As late as 1901, fourteen years after the passage of county chain gang legislation, Zimmerman reports that the counties had not taken full advantage of the law.[76] Some state legislators and perhaps officials in the state government's executive unit apparently saw the 1887 law as one means of helping the state evade the task of building and maintaining the system of state roads. This would be left to the counties. Enabling legislation passed by the legislature in 1901 supports this belief.

The Assembly passed a general road law in 1901 which established a state highway commission. The major responsibility of the commission was not to oversee and build state roads; rather, it was to advise county commissioners in the work of roadbuilding.[77] State officials were directed to instruct county officials as to the most efficient and productive use of convict labor. The state government and the state prison system would play a limited and advisory role in the movement toward a statewide system of good roads. State prison officials were pleased, for they saw convict labor on farms as much more financially rewarding. Nevertheless, the reluctance of the counties to undertake this task rapidly meant that, in response to public pressure, more state convicts were assigned to road work just as farming operations expanded. The eventual direct competition between the state and county systems came only after county officials were almost forced to take more responsibility for construction of the state's roads and after initial county efforts had proven successful.

The State's Attack on the County Chain Gang

After 1890 the number of convicts at the state prison began to decline (see Figure 2). In 1902, as in 1896, the superintendent of the prison criticized the counties' practice of using robust convicts to work on roadbuilding and sending the weak, feeble, and sick to the prison. He also resented the Assembly's continued allocation of large numbers of state inmates to work for private contractors (mostly, but not exclusively, engaged in public works projects), despite the obvious need for convict labor on the farms. He complained that 60 percent of the prisoners under state control were working under contracts to non-state entities.[78] Many contracts may have represented paybacks for political favors. The state could alter its own contracting policies, but the problem of the county chain gangs persisted. He was concerned primarily about the counties' then current practice of retaining all inmates regardless of offense or length of sentence, and about the law that allowed counties without chain gangs to send their convicts to adjoining ones.

The continuing decrease in the size of the prison's population after 1902 led to more attacks by prison officials on the county chain gang system. The 1903–5 Report (pp. 7–8) noted:

> On January 1, 1901, the population of the prison was 860; at this date, January 1, 1905, it is 658, showing a decrease within four years of 202. The county chain gang system, undoubtedly, is responsible for this decrease in population. If the present policy of the State is continued, the population of the prison, within a very short time, will consist mainly of two classes, the larger being the feeble or non-producing class, and the other long-term desperate criminals. With a constantly diminishing number of wage-earners, the problem of self-support is yearly becoming more difficult.

The report also criticized the state's own practice of sending convicts to work under contract on state roads. The superintendent suggested that many of these convicts were dangerous and could escape. "Criminals are imprisoned for the protection of society and the prevention of crime; self-support or financial profit from the prison should be a matter of secondary importance."[79]

By 1906 the financial condition of the prison had worsened. Only 286 convicts were admitted to the prison during that fiscal year. The year's report noted that the state's farms did not yield as abundantly as they had during the previous three years. In 1907 the Assembly, finally giving in to prison officials, passed an act authorizing the issuance of prison bonds to help finance the prison system.[80] The 1907–8 Prison Report recommended that county chain gangs be abandoned,[81] but no legislative action was taken to implement this suggestion. Prison operations continued as usual through 1919. Convicts still worked on the farms, but many also continued to be leased out to road construction companies.

The counties won a major, although perhaps Pyrrhic, victory over the state in 1919. The law of 1887 that permitted county chain gangs was consolidated in a new compilation of statutes that left the powers of the counties unchanged or expanded. Also in 1919, Caledonia farm was put up at auction. It was to lie idle until 1923, when the state again began to use it as a prison facility. The 1919 auction was probably prompted by poor management as well as the continuing decline in the number of convicts assigned to farm labor.

Between 1919 and 1922 both county and state prison operations grew rapidly despite the hiatus in state farming operations. The state's main prison, now known as Central Prison, was only one of fourteen different units in the system. Three farms continued to operate, and camps had been established across the state. Many of these camps later became permanent units within the prison system. The expansion of the state prisons led to much legislative attention to their needs. Prison officials used the growth of the system to renew their efforts to weaken the county chain gang system.

The growth of the state prison population did not signal the demise of the county system. Both expanded rapidly after World War I. This era was characterized by an increase in the crime rate and a concomitant rise in the incarceration rate. It is also likely that the revised criminal statutes of 1919 increased the rate. In any case, both systems expanded. The counties employed more convicts on chain gangs, and young adult units and industrial units for women were established by the state. By the middle 1920s the state prison system had become a formidable competitor of the county system for control of the state's prisoner population. The state had begun to incarcerate larger numbers of inmates who were assigned to work on the farms and at the camps. North Carolina continued to invest substantial resources in its prison operations and began to take steps toward developing a centralized, state-controlled prison system like those already in operation in most other states.

Renovation and Merger

State prison officials complained in 1914 that farm labor in the prison system was composed primarily of convicts whose physical condition prevented their employment on the highways. State public works projects competed with the farms for those able-bodied convicts who had not been retained by the counties. Despite the continuing growth of the prison population, the lack of able-bodied farm workers contributed to a decline in profitability of the farms, although not to the point of causing the prison system to become less than self-sustaining for any length of time during the 1920s.[82]

The state appropriations during this time were primarily for capital expansion, with a number of legislative actions designed to improve conditions in the system. In 1923, the Assembly appropriated $40,000 for the erection of prison quarters at Camp Polk Prison Farm and $50,000 for quarters at Caledonia. An additional $58,000 was spent on the rehabilitation of Caledonia's farming facilities and $25,000 for the rehabilitation of Central Prison. Black and white criminal insane units were also established at two state hospital sites.

Farm and non-farm industries expanded in the 1920s. During 1925, 4,100 acres were under cultivation at Caledonia, and it reported an operating profit of nearly $52,000. All except one of the prison camps showed operating profits with only Central Prison reporting a substantial net loss. The tailor shop, the mattress department, laundry, chair weaving, and other in-prison units showed $55,000 in cash earnings.[83] The 1927–28 report noted a continuing increase in both the prison population and its profits between 1925 and 1928. The total profit for the four-year period was $240,490.[84] The report also noted that fourteen camps were now engaged in rock quarrying and coal mining in addition to road and canal work.

During the biennium ending in 1930 over 7,750 acres were under cultivation at the two state farms. The report for those years contained an important report of a state committee earlier set up to study the prisons' problems, of which the employment of prisoners was a major area of concern. The report made the following recommendations: (1) continue use of farms with improved farming methods; (2) place as many prisoners as possible on the highways and in the quarries and gravel pit so that the road work of the state could be expanded; (3) expand existing prison industries such as the laundry room, the sewing room, and the repair shop for equipment owned by the State Highway Commission; and (4) build a new Central Prison at the smaller farm site. Except for the building of a new prison, the recommendations were implemented over the next few years.[85]

The 1930 prison report also continued the efforts of the state to gain control over the county prison population. A special subcommittee report argued:

> The problem of the State's Prison is only half of the prison problem in North Carolina. There are as many men in the 51 county chain gang camps as there are in the State's prison, and only about ten of the camps in North Carolina can be said to fully conform to the present day standards for caring for convicts. This immediately presents the problem of whether the present is not the time for the county convicts to be transferred to State control, the State to utilize existing county convict camps, which meet the required standards of housing and sanitary conditions, as camps for short term prisoners — say, up to six or twelve months — and all others to be sent to the State's Prison. In other words, since the county is a ward of the State is it not better for the State while planning its prison system to plan to take care of the whole prison population in its enlarged farming program, and upon State road work, and in allied industries producing materials for the highways?[86]

Accompanying this plea for an end to the county chain gang system was an emphasis on improving housing and sanitary conditions at state prison camps and farms. Educational instruction, complete hospital care, separate quarters for various security grades of convicts, and a parole system were urgently recommended. The report also noted a growing problem of housing the increasing prison population.

The agenda proposed in this 1930 report became the blueprint for the renovation of the state's prison system during the early 1930s. In 1933 the state prisons were made a part of the State Highway Commission, and upon authorization by the Assembly, the state took control of all convicts in the state serving terms of thirty days or more.[87] The state assumed authority for running the various county chain-gang camps. Many were closed over the next few years, but most were rehabilitated and became state units. Over 13,000 prisoners were officially transferred from county to state control during that year. Some appear to have been released by state officials because the state was not equipped to supervise such large numbers. Many others were at the end of their sentences. Although the state had won the struggle for control, a large part of the prison system it inherited had been shaped by the counties. The geographic dispersion of the state's prison population and the extensive use of convict labor became prominent features of the consolidated state system, features that were still apparent in the latter half of the twentieth century. That the consolidated prison system was made a part of the state's highway department indicates the enormous influence the county and state chain gang systems had had on penal policy in North Carolina since 1870.

Phases of State-County Relations

In summary, there were four major phases of state-county relations during the period from 1741 to 1934. The first period, from about 1741 until immediately after the Civil War, was one of general cooperation, but is probably best described as a time when both state and county successfully evaded the responsibility of caring for the state's convict population. This was achieved mainly because imprisonment had not yet become a common form of punishment, and the crime rates of the period were generally low. Despite repreated efforts by penal reformers to force the state government to take responsibility for administering punishment after 1791, the counties fully assumed this limited responsibility until after the Civil War.

The second period covers the years 1866 to 1887. Laws passed during this time strengthened both county and state prison operations, requiring their governments to assume some responsibility for the supervision of prison populations. Perhaps more important, the laws enabled or compelled each government to make full use of prison labor. In the earlier years there was little friction between state and county officials. The earlier pattern of evasion of responsibility persisted since prison labor had not yet become profitable, or prison officials had not been forced into the position of investigating its profitability. By the middle 1880s however, some counties were actively seeking to expand their use of convict labor and were successful in securing the passage of enabling legislation for specific uses. Finally, in 1887 the counties, or at least advocates of county-operated prisons, won a major victory when the state legislature approved a general chain gang law for the entire state.

During this period, state prison officials were also laying the legal and bureaucratic groundwork needed to exploit prison labor. They successfully obtained legislative approval for leasing convicts to railroads and other public and private enterprises. At the same time they began to experiment with the use of convict labor on farms. Responding to the good roads movement, they also began to use convict labor for road construction. By 1887 these three operations brought the state into direct competition with the newly empowered counties for control of the state's convict population, although most counties initially avoided assuming the responsibility for the operation of chain gangs.

The third period, 1887 through 1919, was characterized by the expansion of both systems. After initial attempts to evade responsibility, each system concentrated upon maximizing its profits. The counties were somewhat more successful than the state in obtaining a steady supply of healthy laborers. The counties again relied on laws to expand their jurisdiction over the state's convict population. But with most of the major legal battles already won, disobedience of the law and the influencing of judges were probably most effective in increasing the size of the county prison population during these years. By the middle of this period county operations had reduced the size of the resident state prison population for the first time. The recodification of the 1887 chain gang legislation in 1919 solidified the position of the counties.

The fourth period, 1919 to 1933, was the period of most intense struggle as state prison officials began to use their increasing political influence. The eventual success of their efforts to abolish the county system was a result of both the precarious financial position of the state system during many years of this period and the profitability of its operations during other years. The state legislature, which feared the possibility that the state's prisons would become a drain on the state treasury, was by this time also aware of the profitability of prison labor. This mixture of sentiments was effective in convincing it finally to approve legislation to abolish the county system in 1933.

Conclusions

The changing uses of prison labor do not differ markedly in all respects from the patterns of labor use outside the criminal justice system in North Carolina and other southern states during this period. Although it is beyond the scope of this article to provide a full analysis of the larger political economy of

North Carolina during these years, several observations are appropriate to illustrate the interplay between the prison and non-prison economies. After the Civil War, the south was faced with the dual task of rebuilding its war-torn economic infrastructure while also attempting to develop a modern industrial society similar to that developing in the north. On the other hand, the war had left both the north and the south with a severely reduced pool of unskilled and skilled laborers. Both regions resorted to the use of prison labor to fill some of the need for cheap, unskilled labor during the years immediately after the war.[88]

Demographic, political, and economic changes affected the profitability of convict labor during the period. First, by the late nineteenth century, the supply of both skilled and unskilled labor increased as the maturing young filled in the demographic gaps left by the Civil War. Their availability and need for work underlay much of the prison reform sentiment that eventually led to the abandonment of convict labor operations in most northern states during this period. Such sentiments may also have hastened the shift toward the use of convict labor on farms and in other non-industrial occupations in the south. Second, the unskilled labor provided by prisoners and most of the working public during this era became less needed in industries that became less labor-intensive, while at the same time, the unskilled labor supply grew. These changes explain much about changing labor practices in North Carolina prisons from 1870 through 1934.

Railroad construction in North Carolina clearly illustrates this pattern. The railroads drew upon prison labor only during the immediate post-War periods of construction and rebuilding. As the heavy construction work was completed, needs shifted toward skilled labor. The relatively small number of unskilled laborers needed could now affordably be hired from non-prison sources. Thus by 1891, only twenty years after the opening of the state prison, the leasing of convicts to railroads was nearing an end. State prison officials were forced to react to these changes by seeking new sites and types of employment for large numbers of prisoners.

For farming, skill-level changes were caused by the mechanization of agriculture and the trend toward more scientific farming practices, which required more skilled and much less unskilled labor. Most state prisoners who were sentenced to long prison terms and could have been taught new farming skills were not assigned to farm work; farm laborers were short-term prisoners who were released typically before or soon after requisite farming skills were learned. In addition, in later years fewer prisoners came from farming backgrounds.[89] Although such changes had a much greater impact on state prison operations after consolidation, they also affected the profitability of farming during the 1920s.

Road work, too, underwent substantial changes that affected the profitability of both county and state operations. As earlier noted, county governments used convict labor on such state projects as road building and maintenance. Road work was somewhat less susceptible to the vagaries of the marketplace than were railroad leasing and farming, but its profitability was affected by several factors. County governments, even more than the state, could not afford and often did not have the administrative capacity to manage the kind of capital investments that would have led to less reliance on unskilled prison labor. Road work was similar to railroad construction in this respect; unlike railroad construction, however, it continued to require unskilled labor during this period. Nevertheless, road work, like farming, gradually followed a similar pattern of capital intensification as much of the work was mechanized, county administrative capacity grew, and maintenance rather than construction predominated. State highway officials in 1926 suggested that neither convict nor free labor was able to compete with machinery for road grading.[90] In fact, it may be suggested that the counties were ready to relinquish their responsibility for the supervision of the state's prisoners in 1933 because road work had become much less of a benefit than it had been.

State officials might have been forced to take full responsibility for supervision of the state's prisoners in 1933 even if they had not shown a willingness or eagerness to do so. North Carolina was at odds with most of the rest of the nation in its retention of county control of state prisoners, and there was growing pressure to modernize the prison system by centralizing authority in the state. In many respects, a struggle between county and state interests in North Carolina represents a rather unusual episode in the history of criminal justice administration in the state. The post-Civil War political economy of the state, rather than any historically based sectionalism or factionalism, appears to have led to the struggle. Later changes in the political economy of the state led to its cessation. This historical analysis of the North Carolina prison system shows that the state and county governments (and often municipalities) were not at odds over many crucial aspects of criminal justice administration; custody was the critical concern. Once imprisonment had been accepted as the major form of punishment, questions of jurisdiction responsibility and costs were paramount and led to repeated conflicts of interest. These conflicts continued well into the twentieth century. Case studies of other states might reveal similar struggles between states and counties. Historical studies of prisons in other southern states report similar patterns of political economy,[91] but none of the studies analyze state-county relations.

Non-governmental interests, such as penal reformers, labor interests, and civic groups, exerted much pressure on state governmental officials in North Carolina between 1887 and 1933. Many actions of the Assembly toward consolidation of the state's prison system may have reflected such pressures. The state prison system itself was a major actor, however, in the move to dismantle the county prison system. While there might have been some concern on the part of state officials for the inhumaneness of the chain gang as a penal institution and for the fact that county convicts were kept in inferior facilities, these were not the primary reasons for the drive toward consolidation. This is shown by the fact that after consolidation the state's prison system greatly resembled the county system, and penal reformers had to continue their struggle against the chain gang in 1935 after two convicts were mutilated by prison officials.[92] That these reform efforts continued over the next two decades illustrates that the struggle between county and state in North Carolina was primarily economically motivated and did not reflect substantial concern for penal reform or a struggle between competing philosophies of social control, penology, or the role of government in the administration of justice.

Although state prison officials were motivated by economic concerns, the rationality of their persistent push for complete control of the prison population may be questioned. At times they did not seem to appreciate the short- or long-term economic consequences of their actions. The attempts to abolish the county system often resembled a political power play rather than a reasoned move toward increasing profits. This lack of economic rationality was partly the result of the inability of prison officials to anticipate the behavior of other important actors, such as the state legislature, the courts, penal reformers, and the counties. Prison officials also lacked foresight as to the consequences of their own actions. For example, the expansion of the prison population after 1920 led to an increase in the need for construction of new buildings and renovation of existing ones. The central prison, completed in 1884, was in need of major repair by 1920. In addition, the farms and camps were built at some distance from the prison and required new supervisory personnel. Further, since convicts in the camps were frequently moved from one place to another as work needs changed, transportation costs increased. Unlike railroad leasing operations, the state, not private companies, had to shoulder these costs. Farming operations were also greatly affected by the weather and marketing considerations. When a crop failed or could not be sold readily at a good price, prison officials had to restrict needed expenditures in order to avoid the need for new appropriations.

Prison economics was also affected by penal reformers, who pushed for better prison facilities and more social services for the convicts. Officials were forced to provide more space for convicts, better cells and conditions. Reformers also succeeded, during the late 1920s, in forcing prison officials to pay convicts a small daily wage for their labor. This figure was never more than five cents per day, but even such a small sum (in that age of much lower price levels), along with other increasing costs, affected prison earnings.

The Great Depression had a substantial effect on prison administration and economics during the half-decade prior to consolidation and in the years immediately following. Largely due to depression-related increases in the number of persons sentenced for public order and minor property offenses, the resident prison population doubled between 1926 and 1932 (see Figure 2 and Table 2). Admissions to the state prison increased by a third between 1929 and 1931 (see Figure 1). Of course, the Depression also reduced the profitability of the state's farming operations. After reporting a large operating surplus between 1925 and 1929, the prison system experienced a large deficit in 1930 and barely broke even during 1931 and 1932 as prices collapsed (see Table 3).

The actions of the legislature and courts also greatly affected state prison officials. Changes in the criminal code and sentencing practices contributed substantially to the continuing expansion of the state system. For example, after World War I, greater numbers of persons charged with "victimless" crimes were sentenced to prison, and the length of prison terms increased. As is usually the case today, prison officials were put in the position of reacting to the actions of officials in other parts of the criminal justice or governmental systems. Between 1870 and 1933, North Carolina prison officials usually had little control over the number of inmates confined and often did not make the decisions regarding how those who were confined should be employed.

The multi-tiered (federal, state, county, local) approach to government in the United States has been a continuing historical problem, and its importance for understanding the administration of criminal justice has not been fully explored. Historical studies of criminal justice, such as that reported in this article, increase our understanding of this phenomenon in the past and also help us to better understand many current trends. In 1933 the North Carolina state government took over the supervision of an expansive system of previously county-operated prisons. Today the state has more separate prison units than any other state in the country and has a per capita incarceration rate higher than that of forty-seven of forty-nine other states. On the other hand, this extreme decentralization of the state's prison units has helped the state avoid the building of very large, centralized prisons to house many thousands of inmates, such as those found elsewhere. Many other states are now considering the decentralization of their prison systems. Decentralization in North Carolina has also permitted the state to experiment with a program of work release for prisoners in areas near their homes in anticipation of parole; other states are adopting similar practices. These kinds of alternatives to idle incarceration reflect currently increasing cost consciousness among state and federal prison officials.

Chambliss has noted that every historical era has its own set of persistent dilemmas, conflicts, and underlying contradictions, and suggests that the most important of these dilemmas and conflicts derive from the economic and political structures of the times.[93] A contradiction is said to be established "in a particular historical period when the working out of the logic of the social structure must necessarily destroy some fundamental aspect of existing social relations."[94] The establishment and resolution of such contradictions rather than a kind of linear trend toward modernization or centralization characterizes the development of the prison system in North Carolina from 1870 through 1934.

Further historical studies of American criminal justice systems are needed. These studies must not ignore issues of political economy, in particular the economic interests of the various governmental units that are responsible to greater or lesser degrees for the administration of justice. Economic motives may often be more crucial and determinative than concerns of social control, race and ethnic cleavages, and similar concerns examined in previous studies. Of course, one cannot separate economic concerns from issues of racial stratification and social control. An adequate analysis and theory of criminal justice administration must consider these and other various issues.

Notes

I thank Everett Wilson, Richard Simpson, Gerhard Lenski and Nell Painter for their reviews of earlier drafts of this article, and the Department of Sociology at Duke University for permitting me the use of its facilities during the initial phase of my research. Data for this study were collected while I was on a post-doctoral fellowship funded by the Ford Foundation and administered by the National Research Council. Funds were also provided by the University Research Council of the University of North Carolina at Chapel Hill.

1.   Several excellent historical analyses of various aspects of the criminal justice system were consulted in the preparation of this article. Among these were: James A. Inciardi, Alan A. Block and Lyle A. Hallowell, *Historical Approaches to Crime: Research Strategies and Issues* (Beverly Hills, 1977); *History and Crime: Implications for Criminal Justice Policy*, ed. James A. Inciardi and Charles E. Faupel (Beverly Hills, 1980); Alexander W. Pisciotta, "Corrections, Society, and Social Control in America: A Metahistorical Review of the Literature," in *Criminal Justice History: An International Annual* 2 (1981): 109–30; Joel Samaha, *Law and Order in Historical Perspective: The Case of Elizabethan England* (New York, 1974); Thorstein Sellin, *Slavery and the Penal System* (New York, 1976); Michael S. Hindus, *Prison and Plantation: Crime, Justice and Authority in Massachusetts and South Carolina, 1767–1878* (Chapel Hill, 1980): Lawrence M. Friedman and Robert Percival, *The Roots of Justice: Crime and Punishment in Alameda County, California, 1870–1910* (Chapel Hill,

1981).

2. Blake McKelvey, *American Prisons* (New York, 1936; reprint 1977); Hindus, *Prison and Plantation.*

3. Harry E. Barnes, *The Repression of Crime* (New York, 1926) and, by the same author, *The Evolution of Penology in Pennsylvania: A Study in American Social History* (Indianapolis, 1927); McKelvey, *American Prisons;* Hilda J. Zimmerman, "Penal Systems and Penal Reforms in the South Since the Civil War," (Ph.D. dissertation, University of North Carolina at Chapel Hill, 1947); Zimmerman, "The Penal Reform Movement in the South During the Progressive Era," *Journal of Southern History* 17 (1951): 462–92.

4. That is, the primary focus of earlier studies has not been on an examination of the changes that accompanied the centralization of authority in the hands of state governments. This is somewhat surprising given the dispersion of authority (for the administration of justice) in the United States among cities, counties, states, and the federal government.

5. Deil S. Wright, *Understanding Intergovernmental Relations* (Monterey, California, 1982). Wright analyzes primarily relations between the federal government and the states.

6. Barnes, *The Evolution of Penology in Pennsylvania.*

7. Friedman and Percival, *The Roots of Justice,* 3–18.

8. Since there are few historical studies of state prison systems, this conclusion is based on rather limited information. Available studies suggest, however, that other states did not have so expansive a county system as did North Carolina after the turn of the century. In addition, unlike several other states, North Carolina lacks a comprehensive history of its penal system or of other parts of its criminal justice system. Of earlier studies, Steiner and Brown provided a useful summary of the legal underpinnings of the state's chain gang system through 1926, and Zimmerman examined penal reform in the South and presented substantial data for North Carolina. See Jesse F. Steiner and Roy M. Brown, *The North Carolina Chain Gang: A Study of County Convict Road Work* (Chapel Hill, 1927).

9. This issue is partly explored in a paper currently being prepared by the author: Darnell F. Hawkins, "Race and Imprisonment: Extending Blumstein's Stability of Punishment Hypothesis."

10. McKelvey, *American Prisons,* 46–48; Zimmerman, "Penal Systems and Penal Reforms," 19–20.

11. Zimmerman, "Penal Systems and Penal Reforms," 45.

12. Constitution, Art. XI, sec. 3 (1868); and N.C. Public Laws, 1868.

13. See Albert Coates, "Punishment for Crime in North Carolina," *North Carolina Law Review* 17 (1939): 205–32.

14. Steiner and Brown, *The North Carolina Chain Gang,* 14.

15. The 1868 Constitution required that the prison be self-sustaining. An Act of 1889 limited total prison expenses to $230,000 per year.

16. N.C. Public Laws, 1865–66, ch. 35. This legislation was apparently the result of efforts by penal reformers to encourage the counties to adopt imprisonment as the major form of punishment. It was based on an earlier (1741) law that required each county to build a courthouse and jail.

17. N.C. Public Laws, 1866–67, ch. 130.

18. There is evidence that despite the failure of the legislature to authorize the build-

ing of a state prison, many county officials believed that the state should care for the convict population. Much of the opposition to the state prison may have reflected the sentiments of state legislators, who favored state control but feared escalating costs. The first bill to authorize the building of a state prison was introduced in the legislature in 1791.

19. An Act of 1787 allowed free blacks to be sold at auction for various reasons. Punishment for crime became one rationale for such sales. In 1831 the state legislature passed a statute authorizing the hiring out of free blacks and mulattos who were unable to pay fines imposed upon them for having committed a crime. In an important state Supreme Court case, *State v. Manuel*, 20 N.C. 144 (1838), the statute (N.C. Public Laws, 1831, ch. 31) was held to be constitutional. The court went further to delineate justifiable forms of punishment and consequently the case had a great impact on nineteenth- and twentieth-century criminal law in the state. It served as a basis for later revisions of the Constitution to permit hard labor as a form of punishment and also imprisonment because of the inability to pay court costs. After 1870 many whites were sentenced under these provisions.

20. States in the northeast made much more extensive use of convict labor than did the south during this period. Even as late as 1886 the largest numbers of convicts were worked on public works and leasing projects in states outside the south. For example, see U.S. Commissioner of Labor, *Second Annual Report: Convict Labor* (Washington, DC, 1886), 508ff.

21. Coates, "Punishment for Crime in North Carolina."

22. N.C. Public Laws, 1870–71, ch. 124. See also N.C. Legislative Documents, 1873–74, Document 1, p. 28, as cited in Zimmerman, "Penal Systems and Penal Reforms," 82.

23. Steiner and Brown, *The North Carolina Chain Gang*, 27–28; Zimmerman, "Penal Systems and Penal Reforms," 82.

24. Steiner and Brown, *The North Carolina Chain Gang*, 27–28.

25. The leasing of convicts to private individuals and businesses constituted a kind of political payoff or kickback operation. Political allies were selectively given the use of convicts while adversaries were denied such use. These abuses, as well as the competitive unfairness of the system for private industry, led to much criticism of convict leasing.

26. N.C. Public Laws, 1870–71, ch. 251.

27. Steiner and Brown, *The North Carolina Chain Gang*, 6.

28. N.C. Public Laws, 1872–73, ch. 174, sec. 10. County commissioners were given expanded authority to hire out, at their discretion, prisoners sentenced to the county jails. These included all felons and others sentenced to imprisonment or hard labor for one year.

29. Steiner and Brown, *The North Carolina Chain Gang*, 21.

30. Prior to this time, courts appeared to have limited the interpretation of the 1831 law and *State v. Manuel* to permit hard labor for fines, but not court costs.

31. N.C. Public Laws, 1874–75, ch. 113; Steiner and Brown, *The North Carolina Chain Gang*, 21–22.

32. Before this time, violators of municipal ordinances were apparently specifically exempted from work on the chain gangs. Most also were likely sentenced to terms of less than one year.

33. N.C. Public Laws, 1876–77, ch. 196.

34. Charlotte, one of the larger cities in the state, was pivotal in its county's success-
    ful efforts to obtain passage of special chain gang legislation before 1887. In
    fact, only Charlotte Township was willing to levy the special tax needed to
    set up the system, report Steiner and Brown, *The North Carolina Chain Gang*,
    34. City operations do not appear to have been limited to the use of only those
    convicts who had violated municipal ordinances.
35. N.C. Public Laws, 1876–77, ch. 20; ibid., 1879, ch. 39; ibid., 1879, ch. 270;
    ibid., 1880, extra session, chs. 19 and 50; ibid., 1885, ch. 134.
36. Ibid., 1887, ch. 355; 1889, ch. 419; and Consolidated Statutes of 1919, secs.
    1359–61.
37. Zimmerman, "Penal Systems and Penal Reforms," 113–14.
38. Some supporters of the county chain gang system argued that this kind of home-
    custody practice was more humane and rehabilitative for convicts. Perhaps there
    is some validity to this argument; however, it appears that after the turn of
    the century this practice was rare. Most convicts were kept in a movable, cage-
    like building that was pulled from one work site to another. These were
    described by both penal reformers and state officials as unsanitary, overcrowded,
    and without adequate heating during winter.
39. *State Prison Report, 1895–96*, 7–8. The warden's contentions are supported
    by some evidence, though state officials, for political reasons, may have also
    exaggerated the feebleness of state convicts.
40. Steiner and Brown, *The North Carolina Chain Gang*, 37. Zimmerman, "Penal
    Systems and Penal Reforms," 323, reports that in 1901 counties were not taking
    full advantage of convict labor. This was not true in subsequent years, however.
41. *State Prison Report* (Raleigh, 1907–8), 11–13; Steiner and Brown, *The North
    Carolina Chain Gang*, 39–41.
42. Steiner and Brown, *The North Carolina Chain Gang*, 125.
43. *State Prison Report 1928–30*, 19.
44. Steiner and Brown, *The North Carolina Chain Gang*, 5.
45. Ibid., 5.
46. Mecklenberg (Charlotte) and Wake (Raleigh) Counties obtained such permission
    under N.C. Public Laws, 1915, ch. 792. Other counties merely ignored the
    two-year-sentence rule when convenient.
47. State prison officials frequently used this kind of scare tactic to support their
    arguments for the abolition of the county system. In addition, there is evidence
    to suggest that state officials also assigned dangerous criminals to their road
    projects.
48. N.C. Public Laws, 1871–72, ch. 202.
49. Zimmerman, "Penal Systems and Penal Reforms," 86.
50. N.C. Public Laws, 1874–75, ch. 246. All convicts not needed to build the prison
    were to be leased.
51. *State Prison Report, 1874–76*, 5.
52. Zimmerman, "Penal Systems and Penal Reforms," 83.
53. Ibid., 84–85. That is, other states did not require state supervision.
54. For example, see George W. Cable, *The Silent South*, together with *The
    Freedman's Case in Equity and the Convict Lease System* (New York, 1907);
    Steiner and Brown, *The North Carolina Chain Gang*; McKelvey, "Penal Slavery
    and Southern Reconstruction," *Journal of Negro History* 10 (1935): 153–79;
    McKelvey, *American Prisons*; Herbert Stacy McKay, "Convict Leasing in North

Carolina," (M.A. thesis, University of North Carolina at Chapel Hill, 1942).
55. McKay, "Convict Leasing in North Carolina."
56. Zimmerman, "Penal Systems and Penal Reforms," 127.
57. The permanent, full-sized prison structure was completed in 1884.
58. *State Prison Report, 1889–90*, 8.
59. The state prison reports provide much more detailed estimates of the value of convict labor than are provided in Table 3.
60. Zimmerman, "The Penal Reform Movement in the South," 464.
61. There also appears to have been a belief that black prisoners were more suited to railroad and chain gang work than were whites. It was not until farms were established that larger numbers of whites were sentenced to the state prison. See Darnell F. Hawkins, "Race and Imprisonment: Extending Blumstein's Stability of Punishment Hypothesis," in preparation.
62. Zimmerman, "The Penal Reform Movement in the South," 464; *State Prison Report, 1878–80*, 2.
63. *State Prison Report, 1880–82*, 13.
64. Zimmerman, "Penal Systems and Penal Reforms," 182.
65. As a result of public pressure, legislation was later passed to prevent the prison from selling bricks to the public. They could only be used for construction of state buildings. This kind of legislation aimed at preventing the prison from competing with private industry was often passed and then repealed in the state. Even as late as the 1960s prison industries were competing with private economic ventures.
66. *State Prison Report, 1888–1890*, 12.
67. Ibid., 1890–92, pp. 7–8.
68. Ibid., 1894, 5.
69. Zimmerman, "The Penal Reform Movement in the South," 465–66.
70. *State Prison Report, 1907–08*, 7–8.
71. Zimmerman, "Penal Systems and Penal Reforms," 348–50.
72. Ibid., 24–25; Steiner and Brown, *The North Carolina Chain Gang*, 18–20.
73. Zimmerman, "Penal Systems and Penal Reforms," 127; N.C. Public Laws, 1879, ch. 67, pp. 75–76.
74. McKay, "Convict Leasing in North Carolina."
75. *The Raleigh News and Observer*, 8 February 1887, as cited in Zimmerman, "Penal Systems and Penal Reforms," 130.
76. Zimmerman, "Penal Systems and Penal Reforms," 323.
77. N.C. Public Laws, 1901, ch. 50, pp. 195–218.
78. *State Prison Report, 1901–2, 7*, 11–12.
79. *State Prison Report, 1903–05*, 8.
80. N.C. Public Laws, 1907, ch. 152, p. 164.
81. *State Prison Report, 1907–08*, 11–15.
82. *State Prison Report, 1930–32*, 478. This report details population growth and revenue during the preceding decade.
83. *State Prison Report, 1925–26*, 13–14.
84. *State Prison Report, 1927–28*, 7.
85. *State Prison Report, 1928–30*, 10–21.
86. Ibid., 19–20.
87. N.C. Public Laws, 1933, ch. 172.
88. See McKelvey, *American Prisons*, 116–49; U.S. Commissioner of Labor, Report

(1886).

89. For example, in 1928 only 25 percent of white prisoners working at the largest farm came from farm backgrounds. Most blacks were not assigned to farm work at this time. See *State Prison Report, 1927–28*, 12.

90. Steiner and Brown, *The North Carolina Chain Gang*, 102–9.

91. Mark T. Carleton, *Politics and Punishment: The History of the Louisiana State Penal System* (Baton Rouge, 1971); Robert Gunn Crawford, "A History of the Kentucky Penitentiary System, 1865–1937," (Ph.D. dissertation, University of Kentucky at Lexington, 1955); Herman Lee Crow, "A Political History of the Texas Penal System, 1829–1951," (Ph.D. dissertation, University of Texas at Austin, 1964). See also, preface by W. David Lewis, *From Newgate to Dannemora: The Rise of the Penitentiary in New York, 1796–1848* (Ithaca, 1965).

92. Zimmerman, "Penal Systems and Penal Reforms," 421.

93. William J. Chambliss, "Contradictions and Conflicts in Law Creation," in *Research in Law and Sociology*, ed. Steven Spitzer (1979), 2: 3–27.

94. Ibid., 7, citing R. P. Applebaum, "Marx's Theory of the Falling Rate of Profit," *American Sociological Review* 43 (1978), 67–81; and, by the same author, "Marxist Method: Structural Constraints and Social Praxis," *The American Sociologist* 13 (1978), 73–81.

The Chartrand Murder Trial: Rebellion and Repression in Lower Canada, 1837–1839

F. Murray Greenwood

University of British Columbia, Vancouver

Between the two Rebellions of 1837 and 1838 in Lower Canada, there occurred an event of profound significance to contemporaries, an event that historians have tended to ignore: the trial in September 1838 of four *patriotes* from the rural county of L'Acadie, a few miles southwest of Montreal. The four were accused of murdering one Joseph Armand, called Chartrand, a stonemason from St. Jean on the Richelieu River. Chartrand was a lapsed patriote who had joined the militia volunteers and become an informer responsible for the arrest of several suspected rebels during the Rebellion of November 1837. He had been shot to death well away from the scenes of battle two days after the patriote defeat at St. Charles, a defeat that had signalled the end of the Rebellion in the south. For a few hours in a packed Montreal courtroom the prosecution and defence staged a morality play in which the passions generating insurrection and repression engaged once again in pitiless combat. This time there was no catharsis. Rather, the trial and the surprising verdict contributed to the Rebellion of November 1838 and to the drastic decision taken thereafter to try suspected rebels by summary process in courts martial.

The Chartrand murder case is a classic political trial, at once reflecting and acting upon the social tensions of the time.[1] In a modest way it is a Canadian equivalent of the famous *Dred Scott* case extending slavery on the eve of the American Civil War. The Chartrand trial also raises important questions as to the powers and duties of a jury. The verdict in the Chartrand case is one of the few obvious examples in Canadian history of what in the United States is well known as "jury nullification": that is, the intentional disregard of the judge's instructions on the law applicable to the facts (known in Britain as "the rule of law").

Before describing the trial, it is useful to recall the main features of Lord

Durham's penal policy for dealing with rebellion in the Canadian provinces. Soon after his arrival as governor in May 1838, Durham concluded that for most political offences committed by *Canadiens* (French-speaking Lower Canadians), juries would refuse to convict their compatriots. Resisting suggestions for courts martial, packing juries, or Acts of Attainder, he finally opted for clemency.[2] On 28 June 1838 the appointed Special Council, which had replaced the suspended Legislature of Lower Canada, enacted the so-called Bermuda Ordinance, and Durham issued a Proclamation in the name of Queen Victoria.[3] With these documents a general amnesty was proclaimed for the rebels, subject to four exceptions. Wolfred Nelson, the military commander who had led the patriotes to their only victory over British regulars at St. Denis (23 November 1837), and seven other captured leaders were exiled to Bermuda. The rebel leader Louis-Joseph Papineau and fifteen others, then in the United States, were prohibited on pain of death from entering Lower Canada. Also exempted were persons then or thereafter charged with Chartrand's murder or the murder of Lieutenant George Weir, bayonetted to death on the eve of the battle of St. Denis. In each of these cases five suspects were listed by name, but other persons involved whom the government might apprehend and charge were likewise exempt.

Trial Participants

While the Bermuda Ordinance was being debated in the British Parliament—a debate that would result in its disallowance as extraterritorial legislation—the Lower Canadian government set out to prove that its clemency had limits. It would reveal treason as truly the mother of all crime by dramatizing the Chartrand atrocity. In late August the Montreal Grand Jury indicted six men for the murder, and on 6 September four of them were placed on trial.[4] Each of the accused had been exempted by name from Durham's amnesty. Three of them were young illiterate farm labourers. Joseph Pinsonnault, about twenty years of age and his younger brother Gédéon lived with their parents in L'Acadie. In the voluntary examinations they signed in February 1838, the Pinsonnaults stated that on the fatal day they had been threshing grain in their father's barn when René Garant, a local patriote leader, forced them at bayonet point to join the group that later shot Chartrand.[5] Twenty-two-year-old Amable Daunais, originally of St. Cyprien, worked as a hired hand; he, too, was forced to join Garant's men.[6] The fourth accused was François Nicolas, a L'Acadie schoolteacher. A bachelor in his early forties and a captain in the rebel army. Nicolas seems to have been an aggressive idealist, uncharitable to those less committed to the patriote cause than he and a man who entertained thoughts of martyrdom.[7] He was charged with being a principal in the first degree for having actively participated in the shooting. The three younger accused were charged as principals in the second degree for having been present and assisting those who fired on the victim. If proved beyond a reasonable doubt, both charges carried the mandatory death sentence by public hanging.

The presiding judge was James Reid, Chief Justice of Montreal, who believed that the Canadien majority represented a menace and should be anglified as quickly as possible. Assisting him were Justices Samuel Gale and Jean-Roch Rolland. The prosecutors were Attorney General Charles Richard Ogden and Solicitor General Michael O'Sullivan. Ogden, the son of a prominent Loyalist judge, was a competent though not brilliant lawyer whose bias against the Canadiens had made Durham question his suitability for the important position he held.[8] O'Sullivan was a flashy character who had been wounded in a celebrated duel some years before. He was perfectly fluent in French, skilled at manipulating emotions in court, and had a scholarly grasp of the law.

Charles Mondelet, the senior defence counsel, played a dramatic part in the political agitation leading to the 1837 Rebellion. Because of his sensational role in the Chartrand case, Mondelet later was arrested (in November 1838) on suspicion of treason and spent several weeks in jail. Mondelet was assisted by William Walker, who argued objections. Walker had once been a Tory but was in the process of becoming a staunch reformer who would soon advocate responsible cabinet government for Canada. Also assisting the defence, although not a lawyer of record, was Denis-A. Laberge, a patriote activist in Montreal during the summer and autumn of 1837.[9] During the trial, Laberge, who seems to have been mentally unstable, insisted loudly and repeatedly on his right to examine witnesses and make objections. His many interruptions infuriated Mondelet, who asked that he be silenced. The court agreed and ordered Laberge jailed for contempt until the end of term.[10]

Throughout the two-day trial, the courtroom was filled with vocal and opposing groups: English and some Canadien Tories seeking vengeance and a sense of security; patriote sympathizers, mostly Canadien; and a few Irish, pessimistic but hoping the case would somehow vindicate their cause. Among the latter was Louis Delagrave, committed republican and a kinsman of Louis-Joseph Papineau. Delagrave sent Louis-Joseph an interesting and immediate eye witness account of the trial.[11] There were also several reporters in the audience. The rabidly Tory Montreal Herald sent a reporter, as did the moderate Tory French papers, L'Ami du Peuple and Le Populaire.[12] François Lemaître, radical editor of Le Temps and La Quotidienne, sent three persons to take careful notes[13] and published a partisan but comprehensive account in the form of a pamphlet.[14]

Trial Arguments Presented by the Crown

The defence challenged nineteen prospective jurors and succeeded in obtaining a jury composed entirely of Canadiens. In the atmosphere of the times it is virtually certain some of these men were patriote sympathizers. It is even possible, as a knowledgeable government informer later claimed, that four jurors were members of the secret revolutionary society, the Frères Chasseurs.[15] After the indictment was read, the prisoners pleaded not guilty. A desperate attempt at disguise by Nicolas was foiled when he was forced to remove a pair of spectacles and a huge mustache.[16] Solicitor General O'Sullivan opened for the Crown with an address that appeared to reduce Joseph Pinsonnault to tearful hysteria.

O'Sullivan began by dwelling on the gruesome details of the killing, prefacing his remarks with the assertion that never in the annals of criminal proceedings in Canada had there been a crime so barbarous as the one at hand. It was a case of the wolf devouring the lamb with no other justification than superior force. Nicolas had clearly acted as commander, O'Sullivan asserted. It would likely be contended that Joseph Pinsonnault had acted out of fear, but the defence of duress was not available to him. To excuse a crime, threats of bodily harm must have been so terrifying as to induce the strongest-minded persons to obey.[17] As for Gédéon Pinsonnault, his youth furnished no excuse. Indeed in every country it was the young who threatened to overturn the social order, who undermined respect for authority, which it was the jury's duty to uphold. They should pay heed to their priests in such matters and remember that the Bible demands vengeance for the shedding of blood. O'Sullivan concluded by eulogizing the deceased and exhorting the jury to eschew passion for reason. Otherwise, the spirit of Chartrand would escape from the grave to accuse them before the Supreme Tribunal, and their consciences, filled with remorse, would not allow them a moment's peace.

The Crown called twenty-one witnesses, the most important being two accomplices, a teenager named Barthélémi Poissant and patriote Etienne Langlois, the fifth man involved in the Chartrand killing excluded by name from the Durham amnesty. Langlois was then in prison.[18] The testimony for the Crown can be briefly summarized. On the morning of November 27th, 1837, Chartrand went to visit a L'Acadie farmer, one David Roy. His purpose was to collect an advance on wages from Roy, whom he was helping to build a house. At the same time a group of about fifteen patriotes armed with muskets under the command of Garant collected at the nearby house of David Roy's brother Eloi.[19] They discussed marching to help the patriotes at St. Charles or seizing St. Jean. But their small numbers led to the abandonment of these plans. Someone suggested they imprison Chartrand as a traitor and a spy, but Roy would not let them use his cellar. Then someone shouted out that, "Since there's nowhere to keep him, let's kill him" [trans.].

Chartrand was spotted walking on the road to St. Jean. Nicolas, Garant, and another patriote exhorted the party to go after him, which they did. Garant, however, prudently remained behind at Eloi Roy's and took no further part in the affair. Four or five of the patriotes, led by Langlois and Jean Beaulieu, fiery son of the local bailiff, caught up with the quarry – who was then running – about a kilometer from their starting point. Beaulieu gave a verbal order, and Nicolas made a sign with his cane that they escort Chartrand through a gate into a field. All the prisoners on trial, except Nicolas, were armed with muskets. Chartrand was taken across the field into a wooded area where Beaulieu ordered a halt and put Chartrand on his "trial."

Nicolas asked Chartrand if he had boasted of the coming reprisals and if he knew where to find fat pigs and oxen. When the prisoner denied making such statements, the schoolteacher, claiming he had heard them himself, called Chartrand a liar, suggested he make his peace with God, and enquired of his comrades whether the prisoner deserved death. When some answered in the affirmative, Nicolas asked what kind of death would be suitable. Beaulieu responded that he should be shot. Beaulieu, and possibly Nicolas as well, then gave the order to fire. Five patriotes, including Beaulieu and Joseph Pinsonnault, discharged muskets. Chartrand fell, struggled to get up and asked for the coup de grace. Beaulieu took Joseph Pinsonnault's musket, reloaded it, and ordered Pinsonnault in a threatening manner to fire again. Pinsonnault, in a state of hysteria, complied. The shots were fired at a distance of about twelve or thirteen metres; two balls passed through Chartrand's body at the abdomen and his left breast. According to medical testimony, either shot would have killed him. He was not, as some accounts have it, tied to a tree. Chartrand was left to die and the group dispersed. The three younger prisoners were apprehended shortly after the body was found. They had been walking together on a road near Sherrington, possibly heading to the United States. Magistrate James M'Gillivray testified that on 18 January near St. Athanase, he had discovered Nicolas, unarmed, hiding in an attic. The schoolteacher did not resist arrest.

Such was the story told by Crown witnesses. Some also attested to the victim's sterling character. He was a quiet, sober, inoffensive man, with an appealing sense of humor. On cross-examination Mondelet brought out that several in Garant's party had been induced by threats (unspecified) to join and that Gédéon Pinsonnault and Daunais had refused to fire at the victim. Through Langlois, who testified that he had not heard of the battle of St. Charles (25 November), Mondelet was able to leave the impression that the execution had taken place before that decisive patriote defeat was generally known in the area. This was important, for otherwise the jury might have concluded that it had occurred after the Rebellion in the south had ended and could not be given a political justification.[20] Counsel's questioning of François Bourassa, a neighboring farmer, was to prove particularly useful. Bourassa had heard the shots and suspected foul play. The next day he went and discovered the body but did not inform anybody until the Wednesday, when he saw his parish priest. He explained the delay as due to "fear, as there was great political excitement prevailing at the time in that part of the country."

Mondelet also attempted to establish that Nicolas had not given the order to fire. According to Langlois's examination, it had been Beaulieu *or* Nicolas (he could not tell which) who had ordered the discharge. On cross-examination he twice suggested Nicolas was as likely as Beaulieu to have issued the command. He did admit, however, that he was terribly upset at the time. Poissant had testified that both Beaulieu *and* Nicolas had ordered the firing. On cross-examination he repeated this as certain, but then went on to admit that in his extreme agitation he may not have remembered everything accurately and that he had been in the rear of the party. The witness further explained that the two men had not given the order at the same time, and the party had fired when Beaulieu uttered the command. Mondelet later made the point that Poissant's accuracy was open to question, for he claimed there had been two shots after the first round of firing, while Langlois and Bourassa swore there had been only one.

The evidence presented by the Crown witnesses, although damaging to the defence, was considerably less so than it might have been. This conclusion is based on a comparison of what the witnesses said at the trial with the statements they and the three younger accused had earlier made in depositions and voluntary examinations during the weeks following Chartrand's death.[21] It does not appear from these earlier statements, for example, that Joseph Pinsonnault had been hysterical. They also contain information which, if presented in court, might have elicited sympathy on the part of the jurors for the victim.

During the "trial" in the woods, it seems, Nicolas accused Chartrand of having betrayed his sacred heritage. Chartrand angrily denied he had ever betrayed anyone and asserted he was as patriotic a Canadien as his tormentors. He had long been in misery and was prepared to die. His only worry was about his children and his wife, whom he begged the group to inform of his fate. When the first discharge failed to kill him, Chartrand gasped that the good Lord was stronger than they and didn't wish him dead. Then the suffering became unbearable, and he asked for the coup de grace.

From the point of view of the defence, the most useful changes made

by the witnesses in their stories were those that suggested a lack of premedi-
tation and tended to downplay Nicolas's leadership in favour of the absent
Beaulieu. Eloi Roy, for example, had first claimed that a number of men
had called for Chartrand's death, and that he had thereupon asked the
patriotes to leave his house.[22] At trial he swore that only one man had made
the suggestion, and that he, Roy, thought it a joke. Langlois's and Poissant's
pretrial statements indicate that Nicolas had threatened Chartrand with death
before they entered the field and had acted as sole presiding "judge," pronoun-
cing public sentence that the "accused" deserved execution and alone had
ordered the first discharge.[23] In the witness box they either omitted these
facts or related them in a less damaging or uncertain manner. On one point
Poissant directly contradicted himself, first stating it was Nicolas, but at trial
testifying it was Beaulieu who ordered the second firing. These alterations
are remarkable considering the witnesses risked not only charges of perjury
but of murder as well. Very likely their tailored evidence was influenced by
the strong pro-patriote sentiment in L'Acadie. In any case, it greatly assisted
the defence counsel.

Trial Arguments Presented by the Defence

Mondelet prefaced his defence with a passionate, hour-long address that
provoked Tory sneers and elicited patriote smiles. Delagrave was astonished
but pleased that Mondelet dared attack the government. According to the
Herald some of the jurors were visibly won over, though they had not heard
a single word of defence testimony. The address had two major themes: the
prisoners could not have committed murder because at the relevant time and
place the colonial government had been replaced by a de facto government
of the people; and in any case they were not guilty because, while present
at the shooting, they had not aided or abetted the principals.

Mondelet supported the first argument by referring vaguely to British
precedents and supported the second by citing authorities. But he was arguing
an emotional not a legal case; his purpose was to insinuate that the government had been responsible for the Rebellion, that the people had justifiably
defended themselves, and that in circumstances of terror, anarchy, and coercion, the prisoners could not be blamed for acting as they did. Their so-called
crimes, less heinous then those of others the government had pardoned or
merely transported, were being exploited to satisfy government vengeance.
Whatever the precise rules of law, he distinctly implied, it was the jury's duty
to assess the overall morality and politics of conviction or acquittal.

Mondelet began by insisting that the government was acting in a fraudu-
lent manner by charging the prisoners with murder rather than high treason.
This decision had been taken in an attempt to obscure the political nature

of the trial. But the jurors should not be under any illusion. The prisoners' crime, if it existed, was to have taken an active part with the majority of their compatriots in seeking cherished political goals. The trial had "its source in the political and party conflicts of the last twenty-five years and is linked and bound to nothing less than the political demands of the population of this country" [trans.]. Three of the prisoners were very young, of an age when one does not hatch murder plots. Nicolas was older, but no one should be presumed to have a character capable of premeditated murder. Defence counsel then painted a detailed picture of the political situation leading up to the killing of Chartrand. The point was hammered home that the government's authority had totally disappeared in L'Acadie.

The government had entirely lost the people's respect, for it was divided internally, with the popular House of Assembly at loggerheads with the oligarchic Executive and Legislative Councils. The government had trampled on "inalienable rights," daily adopting arbitrary measures, such as the issuance of warrants of arrest against the patriote leaders. Terror was all around, Mondelet asserted. It was thought throughout the county of L'Acadie, as elsewhere, that if the patriote leaders were arrested they would be hanged. And if so, could anyone be safe? The violence in Montreal on 6 November 1837, spawned by the bullies of the English Doric Club and condoned by the authorities, showed that no one's property would be safe. Rightly or wrongly it was widely believed that the government was violating the laws, indeed trying to replace the rule of law with brute force. This generalized terror was so strong that fathers allowed their sons to march to war without knowing whether they would ever return. The jurors themselves were heads of families; they could understand what it took to convince a father to do that.

The government's activities had so lowered it in public esteem that anyone accepting any office whatever was condemned as totally unworthy of confidence. Magistrates and militia officers resigned, and the government was too weak to replace them. There was total anarchy and confusion. The people formed their own government. The patriote leaders established tribunals, and public officers were elected by unanimous choice. The colonial government was not thought about except as an engine of oppression. The people and their leaders had become the de facto government; their authority was palpably felt. Anyone refusing to join with his comrades in defence of the nation was subject to severe harassment. Families that continued to profess loyalty were forced to flee. Without entering into the question of whether the government caused the Rebellion, it is certain that anarchy reigned and that individuals were unable to distinguish between the rights of the de jure and de facto authorities and naturally obeyed the latter. The prisoners, "whose political opinions, attachment to their country's cause and confidence in their leaders were unshakeable found themselves . . . in precisely that situation" [trans.].

It was a well-known principle of the British constitution that obedience to a de facto government — in this case the patriote leaders — was neither treasonable nor a crime of any kind. Those with even a smattering of English history knew this, Mondelet declared. Kings had been overthrown and de facto governments established. Those supporting the existing authority were, quite properly, considered by these laws unable "to determine the legitimacy of one or the other authority" [trans.]. The prisoners' case fell squarely under that principle.

As to the death of Chartrand, it was not as extraordinary as might first appear. He was known as a spy. Was it more horrible, Mondelet asked, to kill a spy in wartime than to have committed, in less troubled times, the excesses of 6 November in Montreal? Or to have urged, as some (English) newspapers had during the winter, that patriote prisoners released by the authorities should be assassinated? Chartrand's death did not differ from the deaths of dozens of British soldiers at St. Denis. The government had allowed some who took part in that battle to go into exile and had released the rest. What justice was there, then, in seeking the death penalty for those who killed Chartrand? By what warrant did the government demand "the blood of those it claims killed one man when it has absolved those who decimated a corps of Her Majesty's troops! [trans.]."

By its own acts of clemency the government had admitted a political justification for killings during the troubles. If the jury believed the government was partly to blame in the whole affair, it was surely not obliged to punish men the government itself had provoked to rise. It was absolutely clear from the works of writers on English law, such as Sir Mathew Hale and Jean-Louis De Lolme, that the jury was master of its verdict: it was the judge of law as well as fact.

Mondelet's second ground — that the accused had not aided and abetted — was not entirely distinct from the first. For even if it failed on its own merits to convince the jury, the more the role of the prisoners in the death of Chartrand could be minimized the more palatable the novel de facto argument would become. Thus if counsel could make a case for coercion — though not itself a sufficient defence — it would illustrate the strengh of the people's government and the very real problems of allegiance men had faced. If Nicolas's supposed leadership could be denied, he could be portrayed as following the orders of others. If counsel could at least cast doubt whether Nicolas ordered the party to fire, the schoolteacher might more easily be excused because of the prevailing anarchy.

Mondelet argued that the testimony of Langlois and other witnesses showed undoubtedly that Garant had been the initial leader, acting under at least a colour of authority. It was he who forced the men to march. More generally, Bourassa's reluctance to inform anyone of the corpse proved how widespread was the fear of displeasing the patriotes. Nicolas could not be described as a leader. He gave no orders at Eloi Roy's. His subordinate status was evidenced from his acting as flagbearer. It was not he who first mentioned Chartrand's execution at Eloi Roy's. Not only Nicolas but others had suggested chasing Chartrand when he was seen on the road. After Garant retired from the affair, Beaulieu assumed leadership. He ordered the men through the gate and gave the command to fire. Only the young Poissant gave positive evidence that Nicolas had joined in that order. The jury could tell from the way he gave his testimony that Poissant was a weak character. He was also contradicted by other witnesses on two important, contemporary points: namely, that Langlois had fired, which Langlois denied, and that there had been two shots, not one, in the second round. Poissant should not be believed.

Obviously, orders had come from some authority to kill Chartrand, but the prisoners were not privy to the plot. The important talk at Eloi Roy's was of marching to St. Charles or St. Jean and not of Chartrand. The four prisoners were present at the death of the latter but did not consent to, let alone voluntarily assist in, the deed. Joseph Pinsonnault was acting under a sense of coercion. He was obviously agitated greatly, and very likely he purposely shot to miss and did miss. Chartrand, Mondelet reminded the jury, had been hit by only two balls. As for Gédéon Pinsonnault and Amable Daunais, they had refused to fire. To support his argument Mondelet cited a number of authorities on aiding and abetting. He quoted from one, Russell's *Treatise on Crimes*, without making it clear that the author was referring to a person who was on the scene by accident:

> In order to make a abettor to a murder or manslaughter principal in the felony, he must be present aiding and abetting the fact committed. . . . But a person may be present; and, if not aiding and abetting, be neither principal nor acessory: as, if A happen to be present at a murder and take no part in it, nor endeavour to prevent it, or to apprehend the murderer, this strange behaviour, though highly criminal, will not of itself render him either principal or accessory.[24]

Mondelet concluded by emphasizing once more the injustice of visiting the death penalty on only four of the hundreds of patriotes who had borne arms, and by reminding the jury again that it was "the sole master of its verdict. . . . [I]t must decide itself and not be guided by anyone" [trans.], including, presumably, Chief Justice Reid and his colleagues on the bench. The Solicitor General had referred to the jury's being haunted by the spirit of Chartrand, but there was another way of looking at it: "The ghosts of these four prisoners would not allow you a moment's peace; their voices would make themselves continually heard; you would be tortured by guilt; you would be miserable; you yourselves would be murderers if you were to condemn these men to the gallows!" [trans.].

The defence called fifteen witnesses. Four had had personal dealings at the relevant time with René Garant, who had gone from house to house recruiting young unmarried men to march in support of the patriotes on the Richelieu. If his commands were not obeyed, they had been told, Papineau would direct that every man, old and young, married and single, be conscripted. One witness claimed: "In the parish they believed those who didn't march would meet with a swift justice. The residents feared for their lives if they didn't obey" [trans.]. By this evidence Mondelet and Walker were offering the jury a concrete example of the power exercised by the de facto "government." Several witnesses attested to the character of the prisoners: Joseph Pinsonnault was a weak, biddable young man of limited intelligence; Nicolas was overly generous, honest, humane, not more severe than other teachers; Daunais and Gédéon Pinsonnault were of mild and quiet dispositions.

Two witnesses attempted to blacken Chartrand's reputation. Pierre Picard, a septuagenarian resident of St. Jean, testified that during the Rebellion and while a guest of Chartrand, David Roy had been severely beaten up by his victim, who had boasted he would do the same to several other patriotes. Chartrand was known as an informer. Jacques Bouchard of L'Acadie told of the great fear in which Chartrand had been held. Throughout the parish it was assumed he would come with fellow volunteers and "put everything to the torch and all to the sword" [trans.]. According to the *Herald*'s report, Mondelet then asked the witness, "if Chartrand *was not esteemed a traitor to the cause of his country.*" This clever question, which momentarily plunged the courtroom into chaos as old hatreds tumbled forth, was ruled out of order on the grounds it was "*indecent.*" In response to another question, the witness declared that Chartrand was thought of as a spy.

Probably the most effective testimony for the defence was given by three witnesses who told of the confused situation prevailing in L'Acadie during November 1837. One Pierre Roy claimed that "no authority was recognized but that of force, and the will of the people who recognized no other government." Notary Laurent Archambault, a lapsed patriote who had resided in the area for seventeen years, testified that the "general excitement and anarchy" was such that "no magistrate could act, or get his orders executed, or give assistance to any one." Many persons left the parish from fear; he himself had been compelled to resign his commission as justice of the peace. Dr. Timoléon Quesnel, a L'Acadie resident for fifteen years, prominent local Tory, and brother of a member of Sir John Colborne's Special Council, but no fanatic on the question of punishment,[25] provided the strongest support for Mondelet's main argument:

> In the part of the country where witness resided there was a great deal of discontent; the parish was in a state of anarchy. The witness was opposed to the political views of the majority. The agitators recognized no authority of the Government. One part of the parish exercised a species of tyranny over the other, and none dared to oppose the will of the majority; they compelled those in office under the Government to resign their commissions; witness was a justice of the peace, and was compelled to resign his commission, after having had his doors and windows broken; knows that young men were forced to leave their parents and join the agitators; the loyal had no protection; none were safe who refused obedience to the orders of the majority. . . .

The Solicitor General's cross-examination of the defence witness was only partially successful. He did elicit statements from Roy, Archambault, and Quesnel that "anarchy" was principally directed against those who held official commissions, but this was not sufficient to counter effectively the testimony given in their examinations. According to Lemaître's pamphlet, O'Sullivan, at the suggestion of Chief Justice Reid, also asked Quesnel how many agitators there were. The witness answered that all the young men were on the march. Quesnel agreed that the agitation had quickly subsided, but only after the news of the defeat of St. Charles. O'Sullivan also concentrated on Joseph Pinsonnault's supposed weak-mindedness. One witness was induced to say that Pinsonnault, whatever his intellect, certainly knew right from wrong, and another offered the opinion that if the prisoner were told to steal or kill he would not do so: "He would not kill the turkey or sheep of his neighbour . . . [or] break his head against a wall to please anyone." Playing to the jurors' religious feelings, the Solicitor General asked one witness how long it had been since Pinsonnault had taken the sacraments. An objection by Walker was overruled, but the witness's answer that he did not know was unhelpful and the question gave the defence ideas. Mondelet recalled a witness who testified that Nicolas's school was under the supervision of the curé, who would not have hired or kept on the prisoner unless his character was irreproachable.

Closing Remarks of the Crown

Attorney General Ogden delivered the Crown's closing address, described by the *Herald* as "a most animated and conclusively argumentative speech, [which] refuted all the cavils and sophisms. . . raised. . . by Prisoner's [sic] Counsel."[26] Ogden was at pains to justify the fairness of the proceedings. The accused, he pointed out (probably correctly), could not have been tried for high treason because of the amnesty.[27] The prisoners had been purposely exempted from the amnesty because a paternal government could not allow to go unpunished the murder of a single Canadien — a man of the same blood as the jurors — whatever the surrounding circumstances. The prosecution had requested that the Crown witnesses be sent out of the courtroom to avoid the possibility of collusion. The Attorney General had not instituted proceedings at the March Assizes because he had feared that being so close to the events the accused might not have had a fair trial. Throughout, Ogden had acted on his own; he was not the political arm of the executive. The jury should remember that nowhere on earth was justice administered as impartially as in Lower Canada.

Ogden analyzed Blackstone, Chitty, and the authorities cited by Mondelet to argue that the prisoners were guilty of murder. They were part of a gang, and those who had witnessed the shooting without attempting to prevent it were as guilty as those who had actually fired. Only those present by accident, that is, innocent bystanders, could be held not guilty. Nicolas certainly had been a leader since it was he who gave the signal to enter the field. The others had been present on their own accord and had done nothing to stop the execution. There had been much talk of coercion, but at the time of the killing the plan to march to St. Charles or St. Jean — which was the reason for the coercion — no longer existed. Indeed, several men in the original group had withdrawn before the murder.

Chartrand was killed with unequalled ferocity, Ogden asserted. Unarmed, he had no chance to defend himself. He was shot in cold blood, then shot again, his mutilated body left in its death throes. He was not even afforded the consolation of a religious preparation for his death. Defence counsel had drawn an analogy between the situation of the prisoners and those rebels who had shot British soldiers; there was absolutely no similarity. At St. Denis and St. Charles it was gun against gun, bullet against bullet, sword against sword. In this case of wanton slaying the gulf with any political offence was unbridgeable:

> Was Chartrand in a [battle] line against adversaries . . . ? Did Chartrand fire? Was there a civil war? . . . No gentlemen! . . . If a kind of council of war had been held by the [patriote] leaders, if the judgment had been pronounced [by the council], but executed by others . . . these latter might have inferred a supposed right to obey. . . . But here it is the same men who apprehend the victim . . . condemn him and who sacrifice him! This is unqualified murder, with premeditation and reflection, and not done . . . in the heat of battle, in the overwhelming need of self-defence. [trans.]

It was the jury's sworn obligation to administer the laws of their country conscientiously, to maintain order, and to support their government, the protector of society. The jury should forget the past, put aside all party feeling, and embrace the great principles of justice, which demand a guilty verdict. I have done my duty, Ogden concluded; you must do yours.

Analysis of the Evidence Before the Jury

It is unfortunate that we do not have a copy of Chief Justice Reid's charge to the jury. The tone, however, emerges from *Le Populaire*'s quotation of the opening sentences:

> Among a people acknowledged to be peaceable, it is rare to see such an atrocious crime committed as that which has just been the subject of our inquiry. The blood of a victim cries out for vengeance and for justice. No doubt the crime will not go unpunished and society will regain confidence from the impartial verdict that you are to render; a verdict you will surely render with all the conviction of conscientious men, who have sworn to leave aside all considerations, all personal feelings, to concentrate solely on their duty to God and their country, however harsh it might seem to humanitarian sentiment [trans.].

According to the brief summaries in *L'Ami, Le Populaire*, and *Le Canadien*,[28] Reid made the following points. The evidence of Joseph Pinsonnault's weak character was quite irrelevant, for he had not resisted firing in the first round. Daunais and Gédéon Pinsonnault were both present and armed. It appears therefore that they consented to the deed, and this consent in law constituted the crime. It did not matter in the least which of the balls fired struck Chartrand. The jurors must confine themselves to the particular facts of the shooting and put out of their minds the larger, political issue, for politics never justified murder. If the jury believed the Crown witnesses, they must find the accused guilty. Although not mentioned in the summaries it seems certain that Reid also commented favourably on the Crown evidence pointing to Nicolas as the principal leader.

There is no indication whether or not the Chief Justice dealt explicitly with Mondelet's conception of the jury as judge of law as well as fact. But it is clear he directed a verdict of guilty despite the legal arguments offered by defence counsel. The question arises whether Mondelet's insistence that the jury bore the ultimate responsibility for interpreting the law as well as the facts was correct. The passage Mondelet cited from Hale's *History of the Common Law* was simply not on the point. De Lolme, however, had taken a very liberal view of the jury's functions:

> And as the main object of the institution of the trial by jury is to guard against all decisions whatsoever from men invested with any permanent official authority, it is not only a settled principle that the opinion which the judge delivers has no weight but such as the jury choose to give it; but their verdict must besides comprehend the whole matter in trial, and decide as well upon the fact, as upon the point of law that may arise out of it....[29]

While the reputation of De Lolme, a Swiss expert on the British constitution, was certainly high, he had erred on this point. Perhaps his confusion arose from the fact that there was no longer, in the late eighteenth century, a sanction imposed by the court on a jury that disregarded its interpretation of the law. In the previous century jurors who apparently followed their own legal insights were commonly fined or imprisoned. Blackstone, who characterized the practice as "tyrannical," noted that it had fallen into desuetude by his day.

Nor was there any redress by way of appeal if a jury acquitted an accused in the face of all the evidence, that is, contrary to law. The jurors then could in fact effectively acquit on legal grounds of their own devising or on intuitive perceptions of equity. But this autonomy was tolerated for policy reasons, not because it was thought that jurors should be judges of the law. They were deemed to be under a *moral* obligation to follow the court's directions as to the applicable law. Lord Mansfield had spelled this out in the celebrated trial of the Dean of St. Asaph:

> No deduction or conclusion can be drawn from what a jury *may* do . . . to what they *ought* to do upon the fundamental principles of the constitution and the reason of the thing, if they will act with integrity and good conscience. . . . The constitution trusts, that, under the direction of a judge, they will not usurp a jurisdiction which is not in their province. They do not know, and are not presumed to know the law: they are not required to decide the law. . . . It is the duty of the judge, in all cases of general justice, to tell the jury how to do right, though they have it *in their power* to do wrong, which is a matter entirely between God and their own consciences.[30]

Did Mondelet have a good legal case on the merits? From the facts presented in court, this writer does not think so, either with regard to aiding and abetting or to the de facto argument.

A principal in the first degree in murder cases was one who actually and knowingly did the deed. It is evident that Joseph Pinsonnault, who fired twice, was a principal in the first degree. No extent of compulsion excused murder. From the testimony presented it was possible to conclude that Nicolas had not ordered the firing, but there was persuasive evidence in the record that he had taken an active role in the affair, and that was to be expected, given his age, education, and officer rank in the rebel army. Even if as Mondelet argued he was not a leader (a very doubtful proposition), he at least had aided and abetted by conducting Chartrand's trial.

Gédéon Pinsonnault and Daunais seem also to have been guilty despite their refusal to fire. The authorities were clear that if a gang of men set out to perpetrate a crime, and one of them was guilty of murder in pursuit of their common object, all others involved were principals in the second degree.

The murder, however, had to be, as jurist Joseph Chitty put it, "within the compass of their original intention."[31] Thus if a gang committing an assault on someone intended to resist anybody who interfered, all were guilty of murder. But if the murder was quite extraneous from the original intention, those uninvolved in the deed were not guilty.

Applying the latter proposition, it might have been argued in favour of Gédéon Pinsonnault and Daunais that although they willingly participated in events originally designed to capture, question, and imprison Chartrand, they could not have anticipated that Beaulieu and the others would commit murder. There had, however, been talk of Chartrand's execution before the party left Eloi Roy's. Even if said in jest, as Roy claimed he had believed, it was enough to alert them to the possibility of murder. In any case they had been given unequivocal notice what was afoot when Nicolas conducted the mock trial, and there is no evidence in the record that they had remonstrated or attempted to dissociate themselves from the group. They had remained where they were and presumably had been prepared to assist in the proceedings, at least to the point of preventing Chartrand's escape, if that should prove necessary.

Mondelet's argument that obedience to a de facto government absolved the prisoners had a certain plausibility. The principle had been clearly recognized as early as Henry VII's reign, when Parliament enacted that upon the restoration of a de jure king acts that had been done in obedience to a de facto King, in full possession of power, were not to be deemed treasonable.[32] The statute was still in force in 1837–1838 and formed part of the law of Lower Canada. It had received a very restricted interpretation following the Civil War of the seventeenth century. Those involved in the beheading of Charles I and some senior officials under Cromwell's Protectorate, such as the military commander Sir Henry Vane, were found guilty of treason and executed. Pleas of obedience to a de facto government were rejected on the grounds that no *king* had supplanted Charles I or his heir, Charles II. As stated by the Chief Baron in the trial of one of the regicides, what the statute of Henry VII did was to protect the king de facto against the king de jure: "It was for a king and kingly government: it was not for an antimonarchical government."[33]

This interpretation was accepted as law by the eminent eighteenth-century jurists William Hawkins and Sir Michael Foster, although the latter did so with evident reluctance.[34] Blackstone, cautiously, did not raise the question. The doctrine that impunity was not extended to persons acting in adherence to nonmonarchical usurpers was roundly condemned early in the nineteenth century by Thomas Bayly Howell, senior editor of the first twenty-one volumes of the British *State Trials* published in 1816.[35] He argued that the 1495 statute was declaratory of the common law and there was no reason to believe the common law restricted impunity to the case of monarchical government. The rationale for the rule in the statute was that ordinary citizens had neither the leisure nor the freedom to decide a question of legitimate title. The same rationale, Howell contended, applied to a situation where non-monarchical usurpers had achieved possession of power. A de jure king not in possession of power could afford the subject no protection and hence the latter owed no allegiance. That principle had cogency whatever the form of the usurping government.

Howell's commonsense viewpoint had become accepted by the time of the Chartrand trial. For example, in an opinion rendered on an Upper Canada case (August 1838), the British Law Officers stated the law in the most general terms and in a context of rebellion aimed at establishing a republic:

> Where an insurrection against a Government had become so formidable as to assume the aspect of an equally-balanced civil war, the laws of war are to be observed between the Government and the insurgents; and native-born subjects could not properly be treated as traitors.[36]

Mondelet's contention therefore was correct in the abstract, but the rule accepted by Howell and the Law Officers did not fit the case. There was no evenly balanced civil war with two organized governments contending for supremacy. The patriotes had not even proclaimed a rebellion. There had been no declaration of independence, no provisional government established, no general call to arms issued. Mondelet argued that in accordance with the resolutions passed at the St. Charles protest meeting (October 1837), the citizens of L'Acadie had elected magistrates and established tribunals. In the weeks following the meeting, the patriote newspaper *La Minerve* carried a great deal of news about the resignations by militia officers and magistrats in L'Acadie. But there was no hint they had been replaced by popularly elected officials. If such elections did take place, the authority of the new officials must have been ephemeral in the extreme. There was nothing that could be called a de facto government that would justify residents in changing their allegiance. In 1745–46 the Young Stuart Pretender had proclaimed his father king and had controlled much of the Scottish highlands, even imposing an excise tax, but this had not prevented his followers from going to the gallows.

The Verdict

While the jury was deliberating, Delagrave and his patriote friends feared the worst. Chief Justice Reid's address seemed to leave no alternative to a guilty verdict. Indeed, Lemaître later claimed that there had never been a charge so completely unfavourable to the accused within living memory. After retiring for about an hour the jury returned and pronounced its verdict: not guilty. "Truly formidable men," Delagrave wrote Papineau, adding that the courtroom erupted in general applause. The judges and Attorney General Ogden, he went on, became deathly pale, fearing a riot. Walker made application that the prisoners not be liberated until provided with a police guard. He had affidavits to prove that their lives had been threatened by extreme Tories. The motion was granted. While descending the stairs of the courtroom, and later when passing Admiral Nelson's monument, the prisoners were hissed at by their political opponents. The large crowd of Canadien and Irish patriotes could easily have taught the Tories a good lesson, Delagrave wrote, but they feared that troops stationed nearby would fire on the patriotes. Escorted by the guard and numerous vocal supporters, the former prisoners made their way without incident to their lodgings. At dusk, fearing the infuriated Tories would wreck the building, they stole away to new accommodation.[37] That night, according to the historian Robert Christie, a contemporary of the events, the "Jury...dined with the prisoners...in exultation of the circumstances as a party triumph."[38]

The reaction of the French-language press to the verdict varied according to political persuasion. In Le Temps, François Lemaître repeated Mondelet's line of argument.[39] The joy of the Canadien community was not that murderers had escaped due punishment, but that the unjust persecution of four Canadiens had finally terminated. They had spent nine months in jail and then had been charged with a political offence when so many others more guilty than they had been amnestied and were at liberty. The most heinous sin one could attribute to the four was to have loved their country too much.

L'Ami was curiously restrained.[40] In a brief note it implied that guilt had been proved beyond a reasonable doubt and left the jurors "to their consciences which no doubt have already spoken to some of them" [trans.]. Le Populaire heaped praise on Reid and Ogden, expressed concern lest the Canadiens be stripped of the right to jury trial, and suggested Mondelet should join Laberge in jail. It also sadly reported that Chartrand's brother had become hysterical when the verdict was announced.[41]

In Le Canadien of Quebec City Etienne Parent, former patriote and normally an advocate of leniency to political prisoners, claimed that the jury's decision was not "the verdict of the Canadien people" [trans.] and might well give the Tories a pretext to deny trial by jury to Canadiens. The killing of Chartrand was an unjustifiable atrocity, of a kind the leaders of the insurrection should have announced would be severely punished. Nicolas was certainly guilty, although the others, perhaps, could have been freed on the grounds of coercion. Even if grounded in an excess of humanity, the verdict was a grievous error, wrote Parent. It sanctioned murder in certain circumstances and such a crime was never justified. The decision thoroughly tainted the Canadien character: "We. . . say that this verdict is the most deplorable event of any met with in our history and the one best suited to compromise the character of the Canadien people, both abroad and among our descendants" [trans.].[42] Parent's words proved prophetic.

The response of the *Mercury* and the *Gazette* in Quebec City was moderate.[43] Both condemned the verdict as partisan and implied that something had to change in the law relating to jury trials. The main burden of the *Mercury*'s comments, however, lay in justifying Durham's Ordinance, while the *Gazette* set itself firmly against any notion of private reprisal. It was in the Montreal newspapers that English outrage and alarm were clearly manifest. The *Transcript* referred to the growing fear that no one was safe from wanton murder.[44] The *Morning Courier* contended that the acquittal once again demonstrated that lower-class Canadiens, normally peaceable, had become through superstition and fear the dupes of an ambitious and unprincipled coterie of leaders.[45] This was not the verdict of twelve particular men but of any Canadien jury "indiscriminately chosen from among the *habitans*." No such jury would have dared challenge the self-proclaimed representatives of a "Nation Canadienne" whose "influence embraces the limits of feudal Canada." It was now established that murder if in any way connected with "revolutionary politics" was legally unpunishable. The verdict proved "beyond question the frightful rottenness of our social system."

Unlike the *Courier*, the *Montreal Gazette* had a specific solution to offer. Only ten weeks before, it had, if reluctantly and with patronizing noblesse oblige, accepted trial by jury on principle. It now changed its tune.[46] There had probably not been a man on the jury who could read or write, or was capable of distinguishing truth from falsehood, reason from prejudice. The verdict proved once and for all the "utter incapability of the French population in this Province to exercise the functions of free institutions, either judicially or politically." The right to jury trial should be confined to those of sufficient morality and enlightenment to use it, that is (an obvious implication), the English.

As usual, the *Herald* took the most extreme line, characterizing Mondelet's speech as "the most extraordinary and seditious harangue, ever heard within the walls of a temple of Justice" and calling for vigilante action.[47] The men of the Thirty-Second Regiment and "Scotchmen" in general were urged to avenge Weir, while all "loyal Canadians" should avenge Chartrand's murder or "die in the attempt." That the *Herald* accurately reflected an important sentiment is clear from a letter written by Lieutenant Colonel Charles Grey from Montreal, two days after the verdict, to his father, the former prime minister. The English, he was shocked to learn, now condemned the Whig administration in London as criminally lenient and talked of taking extralegal steps: ". . . [They] declare openly there is no law in the Land, and that they will now show they know how [to] defend themselves, and that they are independent both of the [imperial] Government and England."[48]

Rebellion of 1838

The astonishing verdict in the Chartrand murder trial was one of three developments enabling the rebels of 1837 to escape punishment. It had been preceded by Durham's general amnesty and would shortly be followed by the news that the Bermuda Ordinance had been disallowed, thus permitting Wolfred Nelson and his colleagues to continue their agitation in the United States. Of the three developments, the Chartrand trial verdict was the most dramatic and pointed. Both governments of Upper and Lower Canada had refrained from dispensing with trial by jury, and, in the latter province at least, it appeared that juries would not convict patriotes, even in extreme cases. There is a considerable body of evidence, albeit indirect, indicating that a sense of impunity encouraged the second rising, which took place in the week of 3–10 November 1838.

In the immediate wake of the acquittals, the *Herald* and *Mercury* carried news that the Loyalists (mostly Canadien) of L'Acadie and the surrounding area reported an alarming increase in "secret midnight meetings and taking oaths" among the habitant farmers. This clearly referred to recruitment into the *Frères Chasseurs*, the secret revolutionary society that intended to and did form the backbone of the 1838 rebel army. According to these newspapers' sources, the clandestine activities were greatly aided by the local patriote leaders, who boasted that "there is now no law or Government, and that every man is at liberty to do what seemeth good in his own eyes."[49] Corroboration of the probable link between the Chartrand trial and recruitment into the Chasseurs awaits detailed research into the massive "Evénements de 1837–1838" series of manuscripts held by the Archives nationales du Québec.

When the second insurrection broke out it was commonplace among supporters of the government that it had been "caused" by what they referred to disgustedly as "mildness," "lenity," "lenience," or "impunity," and which they blamed on Lord Durham or the imperial government, or both. One outraged Montrealer informed Whig M.P. Edward Ellice that the "ignorant peasantry believed that the impunity granted to their leaders originated in fear of them instead of magnanimity."[50] Special Councillor Samuel Gerrard concluded that the "lenity shown the Rebels last summer has encouraged them to a second Rebellion."[51] Lieutenant Colonel Grey was of the firm opinion that executions were warranted to teach "the People. . . that if they escaped punishment last year it did not proceed in any way from *fear* of them, as they had been studiously taught was the case."[52] A letter to the editor of the *Quebec Gazette* blamed the second outbreak on the "imbecile weakness, the dastardly cowardice, the truckling conciliation, the cursed amnesty of the shabby Whig Radical ministry."[53] Similar sentiments were expressed in the pages of the *Courier*, the *Transcript*, the *Montreal Gazette*, the *Mercury, L'Ami du Peuple*,[54] and in a report of the Special Council.[55]

It may be objected that these opinions were merely the fantasies of persons bent on vengeance and ignorant of the facts. But some at least were in an excellent position to make an accurate assessment. Samuel Gerrard was a business associate of Edward Ellice and was well versed about conditions and opinions in Ellice's seigneury of Beauharnois, one of the two principal centres of the second insurrection. Colonel Grey had supervised the examination of hundreds of patriotes in the Beauharnois and L'Acadie areas preparatory to dispatching the most active rebels to the prisons in Montreal.[56] One of the sources of information for *L'Ami* was Pierre-Edouard Leclère, a founder of the paper, Superintendant of Police for the Montreal District, and constant visitor to the prisons.

Another well-placed witness to the November 1838 Rebellion was General Sir John Colborne, Administrator of Lower Canada after Durham's departure, who had access to multiple channels of intelligence and who was neither exceptionally alarmist nor vindictive. The insurgents, he wrote the Colonial Security, Lord Glenelg, in December 1838, had been "encouraged in the second revolt by the recollection of past impunity, and the hope of future amnesty."[57] Given the failure to punish, he told Grey a few weeks later, "nothing could have prevented a second attempt at rebellion this year."[58] More specifically, Colborne was convinced that Mondelet's successful appeal to the jury in the Chartrand trial had greatly increased "revolutionary excitement" and had even helped "produce . . . outrages of an atrocious character" during the 1838 rising.[59]

Also revealing is the fact that even after the special, multiple gallows had been constructed at the new prison and the court martial had begun its grim proceedings in Montreal against the participants in the 1838 Rebellion, many patriote prisoners and their sympathizers remained certain there would be no executions. The Canadien exiles in Vermont and New York, for example, thought Colborne was bluffing, a sentiment reported by William Lyon Mackenzie's *Gazette* published in Rochester and expressed in the private journal kept by Papineau's son Amédée.[60] When complications arose relating to the legality of the court martial and its proceedings, *L'Ami* claimed that "all the rebels, even those in prison, begin to laugh at the government and to insist that all will end in a farce like the exile to Bermuda" [trans.].[61]

According to Lady Colborne, prior to the hanging of Joseph-Narcisse Cardinal and Joseph Duquette on 21 December 1838, nothing would make the condemned prisoners "believe that Sir John would *dare* execute the sentence."[62] It would seem reasonable to conclude from the evidence presented that the impunity enjoyed by the 1837 rebels played a role in encouraging the patriotes to rise again. It is probably not entirely coincidental that in Upper Canada, where there had been three executions as well as numerous sentences of transportation, banishment, or imprisonment, there was no internal uprising in support of the patriote raids on Prescott and Windsor in November-December 1838.

The Chartrand murder trial was to have other momentous consequences. In particular the verdict removed any hopes whatever government officials may have entertained that trial by jury could form part of an effective penal policy for dealing with political offenders. As Attorney General Ogden put it in a report, jury trials had been proven worse than useless:

> The gratuitous assumption of criminal responsibility [on the part of the government] implied by the verdict of the jury, independent of their contempt for the most sacred obligation [of the oath] convince me that similar results must be expected whenever juries thus composed [of Canadiens] are called upon to decide upon matters of similar character or tendency.[63]

The Attorney General's pessimistic prediction was borne out a year later when the government failed to convict François Jalbert for the murder of Lieutenant Weir.[64] Meanwhile, Durham agreed with Ogden's assessment and sent home a copy of Reid's trial notes, later commenting in a dispatch that "trial by jury exists only to defeat the ends of justice, and to provoke the righteous scorn and indignation of the community."[65]

Establishment of Courts Martial for the Trial of Civilians

When the second insurrection occurred, opinion favourable to the government was adamant in demanding radical alteration of the administration of criminal justice. A handful of individuals with legal training advocated jury trials in a district other than Montreal,[66] but their voices were totally inundated by the strident demand that any leaders captured be tried summarily by the military and publicly executed to prevent a third rebellion. Suggestions that there be established a court of judges sitting without juries were likewise submerged.[67]

The atmosphere was captured to perfection by a British traveller to Montreal who wrote home that the English "have been thinking of nothing ever since [the second insurrection] but avenging *imagined* cruelties, and guarding against *apprehended* dangers."[68] Even the once and future beacon of Whig liberalism, editor-politician John Neilson, was caught up in the rush to summary vengeance. His *Quebec Gazette* ridiculed supporters of traditional procedures. Only a military tribunal "divested of the *Jury Chartrand*" could administer "impartial justice."[69]

On 8 November 1838 General Colborne had the Special Council pass an ordinance providing for the trial of rebels by courts martial.[70] It was made retroactive to cover all treasonable offences since 1 November 1838 and authorized the imposition of the death sentence. The ordinance also dispensed with special guarantees to accused in treason trials dating back to the reigns of William III and Anne. These included the right to a list of Crown witnesses at least ten days before trial and the right of counsel to make full defence.[71] In Lower Canada the defence lawyers were able to submit written arguments, but were not permitted to argue orally or to examine or cross-examine witnesses. The drastic nature of the ordinance can be understood by comparing its provisions with those found in the then most recent British precedent, the Coercion Act of 1833, which had established courts martial to suppress popular disturbances in Ireland.[72] That statute had prohibited capital sentences, had explicitly restricted jurisdiction to future offences, and had permitted defence counsel to examine and cross-examine witnesses.

In late November Colborne received word from Lord Glenelg that in view of the Chartrand decision the imperial government no longer insisted on trial by jury.[73] On 28 November a general court martial consisting of fifteen regular army officers began its sittings in the old Montreal court house.[74] From November to May it conducted fourteen trials, ranging in size from a single accused to an unwieldly *pot pourri* of nineteen. One hundred and six prisoners were tried for high treason, some of whom also faced murder charges. Ninety-nine were found guilty. Two of the convicted were banished from the province, and fifty-eight were transported to New South Wales for life, although pardoned in 1844 or shortly afterwards. Twelve were hanged in three sets of public executions. The remainder were released on bail from prison in the autumn of 1839.

The court martial represents one of the gravest abuses of due process in Canadian history. It is not unlikely that the establishment of the court was beyond the powers of the Special Council, which had been expressly prohibited by Parliament from altering any British statute applying to the colony.[75] Read literally, this limitation included the Quebec Act of 1774, which had made permanent provision for the application of the criminal law of England, including "the Method of Prosecution and Trial."[76] Three Canadien judges who adopted this interpretation in two cases involving the Council's suspension of habeas corpus were themselves summarily suspended from office.[77] When asked for a ruling on the legality of the court martial in view of the limitation, the Court of King's Bench (Montreal) expounded the extraordinary doctrine that the constitutionality of colonial statutes was beyond the review of the courts and vested solely in Parliament.[78] The ordinance establishing courts martial also undoubtedly conflicted with fundamental norms of the British legal order in providing for the trial of civilians for capital crimes by military tribunal when the ordinary courts were sitting,[79] and in conferring a retroactive jurisdiction on that tribunal.[80] Prior to the passage of the Colonial Laws Validity Act of 1865,[81] it could respectably be argued that colonial statutes contravening fundamental norms were null and void.[82] This precise position had been taken by several Parliamentary opponents of Durham's Bermuda Ordinance, including Law Lords Brougham and Denman.[83]

The court martial indulged in a number of dubious interpretations of the law, holding, for example, that rebels killing soldiers in battle were guilty of murder; that simple proof of propinquity to rebels placed the onus on the accused;[84] and that *any* resistance to law enforcement during the disturbances amounted to high treason, not riot.[85] One man was executed and another transported on the basis of the court's ruling that aliens entering the province in hostile array to support the rebellion enjoyed the Crown's protection, and therefore, owing temporary allegiance, were guilty of high treason. This ran contrary to the reasoned and well-known position of Chief Justice John Beverley Robinson and the Law Officers of Upper Canada,[86] as well as against the conclusions reached by Lord Durham's Lower Canadian legal advisors.[87]

The court's handling of evidence was patently partisan. In one case the only concrete proof against the prisoner related to his supposed rebel activity on 10 November. Despite establishing through the jailer that he had been under arrest since 7 November and lodged in the Montreal prison, the accused was convicted and later transported to New South Wales. The minatory atmosphere in which trials were conducted is suggested by the recollections of one of the prisoners:

> During these long days of our trial, the abuse and insults levelled at us did not diminish on the part of the rabble which crowded round us on our passage, and invaded the approaches to the Court. Some of our judges even did not spare us gross insults; some of them also amused themselves, during the sittings sketching little figures hanging from gibbets and these caricatures which they passed to one another before our gaze, appeared to amuse them greatly. . . . [trans.][88]

It is of interest that two of the prisoners sent to the gallows by the court martial and by Colborne were François Nicolas and Amable Daunais, accused in the Chartrand case. Nicolas, as a man of the middle class and a rebel officer, might have been executed regardless of the so-called murder. But Daunais surely would not have been. He was an illiterate farm labourer and the only proof against him before the court martial was that he had done sentry duty at Napierville during the second Rebellion. Like Louis Riel after him, Daunais was convicted of one crime and hanged for another.[89]

Conclusion

One hopes the court martial's decisions will never be cited as precedents, but, of course, stranger things have happened. We also hope never again to see the trial of civilians by military tribunals when the ordinary courts are sitting. It should be remembered, however, that such was authorized in Canada (but not implemented) as late as 1918. This was done by regulation under the War Measures Act following the conscription riots in Quebec City.[90] In the United States such a procedure has been declared unconstitutional by the Supreme Court.[91] In Canada the new Charter of Rights and Freedoms now appears to guarantee trial by jury for serious offences, but in an emergency this guarantee could be ignored if Parliament chose to use the power given in section 33 to override fundamental legal rights.

In the Chartrand trial the jury ignored the judge's instructions on the law. There is a considerable recent literature in the United States on the virtues and defects of what is known as jury nullification.[92] Proponents have argued in court and learned journals that the jury should be told it has the right to ignore judicial instructions if enforcement of the law (e.g., the draft) would outrage the moral standards of the community. To date, American law, federally and in almost all state jurisdictions, remains essentially the same as that laid down by Lord Mansfield in the *Dean of St. Asaph* case: juries have the raw power to nullify but the moral duty to obey instructions on the law. And there are good reasons for this conservatism. How is one to have confidence that a jury represents a community's standards? At the time of the Chartrand trial, for example, opinion on the moral question was bitterly divided, even among Canadiens. More generally, the historical record seems ambiguous.

There are indeed cases of nullification that were on the wave of the future. The *Dean of St. Asaph* decision and the controversy it aroused led to Fox's celebrated Libel Act (1792) granting juries paramountcy in criminal libel cases and thus contributing to freedom of the press. Jury nullification in England also undoubtedly accelerated the movement to restrict capital punishment in the first half of the nineteenth century. But how often, even in this century, have white juries in the southern United States acquitted whites accused of crimes of violence against blacks in the face of the evidence and the law?

It is very difficult to argue for jury nullification on the grounds that it would likely further specified social values. If from a law-and-order orientation one believes, as the R.C.M.P. Security Service apparently did, that state necessity should be a defence to crimes committed by policemen or security operatives, one might welcome jury nullification, at least until one reflected that sit-in demonstrators and other civil disobedience activists might go free. If as a women's rights activist one thinks there should be abortion on demand, jury nullification might appear a welcome reform, except that it would also likely result in the acquittal of some men accused of raping not altogether chaste victims. The probable impact of jury nullification, then, seems to cut across any coherent value system, save perhaps that which views the criminal law method of handling social conflict as crude and dangerous. But even holding that value as important, one might not opt for this departure from tradition.

Jury nullification would remove the administration of criminal justice even further from the ideal of equality before the law. Would cases of alleged police brutality, for example, be treated the same in Vancouver and Calgary? Would abortionists be dealt with evenhandedly in Montreal and Chicoutimi? And wouldn't jury nullification widen the scope for prejudice? One of the proponents, writing in 1980, proudly described how he had secured a nullification acquittal in Maryland for a client charged with possession of marijuana. The accused was a young white man, of good family, whose conviction for a felony would prevent his attending dentistry school. One is entitled to ask whether an unemployed black labourer would have fared as well.

Second, jury nullification could result in convictions for behaviour deemed blameworthy but not against the law. It is true that proponents suggest nullification be restricted to acquittals, but it is not apparent that juries that are told their moral judgment is superior to the law would abide by this distinction. If juries did convict on moral grounds, the accused would be punished retroactively, a gross breach of the rule of law. Much of what proponents seek could be achieved if juries were encouraged to accompany recommendations to mercy with reflections on the fairness of the law being enforced.

The Chartrand case, in summary, illustrates well the uses historians can make of legal materials. The trial reports and ancillary documentation provide a clear focus for understanding the tensions between English and Canadiens, and even among the Canadiens themselves, in the period between the two rebellions. The verdict provides a major explanation for the establishment of the 1838–39 court martial, a depressing but instructive chapter in Canadian legal history and one that remained a grievance among Canadien nationalists for over half a century. The verdict also contributed to the outbreak of the second insurrection. The fact that it occurred and failed had important repercussions. In particular, the movements to republican democracy and fundamental, entrenched individual rights were arrested in both Canadas, while French Canada was placed on the route of conservative clerical nationalism from which it would emerge only in our lifetime. The verdict also illustrates a tendency in French Canada that has been clear since the British conquest: a sense that political criminals perceived to be acting, however misguidedly, in the interests of "la nation" should be treated leniently. The movement in the 1840s to repatriate the prisoners transported to Australia, the hostile reaction to Riel's execution, and the generally approved leniency meted out to the F.L.Q. prisoners are other examples of a deep and abiding nationalism. Finally, the Chartrand case provides one of the few clear precedents of jury nullification in Canadian history.

Notes

1. For this subject in a Canadian context, see Kenneth McNaught, "Political Trials and the Canadian Political Tradition," *Courts and Trials*, ed. Martin L. Friedland (Toronto, 1975), 137–61; F. Murray Greenwood, "L'insurrection appréhendée et l'administration de la justice au Canada: le point de vue d'un historien," *Révue d'histoire de l'Amérique française* 34 (June 1980): 57–93.
2. Charles Buller, "Sketch of Lord Durham's Mission to Canada in 1838" [1840], in *Report of the Public Archives of Canada for the Year 1923*, 34–69.
3. Statutes of Lower Canada, 2 Vict. (1838), c.1.
4. The two indicted but not tried were Réne Garant and Jean Beaulieu, both principals in the affair. They had escaped to the United States. Bill of Indictment, 31 Aug. 1838, Evénements de 1837–38, no. 409, Archives nationales du Québec [hereafter E.]; C. R. Ogden, 31 Aug. 1838, Durham Papers, vol. 21, Public Archives of Canada [hereafter PAC].
5. Voluntary examinations, 6 Feb. 1838, of Joseph and Gédéon Pinsonnault, E. 385, 386.
6. Voluntary examinations of Amable Daunais, 6 Dec. 1837, E. 388, 390.
7. *North American* [a patriote paper published by the exiles in Swanton, Vermont], 16 Oct. 1839; *The Queen v. Remi Narbonne et al., Report of the State Trials before a General Court Martial held at Montreal in 1838–9*, 2 vols. (Montreal, 1839), vol. 2; L.-O. David, *Les Patriotes de 1837–38* (Montreal, 1884).
8. Buller, "Sketch."
9. A. W. Patrick Buchanan, *The Bench and Bar of Lower Canada down to 1850* (Montreal, 1925).
10. *Le Populaire*, 17 Sept. 1838; *Le Canadien*, 24 Sept. 1838.
11. Delagrave to Papineau, 7 Sept. 1838, Papineau Papers, vol. 2, PAC.
12. The *Herald*'s report of the trial may be found in the Toronto *Patriot*, 21, 25 Sept. 1838. As most issues of the *Herald* from this period are missing, its stories and editorials can be found only in reprints, summaries, or comments appearing in other colonial, British, or American newspapers. The other newspaper reports of the trial are found in *L'Ami*, 8, 12 Sept. 1838; *Le Populaire*, 14 Sept.–5 Oct. 1838.
13. *La Quotidienne*, 14 Sept. 1838.

14. *Procès Politique: La Reine vs. Nicolas et al.* (Montreal, 1838), PAC pamphlet no. 1–1693. The original court proceedings have not been located, but a copy of Judge Reid's notes summarizing the testimony has been preserved: enclosed in Durham to Glenelg, 23 Sept. 1838, in *British Parliamentary Papers/Colonies/Canada* [hereafter *BPP*], ed. Irish University Press, vol. 10.

15. Confession of J.-B.-H. Brien, 17 Nov. 1838, Jean-Baptiste-Henri Brien Papers, PAC.

16. *Montreal Transcript*, 8 Sept. 1838.

17. The existing records suggest that neither O'Sullivan, Ogden, nor Reid made use of the well-established proposition that duress was never a defence to murder. See Sir Mathew Hale, *The History of the Pleas of the Crown* [1678], ed. W. A. Stokes and E. Ingersoll, 2 vols. (Philadelphia, 1847), vol. 1; Sir William Blackstone, *Commentaries on the Laws of England* [1765–69], ed. Edward Christian (London, 1809), vol. 4.

18. Langlois was convicted of high treason after the 1838 rebellion and transported for life to New South Wales.

19. They had marched from a neighbouring tavern, in military file, with Nicolas in front bearing a red flag with the word "liberté" on it.

20. Given the short distance involved, it is difficult to believe the defeat was not generally known. Jean-Baptiste Mailloux, David Roy's hired hand, later testified that Chartrand had mentioned the battle on the morning of the 27th. It is, of course, possible the dimensions of the defeat were not understood that early. For a few days after St. Charles there remained a number of armed bands of patriotes on the Richelieu.

21. See notes 5 and 6, above, and notes 22 and 23, below.

22. Deposition of Eloi Roy, 5 Dec. 1838, E. 398.

23. Deposition of Etienne Langlois, 2 Dec. 1838, E. 401; voluntary examinations of Barthélémi Poissant, 28 Dec. 1837, 6 Feb. 1838, E. 397, 383.

24. William Oldnall Russell, *A Treatise on Crimes and Indictable Misdemeanours*, 2d ed. (London, 1826), vol. 1.

25. In 1839 Quesnel interceded with Colborne in favour of patriote residents of his neighbourhood who were facing sentences of transportation for life. Quesnel to Colborne, 13 May 1839, S Series, vol. 582, PAC.

26. *Transcript*, 13 Sept. 1838.

27. Ogden was probably correct since the amnesty, in exempting the four accused, described them as "charged with the murder . . . of the late Joseph Chartrand." As an exception, this exemption was properly interpreted in a restrictive manner, i.e., the accused could be charged only with murder. As a general principle, the Crown enjoyed the right to proceed against a traitor for felony: Hale, *Pleas of the Crown; Regina v. McMahon* (1867) 26 U.C.Q.B. 195.

28. 12, 14 Sept. 1838.

29. *The Constitution of England* [1771, in French], printed for G. Wilkie and others (London, 1810).

30. *Proceedings on an Indictment . . . against the Dean of St. Asaph* (1738–84) 21 *State Trials* [hereafter St. Tr.] 847.

31. Joseph Chitty, *A Practical Treatise of the Criminal Law* (London, 1816), vol. 1.

32. 11 Hen. VII (1495), c. 1.

33. *The Trials of Twenty-Nine Regicides* (1660) 5 St. Tr. 947 at 1,114; *The Trial of Sir Henry Vane* (1662) 6 St. Tr. 119.

34. William Hawkins, *A Treatise of the Pleas of the Crown* (London, 1716/1721); Sir Michael Foster, *Crown Cases* (London, 1762).
35. Editorial notes to Vane's trial (see note 33, above).
36. Law Officers to Glenelg, 21 Aug. 1838, *Cases and Opinions on Constitutional Law*, ed. William Forsythe (London, 1869), 199–204.
37. Delagrave to Papineau, 7 Sept. 1838, Papineau Papers, vol. 2, PAC. See also, E. B. O'Callaghan to William Lyon Mackenzie, 7 Sept. 1838, Mackenzie-Lindsey Papers, Public Archives of Ontario [hereafter PAO]; Lemaître, *Le Procès; L'Ami*, 12 Sept. 1838; *Le Canadien*, 14 Sept. 1838.
38. Robert Christie, *A History of the Late Province of Lower Canada*, 6 vols. (Quebec/ Montreal, 1848–55), vol. 5.
39. 11 Sept. 1838.
40. 12 Sept. 1838.
41. 10, 17 Sept. 1838.
42. 17, 19 Sept. 1838.
43. *Gazette*, 10, 12 Sept. 1838; *Mercury*, 13 Sept. 1838.
44. 13 Sept. 1838.
45. 12 Sept. 1838.
46. 28 June, 11 Sept. 1838.
47. *Patriot*, 21, 25 Sept. 1838.
48. 9 Sept. 1838. *Crisis in the Canadas 1838–1839: The Grey Journals and Letters*, ed. William Ormsby (Toronto, 1964), 120–21.
49. *Mercury*, 20 Sept. 1838, reprinting a story from the *Herald* of 18 September.
50. 8 Nov. 1838, Ellice Papers, vol. 13, PAC.
51. Gerrard to Ellice, 18 Nov. 1838, *ibid.*
52. Grey to Earl Grey, 14 Jan. 1839, ed. Ormsby, *Crisis in the Canadas*, 179–83.
53. 12 Nov. 1838.
54. 5, 23 Nov. 1838; 8 Nov. 1838; 29 Dec. 1838; 8, 15 Nov. 1838; 12 Dec. 1838.
55. Minutes of 14 Jan. 1839, Record Group 1, E. 1, vol. 42, PAC.
56. Grey to Earl Grey, 25 Nov., 12 Dec. 1838, Journal Entry, 19 Dec. 1838, ed. Ormsby, *Crisis in the Canadas*, 163–66; 166–70; 144–53.
57. 19 Dec. 1838, *BPP*, vol. 10.
58. Grey to Earl Grey, 14 Jan. 1839, ed. Ormsby, *Crisis in the Canadas*, 179–83 (paraphrase of Colborne's opinion).
59. Colborne to Normanby, 6 May 1839, *BPP*, vol. 10.
60. *Mackenzie's Gazette*, 8 Dec. 1838; "Journal d'un fils de la liberté," 11 Dec. 1838, Papineau Papers, vol. 32, PAC.
61. 12 Dec. 1838.
62. Lady Colborne to _____, 7 Jan. 1839, G. C. Moore Smith, *The Life of John Colborne* (London, 1903).
63. Ogden to Buller, 20 Sept. 1838, *BPP* vol. 10.
64. *Procès politique: La Reine vs. Jalbert* (Montreal, 1839), PAC pamphlet no. I–1759. In this trial Mondelet again made use of the de facto argument. A mixed jury of English and Canadiens could not agree on a verdict, and Jalbert was discharged.
65. Durham to Glenelg, 23, 28 Sept. 1838, *BPP*, vol. 16.
66. E.g., Chief Justice James Stuart to Colborne, 2 Nov. 1838, Colborne Papers, vol. 18, PAC; *Quebec Gazette*, 9 Nov. 1838 (letter from "C").
67. E.g., Glenelg to Durham, 26 Oct. 1838, *BPP*, vol. 10; *Courier*, 5 Nov. 1838.

68. London, *Spectator*, 22 Dec. 1838.
69. 21 Dec. 1838.
70. 2 Vict. (1838), c. 3.
71. 7 & 8 Wm. III (1695), c. 3; 7 Anne (1708), c. 21.
72. 3 & 4 Wm. IV (1833), c. 4.
73. Glenelg to Durham, 26 Oct. 1838, *BPP*, vol. 10.
74. Eleven of the fourteen trials were reported. See note 7, above.
75. 1 Vict. (1838), c. 9.
76. 14 Geo. III (1774), c. 83.
77. Colborne to Glenlg, 14 Dec. 1838 and enclosures, Q Series, vol. 245, PAC; Christie, *A History*, vol. 5.
78. *Courier*, 6, 8, 11 Feb. 1839; Mr. Justice George Pyke to James Reid, 24 Feb. 1839, Collection Baby, vol. 20, PAC. The Lower Canadian Court of Appeal had earlier held a provision in a colonial statute *ultra vires*: *Gillespie et al. v. Perceval* (1829) *Stuarts Reports*.
79. See, e.g., *Wolfe Tone's Case* (1798) 27 St. Tr. 614; Richard O'Sullivan, *Military Law and the Supremacy of the Civil Courts* (London, 1921).
80. See Elmer E. Smead, "The Rule against Retroactive Legislation: A Basic Principle of Jurisprudence," *Minnesota Law Review* 20 (1935–36): 775–97. Even Attorney General Ogden had serious doubts about the validity of the ordinance because of its retroactive application, but kept them to himself. Ogden's "Questions, as to the Operation of the Ordinance 2 Victoria cap:3," 8 December 1838, S Series, vol. 558, PAC. At least two of the men executed had been arrested prior to the date of passage of the ordinance. Several arrested prior to that date were transported.
81. 28 & 29 Vict. (1865), c. 3.
82. D. B. Swinfen, *Imperial Control of Colonial Legislation 1813–1865* (Oxford, 1970).
83. Parl. Deb., vol. 44 (Aug. 1838).
84. Cf. *The Trials of Peter Messenger et al.* (1668) 6 St. Tr. 879.
85. Cf. *R v. Frost et al.* (1839), 4 St. Tr. (n.s.) 85.
86. E.g., Arthur to Durham, 27 June 1838, Q Series, vol. 406, PAC; Law Officers (U.C.) to Arthur, 28 June 1838, ibid.; Robinson to Arthur, 28 June 1838 ibid.; Robinson to Arthur, 6 Aug. 1838, John Beverley Robinson Papers, PAO; *Kingston Chronicle & Gazette*, 5 May 1838; *Patriot*, 13 March, 17 Aug. 1838.
87. Turton and Buller's opinion, — Oct. 1838, Durham Papers, vol. 21. The British Law Officers held to a different opinion (note 36 above), but the main precedent they cited, dating from 1557, was not on the point, and they dealt irresponsibly with statements made by the jurists, especially Coke and Hawkins.
88. François-Xavier Prieur, *Notes d'un condamné politique* (Quebec, 1864).
89. Colborne to Glenelg, 19 Feb. 1839. Q Series, vol. 257, PAC.
90. Herbert Marx, "The Emergency Power and Civil Liberties in Canada," *McGill Law Journal* 16 (1970): 39–91.
91. *Ex parte Milligan* (1866), 4 Wallace 2.
92. See, e.g., proponents: R. J. Stolt, "Jury Nullification: The Forgotten Right," *New England L. R.* 7 (1971): 105–22; A. W. Scheflin, "Jury Nullification: The Right to Say No," *Southern California L. R.* 45 (1972): 168–226; B. L. Becker, "Jury Nullification: Can a Jury be Trusted?" *Trial* 16 (1980): 41–45; and opponents: L. P. Dreyer, "Jury Nullification and the Pro Se Defense,"

University of Kansas L. R. 21 (1972–73): 47–70; G. J. Simson, "Jury Nullification in the American System: A Skeptical View," *Texas L. R.* 54 (1975–76): 488–525; D. A. Harris, "Jury Nullification in Historical Perspective: Massachusetts as a Case Study," *Suffolk University L. R.* 12 (1978): 968–1011.

Conference Assessment:
The History of Crime and
Criminal Justice after Twenty-Five Years

Eric H. Monkkonen
University of California, Los Angeles

The Second International Conference on the History of Crime and Criminal Justice, which took place in Maastricht, The Netherlands, May 17–19, 1984, brought together forty scholars representing eleven countries and three disciplines—law, history, and criminology. The sessions and paper topics (see Appendix A) ranged considerably, though all were loosely united by the general theme of the conference: "Violence in the Atlantic and Mediterranean World Since the Later Middle Ages: From Above and From Below."

Within this larger theme several conceptually tighter foci developed during the course of the conference. Underlying several papers was the work of Norbert Elias on the "civilizing process" in the history of Western Europe. The concern with Elias was in exploring and probing the history of violence in the general context of his observations rather than explicitly testing or reformulating. In addition to Elias's influence, Max Weber's operational definition of the state as that entity which holds the monopoly on violence underlaid papers that focused on state apparatuses for criminal catching, trial, and punishment. These two larger conceptual schemes—the civilizing process and the state—functioned as loose conceptual guideposts.

Interestingly, a more sharply defined, separate, and perhaps ultimately more complex methodological issue appeared. This issue may be crudely defined as contrasting three methods: the anthropological, the quantitative, and that which attends primarily to legal or institutional dynamics of change, the "internalist" analysis. Though none of the methodological approaches nor the two conceptual positions are necessarily mutually self-exclusive, the participants and their papers tended to belong to one position or the other. Curiously, adherents of each of the three methodological positions usually dichotomized all other methods, so that those favoring anthropological approaches viewed all others as one, the quantifiers viewed all others as one, and the internalists viewed all others as one. Although the actual research reported did not follow such dichotomies, it was clear the conferees drew up such divisions of basic stances towards evidence, questions, and research design.

No doubt these themes and divisions, like the multinational aspects of the research reported, would all seem unnecessarily subtle to an outsider in the face of the larger and more dramatic empirical discussions of the conference: torture, prison violence, capital punishment, police violence, blood feuds, spousal violence, banditry, and collective violence. That the conceptual and methodological issues occupied much of the conference demonstrates how the maturity and knowledge of criminal justice history continue to grow. One aspect of this growth is that as conceptualization has become less unambiguous and methodology more precisely demanding, generalization has become more difficult. No conference paper attempted to generalize about the larger scheme of things, and only the extensive comment of M. Sbriccoli raised issues about the general nature of imprisonment.

When one considers that within the span of a year there have been three conferences (one under the auspices of the Past & Present Society at Oxford in July 1983 and one at Warwick University in September 1983 [see Appendix B]) on the history of crime, one must conclude that something has captured the imagination of a wide range of scholars. And rather than summarize the contents of the papers read at Maastricht in this report specifically, I wish to address this larger, if less concrete, phenomenon.

In the late 1950s and early 1960s, social historians made crime a historical topic.[1] The importance of this bold step should not be undervalued, for the work of Louis Chevalier and Eric Hobsbawm changed the angle from which historians considered crime: it had been a historical problem meaningful only in that it was an ancient and essentially objective social problem. By making crime historical, they integrated criminal behavior with society. It became a specific human action located in a human context, both determined by and determining of that context. One can too easily overemphasize the dissimilarities in their works. Chevalier used metaphors of disease to account for crime and its human context in Paris. Hobsbawm located a more narrowly defined kind of criminal behavior in the context of political action in precapitalist states. But both examined crime as social behavior, as behavior that could serve as an empirical entrée into the lives of ordinary people, as behavior that was historically meaningful and could tell historians about the larger world containing the crime.

Law and the institutions that implemented it figured little in their research. The state was present only as an abstraction. The work of Chevalier and Hobsbawm told us about mentalities and rebellions, daily life, and micro events. The history of institutions, of formal organizations, of the law itself seemed trivial and pale in the context of these more universally gripping works. The exciting and stimulating legacy of their work has grown into a major field for a wide variety of scholars, only some of whom were represented at the Second International conference.

In many ways the current research reported on at the conference departs significantly from that which made criminal justice history so exciting in the first place. Although no one conferee directly attacked Hobsbawm or Chevalier, it was almost as though to do so would have made the researchers uncomfortable. Who, after all, can work for years doing research that promises to tell about basic relationships between mind and action, between society and behavior, and then produce results that so qualify the big questions as to make them irrelevant? In the twenty-five years since Chevalier's book we have learned enough about crime to keep our mouths shut instead of calling it a symptom of a diseased society, and we are no longer comfortable in expecting bandits to teach us about rebellion.

If there are any candidates for broad thinkers to have replaced Hobsbawm and Chevalier, one would not have divined their identity at this conference. One might have expected the ideas of Michel Foucault, for instance, to have influenced recent work, but it is apparent that his empirical research is considered so flawed as to be unworthy of criticism. There is a deep irony here. Probably most scholars researching historical crime began their work influenced by either Hobsbawm or Chevalier, while more recently Foucault has made the history of punishment almost a household word.

Thus, a field that has engaged and continues to engage some of the finest historians of the postwar era addresses none of the major issues that originally inspired it. This indicates that although the dynamics and relationships asserted by Chevalier, Hobsbawm, and Foucault may have been serving the important inspirational purpose of providing theories, hypotheses, and models, these quietly dropped at the wayside as they ceased to guide research. Their work gave scholars historical arguments to use as heuristic devices that earlier, less historically concrete thinkers like Weber and Elias had not supplied. Yet one sees an important process of growth and change here: Chevalier and Hobsbawm inspire work that eclipses them in favor of even earlier scholars.

Just because the research of Chevalier and Hobsbawm does not seem to have provoked either a counterargument or systematic confirmation, we should not conclude that their work no longer serves the vital purpose of inspiration and guidance. In actuality, the fundamental contribution of Hobsbawm and Chevalier has not been dropped but has become the bedrock of historical research on crime and its repression. Their fundamental contribution is the notion that crime is an historical phenomenon. As such, crime is not constant, for it varies as do societies and their economic bases. As such, crime is socially produced. And as such, the political mechanisms for its repression express their concrete historical situation rather than any abstract technology.

But what if these bedrock assumptions are wrong? What if crime is like disease and best understood in an atemporal perspective? What if homicides in the Middle Ages differed little from those today?

If these assumptions were to be shown wrong, two major aspects of crime would still remain of great historical importance. First, the crime-control institutions would still provide us with a critical means of understanding the historical development of the state and perhaps the mentality of the non-criminals. And second, criminal records would still be a unique avenue to lives of people usually not retrievable in any other way.

To a surprising extent, much recent criminal justice research does seem to be attentive to one of these aspects of crime and justice. Is it possible then that the abandonment of the assumptions that originally vitalized the historical study of crime has already been quietly accomplished? Those who began their research inspired by Hobsbawm and Chevalier may in fact retain their affection for these exciting authors at the same time that they work under different assumptions. That so many historians are at work, even if the issues on which they work do not appear quite as grand as those originally posed by Hobsbawm and Chevalier, and even if the work may implicitly question some of the basic assumptions that placed crime in a historical framework, suggests that new questions now motivate this historical research. These questions are based on two new primary assumptions: first, that crime control tells us much about the state, and, second, that criminal records allow entrée into past societies.

The central questions now seem to be concerned with explaining how the expanding state has effectively lowered the levels of individual violence and crime. This is much more complex than it may at first appear and seems to involve several components. First, it must be shown how the state itself initially became interested in reducing violence. This is not at all an easy task, as the discussions of Scottish blood feuds and torture demonstrate. That is, it is equally easy to conceive how growing states might have accepted and even sanctioned individual violence, rather than controlled and eliminated it. Second, the research on trial procedures and political policing shows that the criminal justice apparatus was remarkably resistant to innovations, whether such innovations improved, changed, or simply reinforced the existing system. Third, stateless regions or people were often the victims of violence, both organized and random, but there seems to be no way of determining if this was a causal or caused component. That is, were stateless persons chosen as victims and did offenders migrate to stateless areas, or did the ebb and flow of state presence change the local dynamics of crime? Finally, is there an assumption implied here of a constant urge towards violence, violence that only an external organization might temper? Certainly none of the scholars at the conference would accept this, but fewer would accept the notion that human nature has itself changed. Whether one turns to the "civilizing process" or the state's monopoly on violence, the concrete problems in explaining the growth of crime control agencies and the decline in violence seem to be generating a wealth of research questions.

Until there is evidence of stateless places and crime-free situations, the continued analytic metaphor will be that of the state with its organized violence pacifying indigenous, locally violent populations. This metaphor is substantially different from Chevalier's image of a modern urban pathology producing criminals like it produced diseases. It differs also from the world of primitive rebels sketched by Hobsbawm; for the more they look, the more historians seem to be finding common criminals instead of bands of rebels, often to their great disappointment.

Two decades ago one might have predicted easily the burgeoning interest in and research on crime and violence. But the research in crime control, both laws and organizations, would not have been so easily predicted. Nor would the apparent subsidence of interest in crime as protest, as rebellion, have been expected. And finally, the virtually complete absence of criminal behavior conceptualized as symptomatic of social pathology might have been least predictable. Thus, although one might superficially consider the past quarter of a century of research on the history of crime and crime control to constitute a unitary historiographical epoch, the large number of recent conferences and publications demonstrate a subtle evolution in assumptions, concepts, and questions.

Notes

1.   Most notably, Louis Chevalier, *Classes Laborieuses et Classes Dangereuses* (Paris, 1959), and Eric J. Hobsbawm, *Primitive Rebels* (Manchester, 1959).

APPENDIX A

J. P. Balkema, State University of Limburg, Maastricht. "'Penitentiair Tuchtrecht': The Development from a Regime of Punishment to a Regime of Treatment."

John Conley, University of Wisconsin, Milwaukee. "The Problem of Prison Violence in American History."

Pawel Moczydlowski and Andrzej Rzeplinski, Warsaw University. "Group Protests in Penal Institutions — The Polish Case."

Paul Schulten, Erasmus University, Rotterdam. "The Treatment of Criminals in the Roman Empire."

Marzio Romani, University of L. Bocconi. "Crime, Justice et Lumières: Pour un Assainissement du Corp Social dans la Lombardie Thérésienne."

J. C. G. M. Jansen, Centre for Social History, Maastricht. "Jews and Criminal Procedure in Limburg in the 18th and Early 19th Century."

Sibo van Ruller, Free University of Amsterdam. "Servant Girls, Farm Hands and the Ultimate Sanction: Capital Punishment in Nineteenth-Century Holland."

John Langbein, University of Chicago. "The Abolition of Judicial Torture: Revisiting a Revisionist Thesis."

Sjoerd Faber, Free University of Amsterdam. "Torture in Eighteenth-Century Amsterdam: Both a Means of Investigation and a Species of Punishment."

Robert Walinski-Kiehl, Portsmouth Polytechnic. "Judicial Torture, Confessional Absolutism and Witch-Hunting in Early Modern Germany."

J. A. W. Lensing, State University of Limburg. "The Protection of Freedom of Statement of a Suspect During Examination in Preliminary Investigations and the Admissibility of the Suspect's Statements: A Comparison between Some Common Law and Civil Law Countries."

Clive Emsley, Open University. "'The Thump of Wood on a Swede Turnip': Police Violence in Nineteenth-Century England."

Keith Brown, University of Glasgow. "Barbarous Feidis': Putting Blood Back into Bloodfeuds."

Herman Bianchi, Free University of Amsterdam. "State Monopoly of Violence."

Wilbur R. Miller, State University of New York, Stony Brook. "Reconstruction and Resistance: The Limits of Political Policing in the United States, 1870–1880."

Timothy Curtis and Jill Grinstead, Preston Polytechnic. "Violence and Elizabethan Thought."

Herman W. Roodenburg, Free University of Amsterdam. "Beating Spouses: Marital Violence and the Consistory of the Reformed Church of Amsterdam, 1579–1630."

Arend H. Huussen, State University, Groningen. "Family Crime in Frisia (Netherlands) During the 18th Century."

Neithard Bulst, University of Bielefeld. "Collective Violence in the

'Jacquerie' (1358), the 'Tuchinat' (1363–84) and the English Peasant War (1381)."

Jan Sundin, Demographic Data Base, Umea, Sweden. "Bandits and Guerrilla Soldiers, Armed Bands and Violence on the Border between Sweden and Denmark in Early Modern Times."

Florike Egmond. "Bandits As 'Savages': A Bourgeois Stereotype and the Cases of Some Late 18th-Century Robberbands in Western Europe."

Rudolf Dekker, Erasmus University, Rotterdam. "Violence and Ritual in the Revolt in Holland in the Seventeenth and Eighteenth Centuries."

Wayne P. te Brake, State University of New York, Purchase. "Violence in the Dutch Patriot Revolution: Who Needs It?"

Louis A. Knafla, University of Calgary. "The Reality of Violence in Elizabethan England."

Jim Sharpe, University of York. "Understanding Violence in Early Modern England."

Sven Sperlings, Historical Data Base, Stockholm. "Keeping the Social Peace — Crime and Its Control in Stockholm at the End of the 19th Century and the Beginning of the 20th."

Eric H. Monkkonen, University of California, Los Angeles. "The Historiography of Criminal Violence in Britain and the United States."

APPENDIX B

Paulo Sergio Pinheiro and Michael M. Hall, Depto. de Ciencias Sociais, Sao Paulo. "The Control and Policing of the Working Class in Brazil."

Barbara Weinberger, Warwick University. "Police Perceptions of Labour in the Inter-War Period: The Case of the Unemployed and of Miners on Strike."

James Oldham, Georgetown University. "Special Juries: 19th-Century Usage and Reform."

John McEldowney, Warwick University. "Crown Challenges in Criminal Cases in Nineteenth-Century Ireland."

Peter King, Clare Hall, Cambridge. "Prosecution Associations, Courts and Community Concerns in Essex 1740–1800."

David Philips, University of Melbourne. "Good Men to Associate and Bad Men to Conspire: Associations for the Prosecution of Felons in England 1770–1860."

David Neal, University of New South Wales. "Law and Authority in

New South Wales 1788–1840: The Magistracy."

Dennis Davis, University of Cape Town. "Industrial Legislation in South Africa—A Case Study in the Institutionalization of Conflict."

Frederick Cooper, University of Michigan. "Contracts, Crime, and Agrarian Conflict: From Slave to Wage Labor on the East African Coast."

Luise White, Rice University. "Labour Requirements and Malaya Prostitution in Nairobi in the 1930s."

Robert Storch, University of Wisconsin. "'Before the Police': Policing Rural England Before 1856."

Jennifer Davis, Cambridge University. "The Meaning of Theft Prosecutions in London in the Second Half of the 19th-Century."

Martin Chanock, La Trobe University. "Crimes Created and Wrongs Experienced: Perspectives on the Social History of Crime in Colonial Central Africa."

Robert M. Baum, Texas Tech University. "Crimes of the Dream World: French Trials of Diola Witches."

Olwen Hufton, University of Reading. "The Urban Criminal: The Emergence of Stereotypes in 18th-Century France."

Clive Emsley, Open University. "Police in England and France: Continuities and Contrasts."

Richard J. Geary, University of Lancaster. "Welfare Legislation, Labour Law and Working-Class Radicalism in the Weimar Republic."

Ulrich Mueckenberger, University of Breman. "Remarks on the Formative Period of the Modern German Social Constitution."

Joanna Innes, Somerville College, Oxford. "Houses of Correction and Labour Discipline C16–C18."

John Styles, University of Bath. "Controlling the Outworker: The Embezzlement Laws and Industrial Outwork in 18th-Century England."

John V. Orth, University of North Carolina. "M. Dorothy George and the Combination Laws Reconsidered."

Trowbridge H. Ford, Holy Cross College. "Repression, Reform, and Organized Labour in the Context of Peterloo."

Michael Brogden, Liverpool Polytechnic. "Rules, Regulations, and Christmas Boxes—Working Paper on the Policing System of a Mercantile Economy."

Michael Gruttner, University of Hamburg. "Poverty and Crime: The Culture of the Casual Poor in Hamburg, 1880s–1930s."

Jim Sharpe, University of York. "Prosecution and Capital Punishment for Felony in 17th-Century England: Towards a National Pattern."

Peter Linebaugh, Rochester. "'Old Mr. Gory' and the Thanatocracy in the Age of Newton and Locke."

John Beattie, University of Toronto. "The Administration of the English Criminal Law in the Eighteenth-Century: Trial Jury Verdicts and Pardons at the Surrey Assizes."

Louis Knafla, University of Calgary. "The Administration of English Criminal Law in Early Seventeenth-Century Kent."

B. B. Pande, University of Delhi. "Controlling the Working Classes through Penal Measures in British India (1858–1947)."

Wilbert B. L. Kapinga, University of Dar-es-Salaam. "Law and the Control of Labour in Tanzania."

Peter Fitzpatrick, University of Kent, Canterbury. "Legal Compulsion and Wage Labour in Papua New Guinea."

Ken Foster, Warwick University. "The Legal Form of Work in the 19th-Century: The Myth of Contract?"

Richard Evans, University of East Anglia. "Rituals of Retribution: Capital Punishment in Germany 1794–1934."

Randall McGowen, University of Oregon. "Humanitarianism and Criminal Law Reform in Early Nineteenth-Century England."

Victor Bailey, University of Hull. "The Making of English Penal Policy: Delinquency and Juvenile Justice in the 1930s."

Susan Magarey, Australian National University. "The Invention of Juvenile Delinquency in Early 19th-Century Britain."

Charles van Onselen, University of the Witwatersrand. "Crime and Total Institutions in the Making of Modern South Africa: The Life of 'Nongoloza' Mathebula, 1867–1948."

David Sugerman and John Annette, Middlesex Polytechnic. "Taking Stock: Recent Work on the History of Crime and Punishment."

Robin Cohen, Warwick University. "Strategies of Social Control in the Early Stages of Proletarianisation."

Book Review Essay:
Legal History and the History of the Criminal Law

J. C. Levy
University of Calgary, Calgary, Alberta

David H. Flaherty, ed., *Essays in the History of Canadian Law*. The Osgoode Society. Toronto: University of Toronto Press, 1981, Vol. 1, xvi + 428 pp; 1983, vol. 2, xiv + 593 pp.

When I was first asked to review the criminal law essays in these two volumes, the task seemed relatively straightforward. I had already read all the essays at least once, and, as a historically oriented teacher of criminal law of some vintage, I knew instinctively with which essays I was now to be concerned. Gradually, it dawned on me that others might view my selection askance. Some might even ask whether any intellectually defensible vision of the content of "criminal law" as a subject for historical study underlay my selection. I therefore discarded early drafts of this review because they were predicated on the assumption that my own instincts represented a vision of appropriate subject matter that was the common currency of literate humanity.

I next wondered if the essays themselves provided any analysis, express or implied, of the proper subject matter of criminal law. I found that Professor Flaherty, in his introductory essay to volume 1, "Writing Canadian Legal History," posited "the history of crime and criminal justice" as a distinct category of legal history. The footnotes then refer to a select but rich range of recent English and American scholarly writing, together with some unfortunately less well-known Canadian material. If there is a vision of appropriate subject matter here, it is implied and is both undefined and catholic in the extreme. In essence, any author who identifies himself as writing about criminal law in any sense effectively qualifies his subject matter for inclusion in Professor Flaherty's category.

In fairness, Professor Flaherty is concerned to press for a more inclusive, even holistic, approach to legal history generally, and not to define the proper content of any particular subject specialty within the broad discipline. In so doing, he is at least partially identifying himself with the recent legal historical writing that seeks to free the subject itself from the fetters of the legal profession, without simultaneously embracing fetters derived from any one other discipline. Rather, the apotheosis of the legal historian is a synthesizer of truly renaissance proportions. If this is so, we can begin to accept the non-definitional catholicity of Professor Flaherty's "history of crime and criminal justice" citations as an approach, however unintentional, toward a definition of appropriate content for "criminal law." This may be to confound substance with methodology, yet the relationship is surely symbiotic, with neither being the obvious symbiont.

Memory ransacked now led me back to Professor Elton's stimulating discussion — and at least partial resolution — of this definitional problem in his introductory essay, "Crime and the Historian," in J. S. Cockburn, ed., *Crime in England 1550–1800.* His thrust is rather different from that which I have imputed to Professor Flaherty above. Both would seem to agree that nothing can be included properly within a category that is not placed properly there by the era under study. We must not improperly transport definitions through the ages, nor indeed across the oceans. But how do we discern the thinking of a given era in a given jurisdiction on the proper content of "the criminal law" or "crime"? For Elton, the answer is found primarily in the world of legal language and legal usage which, it is assumed, will represent an underlying functional vision shared at least by those in authority. Accordingly, we must look for legal classifications that are capable of rational grouping within the legal framework to make up our definition of "crime." Thus, for the seventeenth century in England, the lawyer of the era would not recognise the action *qui tam* for a penalty as falling into any grouping that also included felonies. Quite so! Since the latter is paradigmatically "crime," it therefore follows that the legal historian cannot properly consider the former in a study of the criminal law.

This is a useful insight, no doubt, but it has its limitations. The key point is that we have to assemble the appropriate content for "criminal law" from legal categories, for "criminal law" is not itself a legally defined category in seventeenth-century England. May it not, therefore, be equally legitimate to have recourse to other groupings appropriate to the era that derive from other environments than the legal professional one? It would be interesting to see, for example, how the classes that typically provided the defendants in actions *qui tam* spoke of their experiences, or whether there is some similarity in legislative rhetoric when enacting statutory felonies and statutory actions *qui tam.* In every case, we would develop a grouping by reference to a contemporary usage. The cohesion that Elton seeks yet may be found in sources external to the legal profession.

Elton is quite clear that, in his view, groupings of legal categories derived from such external sources do in fact destroy cohesion. Yet the argument appears to be almost circular: the legal historian must use legally sanctified groupings of legal categories, otherwise he is not a *legal* historian. That such legal groupings have a necessary place I do not deny. Even for those who do not find them intellectually congenial, they may be of practical utility in selecting and organising specific blocks of material. They certainly represent a perspective that by definition the *legal* historian cannot ignore. The general social historian who merely uses legal material is emphatically not a *legal* historian, just as the lawyer who traces the growth of legal doctrine in a contextual vacuum is not a legal *historian*.

Ultimately, then, the complete legal historian of criminal law will define the boundaries of his subject by embracing the interplay of different groupings of legal categories produced by different frames of reference. Those different frames of reference may derive from within the legal profession itself—which is not always so monolithic in its view as Professor Elton's example might have us believe—or from the perspective of actors in the process who are not of the legal profession. The most obvious of such actors include law enforcement personnel, victims actual and potential, accused persons actual and potential, and what we might nowadays call correctional personnel. All of them will generate their own functional groupings of legal categories related to realities of fact or perception external to those of the legal profession. Perhaps the one unifying thread at the end of the day is that every grouping produced by every frame of reference will involve a notion of patterned, coercive restriction of individual liberty by court process in the interest of some perception of "the public good."

With this framework in hand, we can now return to the essays under review. Of the eighteen essays (excluding Professor Flaherty's introduction), only four seem to me clearly to deal with the criminal law. In volume 1 we find Paul Craven, "The Law of Master and Servant in Mid-Nineteenth-Century Ontario," and Graham Parker, "The Origins of the Canadian Criminal Code"; in volume 2, Constance Backhouse, "Nineteenth-Century Canadian Rape Law 1800–1892," and Paul Craven, "Law and Ideology: The Toronto Police Court 1850–1880." Two further essays, one in each volume, look on the face of it as if they might be concerned with criminal law, but they turn out on closer inspection to be pursuing somewhat different themes: Kathryn Bindon, "Hudson's Bay Company Law: Adam Thom and the Institution of Order in Rupert's Land 1839–1854," and Hamar Foster, "The Kamloops Outlaws and Commissions of Assize in Nineteenth-Century British Columbia."

Craven's first essay on the law of master and servant, reflecting something of the influence of Douglas Hay and the Warwick School, is a masterly review of the interplay of law, politics, and economic interests in the development and enforcement of a statutory regime for dealing with breaches of employment contracts by employers and employees. The fascinating point is the manner in which the legislation ostentatiously treats breaches of the contract by employers as a matter of private law, involving nothing that by any stretch of the imagination can be classified as criminal law, while simultaneously providing a set of remedial mechanisms in favour of employers and against employees that is emphatically public and criminal in its focus. This is a rich and suggestive essay worthy of the most serious attention.

I only wish that I could be as enthusiastic about Craven's second essay on the Toronto Police Court. Again, the foundations of the work are to be found in Douglas Hay's writing, specifically in his celebrated thesis that the criminal law of eighteenth-century England is a system of legitimating ideology keyed to public ceremonial and ritual. What Craven seeks to do is not to show that the proceedings of the Toronto Police Court were themselves contrived to be theatre more than substance, but that the ideological purpose of the law was fulfilled vicariously by the way the proceedings were presented in the press. What the press presents as crime, and the manner in which it is presented, is no doubt a legitimate external perspective relevant to the problems of definition that I explored above. To make it the sole perspective is to play into the hands of those who would emphasize that legal history is a relatively narrow subject keyed exclusively to categories and concepts internal to the legal profession and, simultaneously, to expose Douglas Hay as the author of the founding thesis to unmerited ridicule. I fear, therefore, that this essay — while at the opposite end of the spectrum from those narrow legalistic analyses of doctrine in a hermetically sealed legal system that lawyers are sometimes guilty of — suffers from a fundamentally similar vice. If it is indeed intended as the criminal law essay that it appears to be, rather than an essentially sociological essay on the press, it is really only one-dimensional and sadly lacking in fundamental legal material.

Unlike Craven, both Parker and Backhouse are lawyers. For those who think legal history written by lawyers lacks the diversity of perspective found in the writings of at least the better historians, there can be no more instructive contrast than these two essays. Parker's contribution on the origins of Canada's Criminal Code is nonetheless legal history because it probably could only have been written by a lawyer, and one thoroughly at home with the major doctrines and concepts of the substantive law of crime. The broader social and intellectual climate of the late nineteenth century is reflected only through lawyers and legal literature, although several of the lawyers were also active politicians. There are indeed a few tantalizing glimpses of the lobbying efforts of those outside the charmed circle of the law, but this is little more than a footnote. Nevertheless, the essay is a worthwhile contribution to the ultimate development of a rounded picture, precisely because of the legal focus that has eluded earlier writers in the area.

Backhouse's contribution on nineteenth-century Canadian rape law is anything but a lawyer's document on the law. The law is there, of course, fully researched and accurately stated, but it is the fundamental background to a rich analysis of the interplay between legal doctrine and procedure on the one hand, and social conditions, perceptions, and attitudes on the other. And this is presented as the genuine interplay that it really is—social perspectives influence the law, which in turn influences social perspectives in an endless cycle. A vital ingredient in all of this is that Backhouse constantly seeks to fix in our minds the range of female concerns and perspectives, the absence of which has effectively limited almost all previous writing in the area. Those who feel that presentation of the female perspective in areas dominated hitherto by the male perspective necessarily involves the strident rhetoric of some versions of feminism can be reassured. What little rhetoric appears is not strident and is amply supported by a range of archival material and references to contemporary literature that must compel the scholarly respect of even the most chauvinistic male. So far as I am aware, the richness of perspectives in this essay makes it unique, at least in the world of English-language legal historical writing. This is criminal law history at its best.

Hamar Foster's essay has a title that is redolent of the criminal law, with its reference to "outlaws" and to "commissions of assize." Ultimately, however, this is but the context in which Foster develops a remarkably detailed and documented picture of the political relations between the British Columbia bench (in particular, Chief Justice Begbie and Justice Crease) and the provincial politicians. It is a picture that reflects little credit on any of the participants, including the press. At times the sheer weight of detail causes one to lose sight of the main themes, but the essay can still be recommended most warmly to any legal historian interested in the political torments of the judiciary in a frontier society.

Kathryn Bindon's essay ought to have had a lot more criminal law in it than it actually does, since much of Adam Thom's time as Recorder of Rupert's Land was spent dealing with matters that had criminal content. As a well-documented semibiography of Adam Thom set in the economic and political context of the concerns of the Hudson's Bay Company in the area that was later to become the Canadian Province of Manitoba, this is a useful if essentially conventional account. What is lacking is a legal analysis of the work and achievements of Thom, particularly in the complex area of the jurisdiction of his court in criminal matters, set into the broader economic and political picture.

Overall, these two volumes represent a major step forward for Canadian legal history, and as such they are to be welcomed most warmly. Nevertheless, if Canadian legal history is to take its place in the world intellectual market-place, these volumes have to be seen as a point of departure rather than as the end of a journey. Two essays at least — Craven's on master and servant and Backhouse's on rape — do in large measure meet the wide-ranging vision of the criminal law and the methodology proper to its analysis for which I have contended. They should be of genuine interest to any serious student of the history of the criminal law.

Book Reviews

Elmer Johnson, ed., *International Handbook of Contemporary Developments in Criminology.* Vol. 1, *General Issues and the Americas.* Vol. 2, *Europe, Africa, the Middle East, and Asia.* Westport, Conn., and London: Greenwood Press, 1983. Vol. 1, 319 pp.; vol. 2, 696 pp. Tables, figures, notes, representative bibliographies, indices. $95.

Elmer Johnson, a sociologist at Southern Illinois University, is a well-known authority on corrections. In recent years, he has been the leading force in creating the International Division of the American Society of Criminology. He has arranged with Greenwood Press to put together these volumes of articles, often by natives, on the state and development of criminology in forty countries, the United Nations, and the International Society of Criminology, with an introductory set of general thematic reviews (*e.g.*, women and criminology, radical criminology, general patterns). Each volume is self-contained. I suspect that contributing authors were paid honoraria, which would explain (and commercially justify) a price that will unfortunately restrict the work's circulation. Nonetheless, these chapters can be used effectively in the classroom.

The penultimate paragraph in Johnson's preface begins, "This handbook represents a major contribution to the literature." I agree that it is, not as gospel, but as a starting point for many an inquiry. I wish, for instance, that I had had these chapters to offer graduate students of crime from abroad who have done dissertations about their homelands. Since each chapter on a country addresses the state of its discipline, I would have asked these students to begin their work by responding critically to the portrayal of criminology in their countries and by describing their own place in it.

The *Handbook* offers much grist for inquiry by social and intellectual historians, but care must be taken not to misuse the material. Just as most criminologists are politically naïve about the history of crime and punishment, so I have noticed that historians of crime tend to be politically naïve about accepting social scientists' synchronic and recent historical propositions at face value. If historians can take off political blinders, reports in the *Handbook* offer countless opportunities for historical revisionism; and by cross-cultural comparison, they offer rich empirical foundations for inquiries by those inclined to counterfactual history.

One cannot tell from the *Handbook* alone how well or poorly the reporters represent what is "known" and done about crime and punishment in their countries. But I have no reason to suspect a systematic bias in the selection of the reporters, and on the whole, find the parochialism of criminology around the world to be appalling. Perhaps a recent overdue reading of Foucault's *Discipline and Punishment* has oversensitized me. More likely, my feeling comes from the monotonous regularity with which criminology is reported to deal exclusively in exposing and treating the peculiarities of prisoners as though they represent the universe of criminality. It is distressing to see how thoroughly Euro-American positive criminology has taken hold of the world's criminological imagination, having by now become convinced that wealth and power cause the most and worst crimes, even within statutory limits, to be visited especially upon the poor, and knowing that: underclass young men who inhabit prisons are unrepresentative of criminality; prisons cause more crime than they cure, particularly by showing the rich that they are largely unaccountable for their transgressions; and Third World peoples suffer most from the class injustice that criminalization of the poor itself represents. These criminologists allow police to define the nature of their problems and largely cede the handling of the problems to jailers.

There are outstanding exceptions, which deserve further scholarly attention, in the reports on China, France, the Netherlands, Norway, Poland, and Spain. The Ugandan report begins by describing a legacy of ethnographic work on traditional nonadjudicatory ways of handling disputes, but then jumps to contemporary studies of the standard criminological kind. The Argentinian report, among others, indicates that certain forms of "crime," like chewing on coca leaves, are acceptable in subcultures, but treats the practices as anachronistic deviance to be overcome. The Indian report notes that public order offenses are predominantly rural and that massive unemployment in India generates remarkably few police reports, thus bringing conventional criminological wisdom into question. The Japanese and the Swiss do not seem to be worried enough about crime to support academic programs in criminology at all. Perhaps the most important topic for historical inquiry is the way some countries develop police and prisons without building a totally captive body of criminologists to legitimize their power in all the old familiar ways.

The *Handbook* at least shows that not all criminal justice systems need professional apologists, and that somewhere, somehow, a few students of crime manage to transcend juridical definitions of the problem.

Harold E. Pepinsky
Forensic Studies
Indiana University

Sue Gronewald, *Beautiful Merchandise: Prostitution in China, 1860–1936.* New York: The Haworth Press, 1982. 114 pp.

Sue Gronewald fills a gap in the literature on Chinese women in this work by providing an introduction to the institution of prostitution. Her central argument is that "the purchase of women for prostitution was not qualitatively different from the general trade in women," which is to say that prostitution is an integral part of any society that regards women in terms of the services they render men rather than as persons in their own right. To support this thesis, she amasses evidence from Western-language sources on topics as diverse as female infanticide, marriage customs and attitudes toward sexuality, as well as material relating more specifically to the dynamics of the institution of prostitution. She discusses the changes which occurred in Chinese prostitution in the early part of the twentieth century and attempts to relate these changes to transformations occurring in the larger society. Gronewald suggests that social class is perhaps more significant as a defining characteristic of these women than is their profession—the elegant courtesan, she asserts, had more in common with the lady than she did with the common prostitute. Gronewald has a felicitous prose style, and there is much in the book that is praiseworthy.

Prostitution was legal in traditional China. Officials, both military and civil, were prohibited from visiting brothels, but the necessity of the brothels themselves never seems to have been challenged. But prostitutes were disadvantaged in the eyes of the law. Chinese society was traditionally divided into three legal status groups—officials, commoners, and "mean" people (*chien min*). Both the officials and the mean people numbered a tiny fraction of the total population; the vast majority of the Chinese people were classed as commoners. Among the mean people numbered peddlers, barbers, actors, and prostitutes. The category of "mean" was hereditary: the child of a prostitute (or of an actor or a barber, for that matter) was stigmatized for life. A prostitute born in the ranks of commoners was forced to register as a prostitute and take on the status of "mean." By the late Ch'ing, imperial edicts had greatly weakened the force of the legal impediment, but the stigma probably remained.

In categorizing prostitutes as "mean" and in creating a separate legal status for them (and for other undesirables), the framers of the Chinese legal codes were ascribing to prostitutes a legal status of "other"; they were set off from ordinary people by a clearly demarcated legal boundary. It is interesting to note that one aspect of the opposition to the Contagious Diseases Acts in Britain was that the Acts impelled the registration of prostitutes. Once stigmatized by registration, so the argument went, a woman found it much more difficult to leave a life of prostitution. Registration was a boundary marker. The separation symbolized by the Contagious Diseases Acts, which led to the conceptualization of prostitutes as an "outcaste" group, seems to have existed in China for as long as we have legal codes on the subject.[1]

Some of the most interesting recent work on prostitution in the West— notably that of Judith Walkowitz and Ruth Rosen[2]—focuses on episodes of reform (Walkowitz on the Contagious Diseases Acts in Britain and Rosen on Progressive attitudes in the United States). Walkowitz suggests that the impulse to regulate prostitution may be seen as a part of an increasing state interest in the lives of the "unrespectable poor." The motives various reformers might have had for waging war against prostitution are varied, and an analysis of these various motives might, as the work of Walkowitz and Rosen ably illustrates, tell us much about how society views women and sexuality.

The Chinese case is potentially rich here—the period Gronewald discusses is one in which numerous social reform movements flourished. That Gronewald's analysis is weak is due, at least in part, to her reliance on Western-language sources. There are several groups of reformers whose attitudes on prostitution would repay close study. The Taiping rebels, utopian reformers who devastated much of China in the mid-nineteenth century, took the suppression of women to be a cornerstone of the Confucian hierarchy they were attempting to overthrow. The precise argumentation of their position on prostitution would be interesting to examine.[3] The May Fourth Era reformers also took the status of women as a particular concern. Their views on prostitution are not discussed at any length.[4]

Gronewald suggests that during the 1920s and 1930s, the rate of female infanticide dropped at a time when the life of the average peasant was worsening. This led to an increase, or so she suggests, in the number of women who were forced to turn to prostitution in order to eke out an existence. This, coupled with the sexual demands of the warlord armies, resulted in what Gronewald calls a "brothelization of the countryside" (p. 53). She finds a "dramatic increase" in the number of lower-level houses of prostitution in Peking during this time (p. 65) and sees these prostitutes as women who were "victims of uneven modernization" (p. 69). These sections of the book are fascinating and could be expanded fruitfully by looking at some of the other employment options available to women at this time—for example, in the textile industry. Walkowitz has discussed the argument that prostitution represents an alternative to proletarianization (p. 31); it would be interesting to know what kind of evidence the Chinese case presents.

The study of women's history is progressing at a rapid pace. The books by Rosen and Walkowitz have appeared since Sue Gronewald wrote *Beautiful Merchandise* as a master's thesis. It is to be hoped that she will continue her work on this rich and fascinating topic, not only utilizing Chinese-language primary sources, but also referring to the growing body of material on prostitution in other cultures.

Ann Waltner
University of Utah

Notes

1. Judith Walkowitz, *Prostitution and Victorian Society* (Cambridge: Cambridge University Press, 1980), especially chap. 10.
2. Ruth Rosen, *The Lost Sisterhood: Prostitution in America 1900–1918* (Baltimore: Johns Hopkins University Press, 1982).
3. Vincent Shih, *The Taiping Ideology* (Seattle: University of Washington Press, 1972), 77.
4. Chow Tse-tsung, *The May Fourth Movement: Intellectual Revolution in Modern China* (Stanford: Stanford University Press, 1960), 257–59.

Ehud R. Toledano, *The Ottoman Slave Trade and Its Suppression, 1840–1890.* Princeton, N.J.: Princeton University Press, 1982. $28.50.

Toledano has provided the first comprehensive study of the Ottoman slave trade in the last half of the nineteenth century. Using hitherto unworked Turkish archives as well as the better-known Western sources, he has described the trading network and the largely British pressures to abolish it, and he has done this from the perspective of Istanbul. The present work is a revision of the dissertation completed under the direction of Bernard Lewis. It fills a large gap in the Ottoman, African, and Near Eastern historiography of the nineteenth century.

Toledano begins with two chapters on the slave trade in the middle of the century. He describes the African, Ethiopian, and Transcaucasian sources of slaves within the Empire, but he then settles for a basic distinction between African and white. African slaves cost less and performed more menial chores within the household. Some white women became concubines and wives in well-to-do Ottoman families. This distinction correlates with the abolition story: the Ottoman authorities more easily tolerated British intervention in their African operations than in the white slave trade. The author estimates the volume of the trade at eleven thousand persons per year during the third quarter of the nineteenth century.

Chapters 3 and 4 begin the story of the abolition campaign and carry it up to the late 1850s. The British were able to press Ottoman, Iranian, and local authorities into closing down the Persian Gulf slave trade during this period. Or this seems to be the case, for Toledano does not return to the Gulf zone in the rest of the work. Istanbul allowed some European intervention in the Black Sea trade of Georgians and especially Circassians, but only until the end of the Crimean War crisis with Russia. The Red Sea and Hijaz region were difficult for either Ottomans or British to control, in part because the pilgrimage could easily be combined with the slave trade, and in part because of the proximity of slave catchment zones in Northeast Africa. By contrast, the sub-Saharan slaves fed by caravan into Tripoli and Benghazi and by boat to various Mediterranean ports could be watched. The British succeeded in getting the Porte to abolish the trade in this area in 1857. Toledano suggests that the numbers of slaves on these routes declined sharply thereafter.

Chapter 5 deals with Circassian slavery and slave trade. Istanbul confronted a crisis, beginning in the late 1850s, when the Russian czar decided to force vast numbers of people out of Circassia. Most of these people moved into the Anatolian heartland of the Ottoman Empire. Between 500,000 and one million people probably came into the region, and as many as 150,000 of them may have been agricultural slaves. The influx produced demographic problems and tense relations between Circassian slaves and slaveowners for several decades. In this section, Toledano abandons his focus on the slave trade to enter into a limited discussion of Ottoman slavery and society.

Chapters 6 and 7 carry the story of the abolition of the sub-Saharan and Northeast African trade down to 1890. The author pays considerable attention to the Egyptian role in the Nile and Red Sea trade and chronicles the growing ability of the British to bring pressure on Khedive Ismail as well as the Istanbul authorities. A concluding chapter and epilogue summarize the means used by the British to exert pressure and briefly describe British and Ottoman attitudes toward slavery and the slave trade. Toledano stresses the importance of the household in Islamic society and the critical role that domestic slaves played within that institution.

In the present state of knowledge, it is simply not possible to write an account of the institutions of slavery and the slave trade in the Ottoman Empire of the nineteenth century. Toledano wisely confines himself to the trade (except in Chapter 5) and provides a useful commercial and diplomatic history. It is at this point that the study falls short. A history of the suppression of the slave trade requires a much clearer picture of the world in which the Ottoman authorities made their decisions: the Russian pressure from the north, the British imperial system around the globe, and the efforts at reform at home. The failure to describe British interests especially weakens the book. Toledano often finds himself assessing the degree of humanitarian impulse in a particular consular report or Foreign Office decision. What his theme requires is a picture of the growing "legitimate" trading interests and strategic concerns of the British in or near the Ottoman domains.

Toledano does not deal with the Persian Gulf after the 1850s and hardly touches East Africa at all. In general, he gives little attention to the process of obtaining slaves at the source; the reader will find no information about the situations in southwestern Ethiopia, southern Sudan, and the savanna zones below the Sahara. For the African slave trade, with which I am somewhat familiar, the author has not consulted a number of basic primary and secondary works. These weaknesses, taken together, suggest that Toledano may have moved too quickly to publication. Scholars should nonetheless welcome this work because of the scope and importance of the subject and the gap it fills.

David Robinson
Michigan State University

George Leggett, *The Cheka: Lenin's Political Police*. New York: The Clarendon Press, Oxford University Press, 1981. 514 pp. $34.

There were already before the publication of *The Cheka* several good sources on the history of the Cheka—most notably, Lennard Gerson's *The Secret Police in Lenin's Russia* (see *Criminal Justice History* 1 (1980): 177–79). Leggett notes in his preface that there is "considerable overlapping" between the two studies, but avers that they "are to some extent complementary" (p. viii). Readers already familiar with the topic will be quickly aware of the overlapping in this long book and will wish the author had omitted some of the more familiar material. On the other hand, those who have not read

Gerson's book might find this the only book they need. It is not complementary, but meant to stand on its own and does so quite well.

This is a very thorough work. Until Soviet archives are available, probably few significant facts will be added to the early history of the Cheka. Leggett handles a great mass of information well, separating material on the Cheka's organizational development from more interesting narratives of events and discussions of debates over tactics, politics, and justice. The personalities of Lenin and Dzerzhinsky pervade the book, but Leggett offers a chapter on the Cheka personnel and an appendix of biographical notes that help reveal the nature of the Cheka. His appendix "Deaths Attributable to the Chekas" is probably the most reliable guide through the exaggerations and mistakes that abound.

The most interesting parts of the book are chapters on "revolutionary justice," the Left Socialist Revolutionary (LSR) rising, and the Red Terror. Leggett makes it very clear (as had Gerson and Peter Juviler in *Revolutionary Law and Order*) that there were prominent socialists, including Bolsheviks, who advocated a legal rather than a terrorist approach to rivals and foes of the Bolshevik revolution, but that it was Lenin, Dzerzhinsky, and a few others — who repeatedly insisted on the need for terror — who had their way. The LSR uprising in July 1918, according to Leggett, was not meant to overthrow the Bolsheviks but to demonstrate opposition to specific Bolshevik policies. It helped set the stage for the Red Terror. LSR Chekists, who had opposed the wholly arbitrary means the Cheka had used from time to time, were removed from their posts and became the Cheka's first political victims. Thereafter, the Cheka "immediately extended its exercise of summary justice to include political adversaries of the Communist regime" (p. 110). In the increasingly tense atmosphere of the civil war, the assassination of Uritskii and the attempt on Lenin's life in August were sufficient to trigger the Terror.

As comprehensive as *The Cheka* is, it will not lay to rest the debate about the significance of the Cheka or the nature of the regime and circumstances in which it flourished. As can readily be seen in Leggett's and Gerson's titles, both authors of these most recent histories emphasize that the Cheka was Lenin's creation. In their view, it was not an aberration called forth only by extraordinary circumstances, nor a temporary expedient, the need for which was unforeseen by its creators. It was an organ of terror, revenge, and control whose activities were opposed by many revolutionaries, but which was protected and nurtured by the most powerful leaders of the Bolshevik Party.

It has been argued that terror was inevitable in the circumstances, that Kerensky, the LSRs, and others spoke as Lenin had and, presumably, given the chance, would have likewise engaged in terror. Were the circumstances all that compelling? Can it be that the period of the civil war was that much more horrifying than the preceding world war? Is that sufficient to explain why the Bolsheviks created a powerful organization to extirpate their enemies, real and potential, without legal proceedings? Before and during the world war, the tsarist government imprisoned or exiled its political offenders, usually after trials (in which an embarrassingly large number of prisoners won acquittal). Political prisoners were treated more leniently than criminal offenders. The conditions of their exile were usually relatively easy, permitting them to communicate with one another and to continue their activities in their places of exile. Between 1866 and 1900, there were ninety-four official executions in Russia, while revolutionaries assassinated forty government figures, including the tsar. The Provisional Government had most of the Bolshevik leaders in its hands after the July Days uprising but did not execute them. They, too, were defending a revolution and facing an "intervention" much more perilous than the Bolsheviks ever did.

Maybe the question we need to ask to understand the Cheka and the Terror is: Why was there not civil war in Russia earlier? Civil war did not wait for the end of the world war, so that is not the answer. It was not needed to turn the tsar out; he abdicated. Nor was it required to change the composition of the Provisional Governments. As ineffective as they were, they possessed a certain flexibility, responsiveness, and legitimacy. Civil war broke out against the Bolsheviks who had seized power with force, disappointed their would-be allies by not sharing power, disenchanted their fellow socialists by their policies, and demonstrated their intentions by disbanding the Constituent Assembly. The Terror, if it was "necessary," was necessitated by the fact that the Bolsheviks were an unpopular minority force determined to hold the reins of power whatever the cost. The Cheka killed hundreds of times as many people as the tsarist regime had over a much longer time. Leggett's study illuminates the personalities and thought of the actors who were willing to engage in that slaughter.

Bruce Adams
University of Louisville

Patricia O'Brien, *The Promise of Punishment: Prisons in Nineteenth-Century France*. Princeton, N.J.: Princeton University Press, 1982. xiii + 330 pp. $28.50.

Michel Foucault insists that, despite the humanitarian claims of early penal reformers, nineteenth-century prisons detained and controlled inmates rather than assisted them. More importantly and controversially, he posits that other institutions similarly imprisoned rather than improved society. Thus, the prison, as the most visible instrument of repression, may serve as a model for understanding broader developments. Despite the scholarly interest Foucault has aroused, his view of prisons and of other institutions has not been well documented.

Patricia O'Brien partially fills this lacuna by studying the system of incarceration in France, the nation whose experiences have inspired Foucault's work. O'Brien's book contains eight chapters, each focusing on different aspects of the nineteenth-century French prison. These separate chapters are further subdivided to take up each topic from several vantage points. Such an approach turns her book into a series of essays, and readers will have difficulty putting all the parts together. Sometimes failure to explain connections means that some important links are missed or that two positions that could be resolved appear contradictory. Nonetheless, advantages outweigh the problems of such an organization. Indeed, O'Brien can shed light on various parts of a vast, largely uncharted field while sticking closely to primary sources. In this way, her book gives a general picture of prisons without slighting the primal complexity and richness of the material.

O'Brien organizes her investigation around the theories of penal reformers and the social characteristics and prison culture of the incarcerated — young and old, male and female. O'Brien also examines the work and education of prisoners, focusing not only on the inmates but also on the guards and private entrepreneurs who structured their experiences. The final two chapters explore other forms of punishment — probation and exile to penal colonies.

The range of topics is particularly impressive as O'Brien explains the behavior, not only of the relatively accessible elite who shaped the prison system, but also of the offenders and the intermediaries working in the prisons. These last two groups, especially the inmates, have left little direct testimony, so O'Brien's task of reconstructing their lives is particularly arduous and significant. Not surprisingly, she encounters some problems in this area because she has to base her interpretation of these inarticulate people on works by middle-class observers — particularly those who criticized nineteenth-century penal reform by describing the condition of the prisoners. Difficulties emerge from this. Although we share this critical regard toward that period's system of imprisonment, one must be wary of accepting the arguments of a competing elite. At the least, O'Brien owes the reader an explanation of the beliefs of such critics so that we can evaluate her basis for finding their evidence believable. Placing such commentators in context could have strengthened the reliability of the extraordinarily imaginative chapters on the jailed and jailers.

The breadth of O'Brien's findings, combined with their somewhat disparate presentation, makes it difficult to summarize all the interesting material of this book. Although each separate topic really deserves attention, a survey of two of the subjects can provide an indication of the substantive contribution.

Perhaps O'Brien's most exciting and innovative chapter concentrates on the subculture created by the inmates. The author asserts that despite the efforts of the authorities to discipline prisoners, the incarcerated developed something of an independent world. Men expressed their autonomy through tattooing, and a minority managed against all regulations to maintain a homosexual community. Women exhibited similar sexual behavior, but theirs was combined with a great deal of affection. In the end, O'Brien grimly concludes that the prisoners' independence only reinforced their distance from society at large.

Equally interesting is O'Brien's discussion of prison education. The author shows that teachers were often little more — and sometimes no more — than guards. Underpaid and undereducated, such individuals exploited, not rehabilitated, prisoners. While rudimentary instruction was available in reading, writing, and computation, schooling focused on duty and self-restraint. According to O'Brien, once outside the prisons, they needed to know more than discipline. The education of inmates did more to exclude them from, rather than integrate them into, the outside world.

Other chapters in O'Brien's work join those on education and prison subculture in showing that the penitentiary primarily functioned to isolate its denizens from society. Indeed, this assertion provides the most important common strain uniting the diverse elements of The Promise of Punishment, and it directly addresses Foucault. Inspired by his speculations, O'Brien provides information that goes far toward verifying his vision of prisons as repressive, not rehabilitative, institutions.

Foucault is still on his own, however, when he insists that incarceration typified broader change. While O'Brien's study does not venture far beyond the prison walls, she does not equate the prison with other institutions. Specifically, the observation that prisoners lost by not gaining a real education reveals a belief that education — another institution — could be more than just another form of social control. More generally, her insistence on the way prison undermined the future liberation of the inmate implies that free society offered something to the individual. Thus, although O'Brien confirms Foucault's view of the penitentiary, her more optimistic outlook on modern society disagrees with his thoroughgoing condemnation. O'Brien's implications are not definitive, but any effort to test further Foucault's hypotheses must use her work as the baseline.

Jack R. Censer
George Mason University

J. A. Sharpe, *Crime in Seventeenth-Century England: A County Study.*
Cambridge: Cambridge University Press, and Paris: Editions de la Maison
des Sciences de l'Homme, 1983. viii + 289 pp. $49.50.

In *Crime in Seventeenth-Century England*, "a substantially rewritten version"
of his doctoral thesis, Sharpe ably examines the assize and quarter sessions
records from the period 1620 to 1680 for the county of Essex. He supplements quantification of indictments with data from presentments, recogni-
zances, depositions, literary sources, and the records of the courts of King's
Bench, leet, and archdeaconry. Colorful anecdotes add life to the 8,557 indictments, which Sharpe divides into five major groups (property, violent, drink,
economic, and miscellaneous) and thirty-two subgroups. Sharpe firmly roots
crime and his conclusions in socioeconomic and legal contexts.

Property offenses constituted over a third of all indicted offenses, were
concentrated in the clothing centers, increased during the economic crises
of 1629–31 and 1648–52, but, "contrary to expectations," steadily declined
throughout the period (possibly, Sharpe suggests, because of "the increased
soundness of the English economy," p. 215). They rarely involved violence
and were predominantly committed by the poor, not professionals, as opportunity and need arose.

Assault was the third most frequently indicted offense, and unlicensed
alehouse-keeping was second. Sharpe believes, perhaps correctly, that most
homicides were assaults that went too far and that violence in general was
spontaneous and unpremeditated and resulted from inflammable tempers.
While assaults increased "steadily although gently," homicides decreased.
Sharpe accepts the traditional view of a violent seventeenth-century England,
even though some of his Essex evidence undermines it. Burglars, highway
robbers, and thieves, for example, rarely employed violence.

Regarding drunkenness, there were only eighty-eight indictments because
of the widespread acceptance of heavy drinking, and because the legal definition of drunkenness was nearly total incapacity. As for economic offenses
(such as engrossing), many are discussed as results of "a developing capitalist
economy" (p. 39). The indictments from the 1670s contain evidence that
the assizes began to be used to discipline labor. The thesis that much early
modern crime resulted from movement of squatters into wooded areas is not
confirmed by the Essex material. Finally, Sharpe could locate no upsurge
in the prosecution of moral offenses in the 1640s and 1650s and concludes
that a "puritan" attitude extended beyond these two decades and to all early
modern governments. At almost every turn, Sharpe enticingly invites more
research by adding alternative interpretations of his data.

It would be unfair to criticize Sharpe for not writing this reviewer's book because he did not quantify illegal acts prosecuted in other courts, especially in courts leet. Sharpe never presents his study as anything but an examination of the type and frequency of all indictable offenses at the quarter sessions and assizes. He does not generalize to all offenders or to all of England, although he does point to similarities and differences between crimes in Stuart Essex and modern England. He explicitly states that more detailed village and county studies must be completed before historians can generalize about crime in history.

While superbly and concisely written, the book's greatest asset is the honesty of its author. It is very unusual for a writer to poke as many holes in his data as Sharpe does. He correctly asserts that to quantify indictments is to measure the tip of the iceberg. Sharpe capably discusses various influences on the type and amount of recorded and prosecuted crime: the class basis of some laws, the problem of the ever-changing definition of and sensitivity to certain illegal acts, the "disincentive to prosecution" because of the cost of litigation for victims responsible for initiating legal proceedings, out-of-court settlements, flexible sentencing, and false, misleading, and lost information.

It is commonplace to discuss some limitations of one's sources in an introductory chapter and then proceed as though they did not exist. No historian of crime known to this reviewer has interwoven the limitations of court records into every chapter as well as Sharpe has. He treats as "the fundamental problem" the gaps between committed, reported, and prosecuted crime. Sharpe's tentative conclusions could be firmed up or altered, however, if he examined offenses prosecuted at courts leet where, by his own admission, many offenses infrequently indicted at the quarter sessions and assizes were adjudicated. In any case, Sharpe has cast considerable doubt upon the conclusions of previous investigators who uncritically used indictments to arrive at crime rates in history.

Sharpe is at his best when describing Stuart attitudes toward crime. Applied law was often less severe than called for by statute. Allowing for missing records, Sharpe estimates that about ten persons per year were executed in Essex with a population of about 110,000; the number of hangings decreased after mid-century. He estimates that eighty-six percent of indicted and convicted grand-larcenists escaped the death penalty because they either used or misused benefit of clergy, or because juries reduced the charge to petty larceny by undervaluing stolen property.

Superb as this book is, it has some minor weaknesses. Was violence common to most groups but theft the prerogative of the poor, as Sharpe claims, or were the wealthy and prominent better able to discourage prosecution of theft than of violence? He wrongly claims that leets could only fine offenders (p. 26). In fact, leet officials stocked or occasionally whipped offenders and, according to Edward Coke, could imprison for offenses committed in court. And we are told that indictments at the quarter sessions and assizes for assault numbered 631 (p. 115), whereas two pages later the total is reported as 622.

There are thirty-seven tables, figures, and maps, 1,151 notes, an index, and a useful bibliography. Convincingly argued and extremely well documented, this first-rate book should be read not only for its exceptionally sound conclusions, but also for its balanced and skeptical approach to court records. This is scholarship at its best.

Walter J. King
Northern State College
South Dakota

Jenna Weissman Joselit, *Our Gang: Jewish Crime and the New York Jewish Community, 1900–1940*. Bloomington: Indiana University Press, 1983. xii + 209 pp. Illustrations, appendix, notes, and index. $19.95 cloth ($9.95 paperback).

Jenna Joselit dispassionately examines crime among New York Jews, reaction to it by non-Jews (many of whom were disposed to believe the worst), and responses by Jewish leaders to both crime and related nativist allegations. Though most concerned with the "changing self-perceptions and self-images of the New York Jewish community," Joselit does not slight the "fascinating" history of the underworld.

Her story begins with the "seeming explosion" of lawbreaking among Jews at the turn of the century and ends with the virtual disappearance of Jews from the upper ranks of organized crime after World War II. In between, she discusses: the famous controversy over Police Commissioner Theodore Bingham's charge in 1908 that Jews made up more than half of New York's criminals; institutional efforts to prevent or contain crime, including the Hawthorne School for wayward adolescents; the rise and fall of Herman Rosenthal, Arnold Rothstein, Louis "Lepke" Buchalter, and lesser gangsters; recruitment of thugs to break strikes and protect unions; and Jewish participation in the multi-ethnic Murder, Incorporated.

Our Gang's extensive sources include legislative hearings, muckraking magazines, contemporary sociological studies, and Jewish newspapers (which Joselit often translates herself). Prudently using statistics teased from recalcitrant court records, she shows that Jews, though less law-abiding than community leaders hoped, were underrepresented in most criminal activities, especially those involving violence. The diversion of sacramental wine to illegal consumption during Prohibition, an issue that concerned federal officials and agitated nativists, receives careful attention. Finally, Joselit attributes the decline of crime among Jews to economic mobility and dispersion of the immigrant ghetto.

Some minor errors and questionable interpretations intrude on the text. For example, Joselit takes too seriously tales of women lured into "white slavery," exaggerates Lepke's role in the labor struggles of the 1930s, and seems to think that Henry Ford wrote (instead of merely sponsored) the anti-Semitic series, *The International Jew*.

Our Gang invites comparison to Albert Fried's *The Rise and Fall of the Jewish Gangster in America* (1980). Both discuss many of the same criminals, stress the impact of Prohibition, perceive continuity between the underworld and legitimate business, and note dishonesty's contribution to upward mobility. Joselit's and Fried's books, contributions respectively to the "new" and "old" social history, highlight the strengths and limitations of their genres. While Joselit presents a detailed picture of lawbreaking in New York City, Fried's breezier volume takes the action as far as Hollywood and compares Jewish criminals with their counterparts in other ethnic groups. More willing than Joselit to make moral judgments, Fried shows healthy skepticism about the motives and methods of such gangbusters as Thomas E. Dewey. In short, Joselit's able book supplements but does not replace Fried's.

Leo P. Ribuffo
George Washington University

Submissions, Subscriptions, and Professional Notes

Notes on submissions:

The general rule guiding authors and editors is that submissions should follow as closely as possible the formats of the most recent publication. Therefore, previous volumes of *Criminal Justice History* should be consulted for guidance.

Submit two copies—original and xerox or good xeroxes, the original made with a good ribbon. Submissions should be carefully proofread by authors.

Double-space throughout—text, indented quotations, and end notes. No part of a typescript should be single-spaced. Margins should be at least 1¼ inches, or 32 millimeters, on all sides.

Use text and end notes; no footnotes. End notes should be in a separate section (but with continuous pagination) following the end of the text. End notes should be numbered in the margin to the left of the first line of the particular note, a period following the number. (Do not hang end note numbers above the line, nor omit periods; this should be done only with note numbers in the text.)

Use upper and lower case throughout. Do not capitalize or underline titles or subtitles of the essay text. (If special emphases are desired, convey them in the covering letter.) The abbreviations *cap*, for capitals, and *ital*, for italics, may be written at appropriate places in the left margin if the author is convinced they are necessary. Use quotation marks for quotation marks; do *not* use apostrophes as quotation marks, except, of course, around a quotation within a quotation. Originally foreign phrases now common in English usage should not be underlined.

If there are tables, charts, graphs, or other illustrations, they should be submitted camera-ready and on separate sheets. A space may be left in the text with indication of the specific matter that belongs there. In general, however, it will be simplest and most feasible for illustrative material to be grouped in an appendix following the text, with text references to each item by number.

In end notes, the first citation of a source should be complete. Later citations of it should use short titles (not "op cit."). "Ibid." is acceptable.

Sensible abbreviations of sources often referred to, after the first full citation, are acceptable and desirable.

Editorial correspondence and submissions:

Professor Louis Knafla
Department of History
University of Calgary
Calgary, Alberta
Canada T2N 1N4

Books for review, proposals to review, and reviewer registrations should be sent to the appropriate review editor:

U.S.A. and Canada:

Professor Ellen Dwyer
Department of Forensic Studies
Indiana University
Bloomington, IN 47405
U.S.A.

Other areas and transnational:

Professor James Cockburn
Department of History
University of Maryland
College Park, Maryland 20742
U.S.A.

Subscriptions

Subscriptions at $49.50

Criminal Justice History
Meckler Publishing
11 Ferry Lane West
Westport, CT 06880

Professional notes

Criminal Justice History plans a register and notes on research in progress to acquaint readers with current trends and allow persons doing related research to make contact. Researchers are requested to forward information as follows, using separate pages for each project:

1. Name
2. Address
3. Telephone
4. Discipline(s)
5. Short title of research project, specifying book, article, or other
6. Description or abstract (separate attachment preferred)
7. Stage of preparation and expected date of completion

If more than one research project is in preparation, use separate pages for each. Forward to:

Professor Cyril D. Robinson
Crime Study Center
Southern Illinois University
Carbondale, Illinois 62901 U.S.A.
(618) 453–5701

CRIMINAL JUSTICE HISTORY

AN INTERNATIONAL ANNUAL

Meckler Publishing

CRIMINAL JUSTICE HISTORY:

An International Annual established to publish papers and articles on the history of crime and criminal justice. An extensive book review section is also found in each volume.

Articles are so relevant to modern discussion that it would be a shame not to have them available ... The first two volumes of Criminal Justice History also review more than 30 books, which would help develop collection in criminology.

CHOICE

Unlike many American publications, this anthology offers a truly international introduction to the burgeoning field of the social history of crime and criminal justice institutions ... Essays of substantial value to both social and legal historians.

AMERICAN JOURNAL OF
LEGAL HISTORY

Contents: Volume One/1980

Contents: Volume Two/1981

Contents: Volume Three/1982

Contents: Volume Four/1983

Cover: *Figura Condemnationis Reorum* from Jean Milles de Souvigny, *Praxis Criminis Persequendi* (Paris, 1541). See Mentzer, "The Self-Image of the Magistrate in Sixteenth-Century France," *Criminal Justice History*, Volume Five/1984.

Contents: Volume Five/1984

Order Information

Price: (each volume) $49.50
Size: 6x9; cloth

ISSN: 0194-0953

ORDER FORM

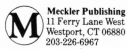

Meckler Publishing
11 Ferry Lane West
Westport, CT 06880
203-226-6967

Please enter my order for the following volumes of CRIMINAL JUSTICE HISTORY:

	No. Copies	Price	Total
☐ Volume One/1980 **ISBN:** 0-930466-67-5	_____	@ $49.50 ea.	_____
☐ Volume Two/1981 0-930466-68-3	_____	@ $49.50 ea.	_____
☐ Volume Three/1982 0-930466-69-1	_____	@ $49.50 ea.	_____
☐ Volume Four/1983 0-930466-70-5	_____	@ $49.50 ea.	_____
☐ Volume Five/1984 0-88736-019-X	_____	@ $49.50 ea.	_____

☐ Please make this a standing order.

_____ Payment enclosed (10% discount allowed)   _____ Bill me   _____ Bill my organization

_____ Charge to the following credit card (circle one):   AMEX   VISA   MASTERCARD

Card number _____ Expires _____

Signature _____.

Name _____ Organization _____

Address _____

City _____ State _____ Zip _____